NETWORKS FOR WATER POLICY:
A COMPARATIVE PERSPECTIVE

Networks for Water Policy

A COMPARATIVE PERSPECTIVE

edited by

Hans Bressers,
Laurence J. O'Toole Jr
and Jeremy Richardson

FRANK CASS • LONDON

First published in 1995 in Great Britain by
FRANK CASS & CO. LTD.
Newbury House, 900 Eastern Avenue,
London IG2 7HH
England

and in the United States of America by
FRANK CASS
c/o ISBS
5804 N.E. Hassalo Street
Portland, Oregon 97213-3644

Copyright © 1995 Frank Cass & Co. Ltd

British Library Cataloguing in Publication Data

Networks for Water Policy: Comparative
Perspective. – (Special Issue of
"Environmental Politics", ISSN 0964-4016;
Vol. 3, No. 4)
  I. Bressers, H. II. Series
  333.910941

    ISBN 0-7146-4642-3

Library of Congress Cataloging in Publication Data

The group of Studies first appeared in a Special Issue:
'Networks for Water Policy: A Comparative Perspective' of
Environmental Politics, Vol.3, No.4, published by Frank Cass
& Co. Ltd.

Typeset by Regent Typesetting, London
Printed and bound in Great Britain by
Antony Rowe Ltd, Chippenham

Contents

Networks as Models of Analysis: Water Policy in Comparative Perspective

HANS BRESSERS, LAURENCE J. O'TOOLE JR,
and JEREMY RICHARDSON

Network models for analysing public policy have become widely used in recent years. This symposium assesses the network idea by applying a common perspective on network analysis to the constellations involved in water policy formation and implementation in several countries and the European Union. Water policy is an important and increasingly salient subject, and the networks involved in the sector have altered recently in important fashions. Thus the topic is suitable for investigations of network dynamics and their impacts. In this article, some of the most significant lines of contribution to network research are reviewed, and the network concept is clarified. Preliminary assessments of the utility and limitations of network analysis are presented. In particular, it is argued that the network emphasis offers some analytical advantages in understanding policy processes. Network characteristics and some dimensions of network variability are sketched. Particular attention is paid to the dimension for which policy communities and issue networks constitute polar cases. A rationale for the comparative analysis of water policy networks across different settings is presented.

Introduction

Over a 20 year period and on both sides of the Atlantic, political scientists, policy specialists, and sociologists have been developing and refining network-based models of policy making and policy implementation. Literatures have emerged on issue networks, triple alliances and pluralistic structures, public-private cooperative arrangements, policy communities, and other similarly-labelled entities.

Indeed, the profusion of terminology has sometimes confused more than it has clarified. There have been many reformulations and redefinitions.

Hans Bressers is Professor of Policy Studies and Director of the Centre for Clean Technology and Environmental Policy at the University of Twente, The Netherlands; Laurence J. O'Toole, Jr is Professor of Political Science at the University of Georgia, USA; and Jeremy Richardson is Director of the European Public Policy Institute and Professor of European Integration, University of Warwick, UK.

Numerous case studies have used variations of the network concept in a heuristic, sometimes even vaguely metaphorical way. (These cases have usually been sectoral – that is, within one substantively-specific field of policy – and mostly at the national rather than the comparative cross-national level.) At a minimum, however, network analysis has enabled scholars to order a mass of empirical material in a useful way and in a fashion which is often readily recognised by the actors under study. And it has prompted theoretical speculation regarding intriguing social-scientific questions.

This symposium is intended to contribute to the assessment of the network concept after two decades of usage. Has the application and development of network analysis gone beyond its intellectual shelf life? Or can an appropriately-formulated network perspective advance further our understanding of important policy issues? To answer these questions it is essential to identify the most important features in the literature on network analysis, especially as developed in political science and public administration. Just what, if anything, *is* being claimed when it is argued that policy networks exist and play an influential role in the policy process? What *can* be claimed?

This collection is also designed to contribute to an understanding of the policy dynamics in a particular field – water – that is now closely linked to, though certainly not synonymous with, the environmental policy sector. To what extent can water policy be explained by the use of network analysis?

Furthermore, through this compilation and most explicitly in the concluding article, we strive to facilitate the *comparative* analysis of water policy. While some other studies have pointed to questions of network variation (see, for instance, Marsh and Rhodes [*1992*]), the present set develops and documents the range and types of variation as part of a carefully-coordinated joint effort.[1] All settings analysed herein face generally the same basic water policy goals – primarily, to dispose of waste safely into the hydrological system and to provide pure water in sufficient quantities for both domestic and industrial uses. Clearly, the hydrological and demand conditions vary considerably both within and between nations, and this variety could be expected to produce quite different policy outcomes. What is less clear is whether policy outcomes are also affected, and if so, to what degree, by the range and nature of participation in the policy process and by different configurations of actor relationships.

In this regard, water policy constitutes a particularly interesting subject for investigation. For the starting point of our analysis is an assumption that water policy (or at least some aspects thereof) has, for several reasons, been subject to significant pressures in recent years by forces both technical and political. The results in some settings have been, first, a proliferation of actors in a field known hitherto for its rather low salience and technical character and secondly, shifts in the structures of their interdependence. Water policy appears to be an intriguing example of the difficulties of managing a multi-actor policy environment in which new players have introduced both new values and behavioural norms, and in which altering network patterns may have shifted the *loci* of influence and the ability of *any* actors to effect the outcomes they desire. How such altered circumstances might themselves influence policy results is a consequential albeit intricate question.

In this introductory contribution, we set the stage for the succeeding network investigations and their comparative analysis by addressing several issues. In the following section the discussion offers a review of some of the more important tributaries to the stream of literature on networks and policy and elaborate on the network concept. The summary shows that the network notion has been increasingly prominent in scholarship on both policy-making and policy execution. It also suggests that the theme refers to a cluster of somewhat different ideas. Therefore we stipulate how the network concept is used in the set of studies comprising this symposium, especially with regard to the question of which kind of actors makes up networks: persons or organisations.

Then we offer some preliminary assessments of the utility and limitations of network analysis. In this section we present two lines of argument. The first is that the world itself is increasingly networked. The second is that the network emphasis offers some analytical advantages when one is trying to understand policy processes.

Networks can vary greatly in a number of respects and those variations can be expected to matter for policy results. So researchers need to get beyond the general network metaphor and tackle the more complex issues of network characteristics – along with their causes and consequences. This is done in the fourth section of this article. The conceptual differences and some of their theoretical implications are illustrated more specifically through treatment of one important dimension of reported network differences: that of intra-network exchange- and norm-based integration. This is the dimension alluded to in the literature on policy communities and issue networks for policy formulation. The coverage here also provides an appropriate backdrop for investigating the theme of policy development and change. Aside from this dimension some other network characteristics are mentioned.

In the fifth section we suggest a rationale for the comparative analysis of water policy networks across different settings, and in so doing provide context for the six cases being treated in this collection. We also offer some brief comments on the selection of the cases and the comparative methodology. The concluding section of the collection offers a short preview of the rest of the symposium.

The Network Concept

Governments have long had to deal with numerous actors in the course of seeking to develop and implement public policy. Effective public problem solving in late welfare states, it is clear, requires the cooperative efforts of numerous individuals and institutions: public, private, and third sector (not-for-profit). Often, no organisation of government possesses sufficient authority, resources, and knowledge to effect the enactment and achievement of policy intentions. Instead, policies require the concerted efforts of multiple actors, all possessing significant capabilities but each dependent on multiple others to solidify policy intention and convert it into action. Indeed, it is often difficult for any one actor, or group of actors, to manage, or manipulate, the flow of problems and solutions onto the political agenda in the first place. Thus, there are complex multi-actor processes for both the identification, definition and resolution of policy problems, and for the implementation of policy.

Social theorists have come to place great emphasis on the cross-institutional, networked features of large-scale social action. We recognise three fields of social science that share this emphasis and have in turn contributed to what could be labelled a network concept: first, interorganisational theory; secondly, classic and more recent descriptions of 'iron triangles' as 'real life' phenomena; and thirdly intergovernmental relations. In the paragraphs below we touch lightly on these fields.

First, the field of interorganisational theory or interorganisational relations has burgeoned during the last generation (see for instance the multiple reviews in Nystrom and Starbuck [*1981, esp. pp. 383–530*]). Even formal social theorists, using such diverse modelling strategies as mathematically-based social exchange theory [*Coleman, 1986*] and game theory [*Weissing and Ostrom, 1993*], have sought to ground the investigation of complex, networked interdependence in robust and rigorous approaches. Beyond the distinction between formal and more inductive perspectives, important theoretical differences continue to separate the approaches taken, most especially between power dependence and exchange theories; and sociologists still struggle with basic issues of conceptualisation and measurement (see Cook *et al.* [*1983*]). But interorganisational studies have become a fertile subject of scholarship.

Secondly, in the study of government more directly, real-life network arrangements have been objects of systematic scholarly attention for some time, albeit under varying terminology and conceptualisation. The classic American notion of the triple alliance or iron triangle – the symbiotic relationship among administrative unit, legislative oversight committee, and supportive interest group – had been developed extensively in the 1960s and even before [*Freeman, 1965*]. Later critiques of this portrait of networked policy-making and execution – like Heclo's very different conceptualisation [*1978*], see the discussion later in this article as well as in others in this collection) – stimulated important revisions in the theoretical discussion. However, respected analysts, including those based in the United States, continue to give the tight and mutually supportive pattern of interaction its place in empirical accounts [*Lowi, 1979; Wilson, 1989*].

Thirdly, especially in the complex relations among governments within the same national system, the field of intergovernmental relations has seen considerable attention in recent years. While the complexities of interdependence in federal systems have received special attention (for instance Beam, Conlan, and Walker [*1983*], in the United States; Scharpf, Reissert, and Schnabel [*1976*], for Germany), unitary states have not been exempt from this scholarly trend (see Friend, Power, and Yewlett [*1974*] for an early British instance; and Toonen [*1987, 1990*] and several selections in Hufen and Ringeling [*1990*] for coverage of the Netherlands). Indeed, recent government cutbacks in subsidies and intergovernmental transfers have only increased the investigations of mandating, privatisation, and networked indirect influence (see Kettl [*1993*]). The emergence of the European Union (EU) has provided further impetus (see for instance Scharpf [*1988; 1994*]).

Recent studies of these phenomena echo, in turn, scholarly investigations – dating at least since the 1970s – of the welfare states' crisis, the challenges of implementation, and the problems of governmental steering in complicated systems of interdependence. The theme of welfare state crisis – a portfolio of challenges to *all* policy sectors, one tied to serious expenditure constraints and apparent limits on state capacity to set policy goals and achieve them, so as to satisfy the demands and expectations of the populace – has been a central motif both of the scholarly left since the 1970s (see Offe [*1984*] for instance) and also of neoconservative social thought. In some of its most influential versions, the argument is tied directly to the issues of social interdependence and the complications of government – or any institution – seeking to control or direct concerted action when such action is crucially reliant on the concerted efforts of many. These theoretical efforts serve as background for the empiric-theoretical effort in this collection.[2]

For present purposes, we employ the term *policy network* to denote the large class of multi-actor arrangements of interdependence in these varied phases of the policy process. Following the notions employed by Jordan [*1990*] and others, we use the concept of policy network in a generic sense to encompass the variety of structures of interdependence identified, sometimes only vaguely, in the burgeoning scholarship. In the fourth section we introduce further differentiation among network types.

Treating the network concept as a generic referent for multi-actor structures of interdependence raises the further question: who are the actors in policy networks? In particular, are networks comprised of individual persons or organisations? This issue touches upon longstanding debates in social science. The next two paragraphs clarify how the composition of policy networks is considered for purposes of this symposium.

As proposed by the criteria of methodological individualism, we treat persons rather than organisations as basic actors. In their actions, persons represent their organisation(s) and also themselves (or their perspectives and interests). These influences may point in different directions, of course. Still, when one examines a policy network, one observes behavioural patterns among the individuals; and the organisations are only visible via the form in which they are represented by and through the individual actors.

Nevertheless, most network participants are present because of their organisations' interests in the issues at stake, and the behaviour of the individuals within networks is likely to be shaped heavily by the institutional arrangements that drive the perspective of the actors and the composition of the network. 'Miles's Law', as it is sometimes called, is operative: where one stands depends on where one sits. Thus it is inappropriate to exclude organisations and organisational identities from the picture; indeed, they help to drive policy processes and results. Accordingly, for shorthand and emphasis we typically follow the convention of referring to network actors in terms of (or as representatives of) their organisations. These refinements clarify but do not negate the basic perspective of persons as the actors in network processes. Indeed, in some cases in the water policy sector, individual persons, like academics, become involved primarily because of the knowledge they possess rather than the organisations with which they are affiliated.

The Utility and Limitations of Network Analysis

Why and how do networks matter? In this section we present two lines of argument. The first is that the world itself is increasingly networked. The second is that the network emphasis offers some analytical advantages when trying to understand policy processes.

For the reasons sketched earlier in this article, network structures are increasingly important in substantive terms, and an adequate understanding of policy action (and inaction) in many nations requires a recognition of the causal impact of these multiunit structures. Differentiation, states this argument, has dispersed problem-solving capacity (involving knowledge, power, and financial resources) across sets of actors whose cooperative efforts are nonetheless needed for policy success – that is, problem solving on issues of mutual interest (see, for instance, Hanf and Scharpf [1978]; Hanf and O'Toole [1992]). The social and political as well as technological features of policy context thus create, even guarantee, the development of conditions for highly complex and interdependent decision-making; the result is the challenge of joint action and its implications. In some parts of the policy process, for instance formulation efforts, the emergence of networks has been stimulated primarily by the *political* functions served through interdependent action. For policy implementation, the explanation can be extended to include technical requisites: functional differentiation vitiates straightforward co-ordination and integration and creates challenges to collective action; thus, it follows, the enhanced importance of network arrangements as integrative structures for practical policy action [*Hanf, 1978; Mandell, 1992; O'Toole, 1988*]. This functional differentiation includes not only various governmental and semi-governmental agencies but also active participation by members of target groups and their representatives in implementation structures [*Bressers and Klok, 1988*]. Some researchers and theorists point to both developments (for example, Scharpf, *1978*).

In the investigation of environmental politics and policy a consideration of the network theme is particularly relevant. In many developed nations, the unanticipated consequences of complex patterns of interdependence have resulted – through the emergence of environmental movements, policies, and institutions – in efforts to reorient and restructure extant patterns of action on behalf of previously-neglected values. Furthermore, the flaws evident in many early approaches to environmental issues – for instance, the lack of due consideration given to cross-media transfers of pollutants (still typical in the US structure for environmental issues at national and subnational levels) – have added a further impetus to networking and coordination across institutional niches: interorganisationally within governments, intergovernmentally within and across nations (note the emergence of important environmental regulation at the level of the EU and even now in a very limited way via the North American Free Trade Agreement), and between public and private spheres. In some nations, notably the Netherlands, policy now stipulates that the comprehensive and systemic character of the environmental issues requires in turn comprehensive approaches and institutional arrangements for policy and its execution: a networked environment, in short, necessitates a networked approach. The developing cross-sectoral links thus pose challenges to the stability of sectoral and sub-sectoral structures and may, indeed, signal eventual shifts in the scale of networked arrays: towards many more actors tied across broader policy spaces.

The foregoing discussion documents that there are plausible if not compelling reasons to expect networked patterns of interaction to matter in contemporary policy activities. The question can now be asked: do network-based examinations of policy activities produce any added value, beyond what scholars are likely to garner through other, and perhaps more traditional, approaches to social theorising and empirical observation? For even if networks exist, it is nevertheless not obvious that approaching the analysis of policy settings via a network *perspective* – with the concept of networks a prominent one in characterisation and explanation – provides better or more thoroughgoing explanations and predictions.

The demonstration of the proposition is dependent on testing through systematic research. This symposium marks one effort to see if the network idea offers a contribution – and perhaps more interestingly, what the limitations of such a contribution are likely to be. In this initial discussion, some preliminary thoughts can be offered regarding both the utility and limitations of network analyses.

In a sense, the utility of network approaches has been suggested in the foregoing coverage, at least by implication. For the apparent ubiquity of network-based discussion and theorising has not been driven primarily by some mindless fashion among social scientists, but rather from the inadequacies of alternative perspectives. As Hjern and Porter observed with regard to the investigation of policy implementation, the 'lonely organisation syndrome' – the set of approaches neglectful of the networked features of the implementation context – had restricted insight, limited predictive power, and even generated weak and counterproductive practical recommendations [*Hjern and Porter, 1982*]. In the study of both policy implementation (see Sabatier [*1986*]) and also policy formation [*Kingdon, 1984*], the increase in attention to networks has itself derived from the need to incorporate the network insight systematically into analysis.

A few additional and somewhat more specific points can be made about the advantages (and also limitations) of focusing on networks in policy. A network perspective in policy research is further justified by reviewing several observations about settings for policy research. Most modern approaches conceptualise policy formulation and implementation as multi-actor interaction processes, the course and results of which can only be understood from characteristics like the goals, information and power of the set of actors involved. A network perspective is also consistent with this conceptualisation, but these features alone do not mark this perspective as distinctive. Rather, a set of additional observations comes into focus once one adopts a network approach.

A first observation from a network perspective is that the actors involved in the policy subject interact not only during the research period, but also before and after. The interactions under observation in any policy research, therefore, are influenced by the history and predicted future of these intersections.

A second and related observation is that the actors often interact not only in the processes under study but also in other fields as well. Acknowledging that the process under investigation is not the only venue for interaction among those under study, even during the period under investigation, means that the analyst is better able to understand some of the activities and inter-actions in the process under study that, almost inevitably, are inducted by experiences in our expectations of other processes of interdependence (for an elaboration of these two observations in an implementation setting, see Arentsen and Bressers [1991]).

A third observation from a network perspective is that the actors involved in the process under study not only act on their own or in reaction to each other, they are also influenced by background actors who play no direct role in the observable interaction but are connected through a network. One can expect to find that some organisations in a policy network nearly always remain in a background position, but these can be important when they are a source of indirect influence upon others (for an interesting example in trans-port policy – the role of consumers – see Dudley [1994]). One obvious role could be as trusted or authoritative advisers. Another, more subtle channel of influence by background actors occurs when those in the core of overt decision-making respond in advance to the expected positions and pressures of certain others in the broader array, as suggested in a different context by Friedrich's 'law of anticipated reaction' [1940].

Finally, and again relatedly, this point about indirect influence can be broadened. An advantage of a network perspective is that it can be used to direct attention to the larger structure of interdependence. Instead of assuming that influence takes place only through direct and observable inter-actions, whether as personal relationships or among representatives of institu-tional interests, a network approach – applied at portions of a policy process as varied as formulation and implementation – can investigate how the larger structure can have systematic effects on the behaviour of individual actors as well as on the content of decisions, policy responses, and implementation efforts. A network approach thus offers the chance to combine both inter-personal and structural explanations for policy-relevant events.

In total, these observations explain why the course and product of a policy process can seem to have a rationale different from what might be expected from the immediately-observable interactions of a set of separate actors. Accordingly, then, one could expect a network perspective to provide insights helpful in the analysis of policy.

Of course, one must be cautious. To confirm the existence of networks of some kind may say no more than that there *are* networks! The network perspective can lead to an overemphasis on the who compared with the what. The activities and interactions within the network then tend to be viewed as one giant garbage can, largely immune to careful analysis. In the extreme form, all processes under scrutiny merge into one, which seems to process and produce nothing, but only reproduces itself. The analyst might then conclude, incorrectly, that this perspective constitutes the state of the world, while in fact it may be an artifact of one's failure to make clear distinctions among the various processes being examined. Furthermore, the degree of involvement, and the goals, information and power of the network actors often vary considerably from one process to another. Whenever this circumstance obtains, it is useful to analyse these processes separately, albeit not in isolation from the others in which the network actors are also engaged. We are conscious, therefore, that network analysis has both advantages and limitations.

Network Characteristics

A very general formulation of the policy networks notion is helpful as a starting point but means little in terms of explanation and prediction. For such purposes, a characterisation of the systemic, patterned network arrangement – and its causes and hypothesised consequences – is necessary. Among policy researchers focusing on processes of policy formulation, in particular, some efforts have been made to develop characterisations in terms of the degree of exchange-based and normative integration observable within the network.

For instance, Richardson and Jordan, writing of British policy making in the late 1970s and attempting to de-emphasise the traditional political science accent on formal institutions, made use of the term policy *community* [*1979*]. It was meant to convey a very close and stable relationship between policy actors, akin to the dictionary definition of community – 'joint ownership of goods, identity of character, fellowship (. . . of interest)' [*Oxford Dictionary*]. This formulation was in turn prompted by Heclo and Wildavsky's study of the spending community in Whitehall, which they likened to village life [*1974; 1981*].

Use of the community notion carries with it, therefore, some reasonably explicit notions of appropriate *levels of analysis*: if policy actors are brought together in a long-term and stable relationship which presents the prospect of both significant normative agreement (perhaps manifested through the folkways of the community-like pattern) and relatively smooth exchange ties, then this type of pattern is likely only at the sub-sectoral or even micro level.

Jordan emphasises both the *stability* of policy communities and the existence of *shared views*. Such an arrangement, he argues, 'has advantages in encouraging bargaining in policy resolution' [*Jordan, 1990: 327*]. The explicit hypothesis (or sometimes assumption) of stability of relations and of actor participation (almost exclusiveness) is also evident in more recent work incorporating the concept of policy community. Thus, as Judge points out, Rhodes repeatedly states that 'policy communities are networks characterised by stability of relationships, continuity of a highly restrictive membership, vertical interdependence based upon shared delivery responsibilities and insulation from other networks and invariably from the general public (including Parliament)' (quoted by Judge [*1993: 122*]; see, for instance, Rhodes [*1985: 15*]; Rhodes and Marsh [*1992: 182*]).

This usage is more restrictive than earlier formulations in that it seems to emphasise insularity almost as an overriding feature and thus appears to reject the notion that new members might be admitted and absorbed relatively easily. Also, it implies great, nearly exclusive, emphasis on a shared *community of views*, suggesting that policy communities do not exhibit much conflict. The formulation neglects exchange as a potential binding force and thus may underestimate the potential for policy communities to remain vital and coherent despite quite serious disputes and despite having to admit new members. Further, these definitions also significantly underestimate the linkages between different policy communities, now a very common feature of the policy process in some national settings (see, for instance, Jordan and Richardson, [*1982: 89–90*] for evidence on the British case).

This particular shift in emphasis in Britain – from a world of policy-making rather dominated by policy community politics to a more loosely organised and therefore less predictable policy process – was also reflected, somewhat earlier, in the US (see Campbell [*1989*]). Indeed the seminal work (on either side of the Atlantic) is still Heclo's US-focused analysis which began to re-direct attention towards policy *dynamics* – the impact of network arrangements on shifts in policy processes and results. Just as many writers were identifying stable policy communities, Heclo had observed a trend: policy decisions often escape the confined and exclusive 'worlds' of professionals and are resolved in a much looser configuration (if indeed such a structured term can be used) of participants in the policy process. 'Professionals' here refers to those with advanced training, preference and capacity for self-governance (thus limited access by outsiders), and specialised knowledge within the sphere in question. Heclo argued that the nature of power in Washington had begun to change – politics was less 'clubbable' because more and more groups had entered the policy process [*Heclo 1978: 94*]. Thus 'as proliferating groups have claimed a stake and clamoured for a place in the policy process, they have helped diffuse the focus of political and administrative leadership' [*Heclo 1978: 94–5*]. Existing conceptions were not well suited to the loose-jointed play of influence that was emerging.

In a now classic formulation, he argued that

> Obviously questions of power are still important. But for a host of
> policy initiatives undertaken in the last twenty years it is all but

impossible to identify clearly who the dominant actors are. Who is controlling those actions that go to make up our national policy on abortions, or on income redistribution, or consumer protection, or energy? Looking for the few who are powerful, we tend to overlook the many whose webs of influence provoke and guide the exercise of power. These webs, or what I will call 'issue networks', are particularly relevant to the highly intricate and confusing welfare policies that have been undertaken in recent years [*1978: 102*].

Even Heclo, however, was reluctant to accept a thesis of total disorder. He added significant qualifications to the model of diffuse power and lack of accountability. He pointed out a paradox (which will be considered again in the concluding article in this collection) of disorder *and* order when he argued that a second tendency could also be distinguished in issue network settings, one cutting in the opposite direction to widening group participation. In the midst of the emergence of the loose issue networks he could also identify what he called 'policy as intramural activity'. He points to 'the development of specialised subcultures composed of highly knowledgeable policy-watchers' with a 'detailed understanding of specialised issues that comes from sustained attention to a given policy debate' [*1978: 49*].

He deftly linked the two apparently contradictory trends by noting that

Whatever the participants' motivation, it is the issue network that ties together what would otherwise be the contradictory tendencies of, on the one hand, more widespread organisational participation in public policy and, on the other, more narrow technocratic specialisation in complex modern policies [*1978: 103–104*].

Can sense be made of these contrasting images of networked arrangements and their impacts in the policy process? The suggestion by Rhodes and Marsh that policy communities and issue networks are part of a continuum, indeed anchor its poles – and that policy networks should be used as the generic term — is a useful reminder that more than one kind of multiactor arrangement may be present and thus more than one model of policy making may be applicable in networked settings.[3]

This continuum, one based on tightness of coupling (through both exchange relations and normative ties) and perhaps also on a shared familiarity with the subject matter, is of considerable interest. The preceding paragraphs make clear that the theme has been exceedingly prominent in scholarship on networks for policy-making, that it bears on theories of policy development and change, and that it cannot be simplified merely into distinctions among networks based on national systems of policy (for instance, British networks as communities and the American variant as issue

NETWORKS AS MODELS OF ANALYSIS   13

networks). Although considerably more research is required on the topic of this dimension of network characteristics, therefore, the questions raised by it are of sufficient interest and importance that they receive attention in the current collection. Each of the studies that follow offers some observations regarding how the water policy networks in the context in question can be placed on this dimension. (Several of the cases also characterise the networks on additional dimensions.)

Each deals with the link between this dimension of network structure and policy dynamics as well. Placing networks on this continuum enables us to focus on the possibility of observing *changes* over time in the relevant network characteristics – the nature and range of participation as well as the structure of participants' interdependence – and determining whether these are related to patterns of alteration in the associated water policy processes (and perhaps outputs and outcomes). Further, it may be that at any given time *several* types of networks are in operation. If so, the interrelationships (if any) between these require examination.

The continuum is also helpful in analysing different *stages* of the policy process, particularly formulation and implementation. On the relationship with the policy formulation stage it can be hypothesised that the initial characteristics of the network will tend to reproduce themselves by means of the choice of goals and policy instruments [*Bressers, 1993*]. In tightly-coupled networks, policy instruments will tend to be selected so as to strengthen the networks' coherence. This hypothesis is explored further in the Dutch contribution to this volume.

As suggested earlier, policy ultimately requires delivery or implementation. The requisite actors have to be mobilised and co-ordinated. Research on the implementation task has often emphasised the network features of the implementation context (see, for instance, O'Toole and Montjoy [*1984*]; O'Toole [*1986*]; Hanf and O'Toole [*1992*]). However, relatively little attention has been devoted to how more successful mobilisation and more concerted co-ordination may be achieved (for early efforts, see O'Toole [*1988*]; Mandell [*1992*]; O'Toole, Hupe and Hanf [*1994*]). And virtually no examination has been attempted of the relationship between the challenge of successfully managing the implementation process in networked contexts, on the one hand, and the placement of network type on the dimension under discussion in this section, on the other.

It might seem that, *ceteris paribus*, more successful implementation management in networks is related to tighter, more community-like network characteristics among those required to cooperate in the execution effort. However, a more complex hypothesis might be offered by distinguishing among dependent variables. Community-like implementation networks may be expected to be associated with smoother execution processes during the implementation phase. However, they may not necessarily be related to more successful outcomes. Building and maintaining communities for implementation may require some restriction of access, which in turn can hinder overall achievement by excluding some necessary participants from the coordinated effort. (For coverage of some of the complexities of plausible implementation hypotheses in multi-actor (network) contexts see O'Toole [*1989*]; Goggin, Bowman, Lester and O'Toole [*1990*].)

Nevertheless, despite the obvious importance of the community-issue network dimension for implementation processes (and results), thus far these two bodies of scholarship – that on the network dimension under discussion here and that on the requisites for implementation success – have developed in almost complete isolation. While this symposium is not the place for a full synthesis of the two, the contributions do provide some opportunity to consider possible links between these separate network literatures.

A comparative symposium on networks for water policy may be particularly propitious for such an inaugural effort. It can be argued that well-integrated implementation arrangements may be especially crucial in policy areas – like water and associated infrastructure – which involve complex *physical* networks, sometimes operated by multiple professions. Where the physical system is interdependent, we might likewise expect actor interdependencies to be quite marked. This circumstance raises the possibility of a model of policy-making which both emphasises the fluidity of issue networks – perhaps even more fluid than Heclo's original formulation which still envisaged a 'shared knowledge group' [*Heclo, 1978: 103*] – and also emphasises the importance of rather specialised and technical 'policy communities' in the model suggested in some of the literature reviewed earlier.

In the discussion so far we have focused on a set of characteristics that is helpful in placing various networks on a continuum. But of course these are not the only characteristics that can be expected to matter for policy results. There is no shortage of network dimensions of potential interest to scholars of policy. If researchers were to try to consider them all, empirical designs would face a degrees-of-freedom problem, since the number of dimensions would rival the number of networked settings that could reasonably be subjected to careful examination. Among those that have been suggested as potentially important for systematic investigation are: number and type of network participants; degree of stability or institutionalisation; level of formalisation; degree of complexity; type of interdependence (for example, Thompson's distinction among pooled, sequential, and reciprocal patterns [*1967*]); degree of overlap; extent of centralisation or concentration; degrees of dominance, accessibility or openness, and coordination; type or scope of issue or coverage; as well as phase of phases of policy for which the network is engaged. Other plausible possibilities could be mentioned. (For treatments of some putatively important dimensions of policy networks see Jordan and Schubert [*1992*]; Pappi, Knoke, and Bisson [*1993*]; Parks [*1985*]; van Waarden [*1992*].)

It is clear that previous empirical research has been unable to clarify this bewildering array of network features. As but one collection comparing networks in the single field of water policy, this volume cannot hope to provide a definitive classification of network characteristics. In the concluding essay, however, we seek to make a modest contribution to the characterisation of networks in more analytically-meaningful terms. Accordingly, our approach contains two components.

First, the research reported in the next several articles has been conducted by investigators who have coordinated with each other in several respects, not least in considering collectively which network dimensions seem most significant in each case as well as collectively. Consequently, although none of the investigations offers a complete characterisation of the policy networks studied, each treats relevant dimensions.

Second, to ensure some consistency across the studies and to offer a small step forward in developing meaningful network distinctions, *all* of the investigations report on *one* potentially-important network dimension, that indicating extent of exchange- and norm-based integration within the network in question. This is the network feature implicitly referenced in the literature on policy communities and issue networks discussed in this section.

Comparing Networks for Water Policy

This volume offers a contribution to the study of policy networks by developing comparative characterisations of a set of such arrangements within an important common policy sector – water – across several nations and at the level of the European Union.

Studying the water policy sector is useful for a number of reasons. Handling public functions related to water involves some of the oldest responsibilities of government. Indeed, in some nations, such as the Netherlands, water management tasks have been handled for centuries by water boards (*Waterschappen*) whose existence predated the state. Furthermore, better technical knowledge and the increased salience of environmental issues in recent years mean that water policy has acquired renewed importance. Investigations in this field also provide opportunities to conduct policy research in a context of dramatic policy and institutional change. In this sector and among the settings scrutinised in this set of studies, these dynamics include: experiments in privatisation, the challenges of unification (in Germany) in a field where institutional-technological incompatibilities render coordinated change especially problematic, tightened and increasingly complex regulatory standards, and the emergence of the EU as a supranational policy actor – or network of actors. Accordingly, the study of networks in the water policy sector deserves special attention.

The varying types of turbulence referred to above mean that network structures and relationships are not necessarily stable over time. They can be subject to both endogenous and exogenous change, reflecting shifting conditions (for water networks, these include hydrogeological, financial and legal circumstances), values, and participation in the various stages of the policy process. These 'disturbances' can be expected to be especially noticeable in situations where scientific and technical knowledge emerges in the context of growing political salience. (There is also the possibility that new knowledge will itself *raise* political salience, of course.)

In the case of water policy, a number of factors appear to be at work which have led and may continue to lead to disturbances of established patterns of behaviour in the relevant networks. For example, water supply shortages in certain regions, tightened regulatory standards on waste disposal and clean water systems for both domestic and industrial use, severe resource constraints, and much greater knowledge of the intra- and international effects of pollution – both to wildlife and humans – all have suggested that existing policy arrangements may need to change quite radically. In addition, water policy has become caught up in broader questions of environmentalism, thus raising the political salience of aspects of the policy area enormously. In some of the countries under study here the matter is even more complex because of broader currents of political and ideological change, plus what we might call (following Dror [1968]) 'metapolicy': policies and framing assumptions about policies. One such additional influence is the push for privatisation experienced in several nations; this impetus too can present a seismic shock to sectoral politics. Thus, in the British case, as documented in the article by Maloney and Richardson, the policy sector has been subject to major stress for all of these reasons – with yet further complications because of Britain's membership in the EU. In the German case, as Rüdig and Kraemer show, the impetus to privatise has been weaker, but the policy dynamics are complicated in a different fashion by the severe pressures attendant to political unification. In Hungary, of course, political upheaval has combined with intergovernmental differentiation and large-scale privatisation to create massive changes in the water field, as well as in many others.

In almost all of the countries under study, the researchers whose work is included in this symposium examine what – decades ago – used to be a rather quiet, well managed and consensual policy process but which has become much more salient in political terms; is facing considerable financial pressures; and is experiencing pressure from new actors (for example, environmentalists, consumers) who have begun to demand access and influence (the US case is somewhat more complicated, as is clear in the detailed study included in this collection).

In some cases the agenda setting process may have 'escaped' the traditional confines of the sector or sub-sector, and observers may be witnessing the defensive response of traditionally-powerful actors to agendas set elsewhere. However, at some point governments – local, regional, national, or even supranational – must seek resolution of conflicting objectives, differing values and diverging demands. At its most basic, wastewater must continue to be disposed of and usable water supplied. Some collective means must be found for devising solutions which are acceptable (in the sense that key actors acquiesce to the policies and relevant implementers cooperate in executing them) and which will actually work. Shifts in network membership and structure, which are consequences of the kinds of disturbances sketched above, are therefore likely as a means of dealing with these functional-technical and political pressures. Changed systems of interdependence with altered memberships are likely to see shifts in shared assumptions; new patterns of alliance and conflict; transformed vocabularies, core values, and perceptions (see Sabatier and Jenkins-Smith, [1993]). All these modifications, it can be hypothesised, can have independent effects on policy and implementation processes and on policy results (compare the treatment of the influence of the policy community-issue network dimension in the discussion above).

In the field of water policy, there can be no doubt that policy and implementation processes have taken on new characteristics in numerous national settings during recent years. And it is even more obvious that during the same period policy results – in terms of both outputs and also outcomes – have changed greatly in most developed settings. As policy researchers know all too well, nevertheless, it is much more difficult to attribute causality in these complex processes. For all their differences, theories of policy processes built on the notion of networks as a central concept either assert or assume that the networks *per se* make a difference in what happens. Whether and how they do in actual empirical instances is a most difficult but extremely important set of questions for scholars of public policy. These are questions that the individual country investigations included in this collection address and try to answer. And the issue is considered again in the concluding article of the symposium.

This collection includes analyses of water policy networks in six settings: Germany, Hungary, the Netherlands, the United Kingdom, the United States, and the European Union. This last instance adds another level of analysis and also helps to place most of the single-country European instances into context and systematic comparison. Comparing policy networks in this way offers particular advantages. Until recently, cross-national comparisons of policy networks have been rarities. However, such investigations may be necessary to advance the study of such networks (see Schneider [*1987*]; Hanf and O'Toole [*1992*]).

The selection of cases comprising this collection has been based on settings which, as a group, encompass sufficient diversity so as to allow an approximation to a most different case comparative design. An investigation of the EU networks themselves was deemed warranted on the basis of the increasing importance of the European level in water policy matters specifically, and environmental policy generally. While all the national settings included in the symposium face roughly similar water challenges, their hydrogeological conditions and institutional arrangements – including the financial and legal factors mentioned earlier – are sufficiently varied so as to allow an investigation of quite diverse contexts. An advantage of such a comparative design is its potential to identify important cross-case similarities. That is, if in very different kinds of cases water policy networks exhibit similar characteristics, or if their features seem to be shaped in similar ways, or if they demonstrate parallel impacts on policy process or results, such findings may be strikingly suggestive. Indeed, such cross-case correspondence can be identified in the cases treated in this collection, and some general patterns are examined in the concluding article in the symposium.

While each researcher or team of investigators was free to employ the methods that seemed most appropriate to the conditions and constraints prevailing in the given setting, all cases reported here derive from extensive examination of the relevant literature produced earlier in each context, plus a review of reports developed by governments and other groups, and – especially – interviews with many of the participants in the networks under investigation. More precise details of method are provided in each article.

Overall, this contribution to the comparative study of water networks focuses on several research questions, all derived directly from the perspective advanced above. Consequently, the first question is descriptive. The second treats networks as a dependent variable. The third involves networks as an independent variable. The research questions that emerge on this basis are the following:

How can the networks involved in water policy be characterised?

The *foci* of this question are the network properties identified earlier. In each investigation conducted as a part of this coordinated effort, some coverage of *both* water supply and water quality has been attempted; furthermore, each has treated – at least to some extent – not only policy formulation but also implementation. Each investigation thus reflects an effort to cover the waterfront, as it were, within the context in question (nation or EU). Individual investigations in several cases emphasise one or more of these topics (for instance implementation, or policy formulation for water quality); in each case, such skewing of the presentation is based on the scholars' judgment as to the network issues of special importance for the case in question. Each contribution in this symposium identifies the principal actors in the network(s), and the network setting as a whole is characterised. In each case, the network setting is described in terms of the policy community-issue network dimension discussed earlier; additional network features are also included in the characterisations in several of the articles.

What are the dynamics of change in the network or networks?

How have the networks under investigation assumed the character they now have? Are they now in rapid flux, or static? Why? This coverage necessitates some inclusion of historically-relevant information. The scope of longitudinal coverage has been left flexible so that the authors can select the most appropriate range in terms of what best helps to explain the current and recent characteristics of the network(s) and their dynamics of change.

What is the importance of the water policy network(s) to the nature of the policy process, outputs and (if it is possible to say) outcomes in the case in question?

Can features of the policy network(s) being examined help to explain how policy gets made or implemented, or why water policy has the features it has, or why it has changed in particular ways? If possible, the investigators are asked to offer at least tentative answers as to why knowing about the policy network(s) may provide information of some import for policy making and its execution.

Prospect

The network characterisations developed in this volume identify a number of findings of interest and raise issues of theoretical consequence. The research demonstrates, for instance, that a policy community – a particularly well-integrated arrangement – has operated at the core of the British networks for water policy formulation and also implementation. However, this core has been set aside, at times, and now has to operate in the context of a much broader and more open *mélange* of actors. In the United States, by contrast, the network structure had long been more variable and diffuse. Here too, however, signs of further broadening are now evident. In the EU and in Hungary, to take two additional instances, the participants themselves may, at present, find difficulty in predicting the ultimate structures of their interdependence, which they are in the midst of crafting. In each of these cases, and others covered as well, elements of policy network composition and structure can be related, at least tentatively, to some attributes of policy process. As it turns out, nonetheless, the ability of scholars to develop clear evidence regarding the attributes and importance of this link between network structure and policy results is bounded in some important ways, which are themselves a subject of analysis in the concluding essay of this collection.

Further, the detailed analyses of this collection demonstrate the impact of multiple factors on characteristics of policy networks. Through coordinated network investigations, including an explicitly-comparative concluding chapter, the studies show the range of variation observable across the set of networks.

The overall product, we believe, offers a contribution to both the comparative study of policy networks and also the operations of one important and dynamic field of modern policy with substantial implications for the environment.

NOTES

1. Thanks are due to the Council for European Studies, the Anglo-German Foundation, and two host universities (Twente in Enschede and Erasmus in Rotterdam, The Netherlands) for support enabling the group and editorial meetings resulting in the coordination of these parallel studies. The editors also acknowledge the helpful comments by the other contributors to this symposium to earlier versions of this introductory article. The responsibility for any errors of fact or interpretation in this article, nevertheless, rests with the authors.

   The research is the product of an ongoing cross-national comparative water policy-network study among researchers located in the nations under investigation. Following an initial planning meeting, the researchers convened several times during 1992–1993 to coordinate analyses. Earlier research from this project is reported in Bressers and O'Toole (1992).

2. For instance, the work of Scharpf and colleagues has highlighted the networked character of social action deriving from technical-functional and political imperatives in late welfare states [*1977; 1978; 1993*]; (see the discussion later in this article). And the efforts of Luhmann and other theorists (see Luhmann [*1990*]; Teubner [*1993*]), while quite different and arguably more pessimistic, carry intriguing implications for how policy might be made and executed in networked systems characterised by autopoiesis, or self-referentiality. What kinds of guidance can policy makers and implementors provide, what kinds of steering may be possible, if direct chains of control or even influence are inherently unmanageable and unpredictable? Such important questions, while beyond the direct focus of this symposium, provide clear evidence of the broader theoretical and practical issues that frame and fuel the study of networks in political and social action.

3. They draw on Benson's 1982 definition of a network as 'a cluster or complex of organisations connected to each other by resource dependencies and distinguished from other clusters or complexes by breaks in the structure of resource dependencies' [*Benson, 1982: 148*]. However, they go on to distinguish five types of networks '. . . ranging along a continuum from highly integrated policy communities to loosely integrated issue networks'. [*Marsh and Rhodes, 1992: 13*].

REFERENCES

Arentsen, Maarten J., and Hans Th.A. Bressers (1991), 'The Relevance of Power in the Process of Policy Implementation'. Paper presented at the World Congress of the International Political Science Association, Buenos Aires, Argentina. (Also published in Dutch: (1992) *Beleidswetenschap* Vol. 6, No. 4, pp.103–125.)

Beam, David R., Timothy J. Conlan, and David B. Walker (1983), 'Federalism: The Challenge of Conflicting Theories and Contemporary Practice'. In Ada W. Finifter, *Political Science: The State of the Discipline*, Washington, D.C.: American Political Science Association.

Benson, J. Kenneth (1982), 'A Framework for Policy Analysis', in D.L. Rogers, *et al.*, *Interorganizational Coordination: Theory, Research, and Implementation*, Ames: Iowa State University Press, pp.137–201.

Bressers, Hans Th.A., and Pieter Jan Klok (1988), 'Fundamentals for a Theory of Policy Instruments', *International Journal of Social Economics*, Vol. 15, Nos. 3–4, pp.22–41.

Bressers, Hans Th.A., and Laurence J. O'Toole, Jr. (eds) (1992) *International Comparative Policy Research: Preparing a Four Country Study on Water Quality Management*, Enschede: University of Twente Press.

Bressers, J.Th.A. (1993), 'Beleidsnetwerken en Instrumentenkeuze', *Beleidswetenschap*, Vol. 7, No. 4 pp.309–330.

Campbell, J.C. (1989) 'A Note from the Guest Editor', *Governance*, Vol. 2, No. 1, pp.iii–iv.

Coleman, James S. (1986), 'Social Action Systems', in J.S. Coleman (ed.), *Individual Interests and Collective Action*, Cambridge: Cambridge University Press.

Cook, Karen S., R.M. Emerson, M.R. Gillmore, and T. Yamagishi (1983), 'The Distribution of Power in Exchange Networks: Theory and Experimental Result', *American Journal of Sociology*, Vol. 89, pp.295–305.

Dror, Yehezkel (1968), *Public Policymaking Reexamined*, San Francisco, CA.: Chandler.

Dudley, Geoffrey (1994), 'The Next Steps Agencies, Political Salience and the Arm's Length Principle: Barbara Castle at the Ministry of Transport 1965–68', *Public Administration*, Vol. 72, Summer, pp.217–238.

Freeman, J. Leiper (1965), *The Political Process: Executive Bureau-Legislative Committee Relations*, rev. ed. New York: Random House.

Friedrich, Carl J. (1940) 'Public Policy and the Nature of Administrative Responsibility', *Public Policy*, Vol. 1, pp.3–24.

Friend, John K., John M. Power, and Chris.J.L. Yewlett (1974), *Public Planning: The Inter-Corporate Dimension*, London: Tavistock.

Goggin, Malcolm L., Ann O'M. Bowman, James P. Lester, and Laurence J. O'Toole, Jr. (1990), *Implementation Theory and Practice: Toward a Third Generation*, Glenview, IL: Scott Foresman/Little Brown.

Hanf, Kenneth I. (1978), 'Introduction'. In Hanf and Fritz W. Scharpf (ed.), *Inter-organizational Policymaking: Limits to Coordination and Central Control*, London: Sage: pp.1–15.

Hanf, Kenneth I., and Laurence J. O'Toole, Jr. (1992), 'Revisiting Old Friends: Networks, Implementation Structures and the Management of Inter-Organizational Relations', *European Journal of Political Research*, Vol. 21, pp.163–80.

Hanf, Kenneth I., and Fritz W. Scharpf (eds) (1978), *Interorganizational Policymaking: Limits to Coordination and Central Control*, London: Sage.

Heclo, Hugh, and Aaron Wildavsky (1974, 1981), *The Private Government of Public Money: Community and Policy inside British Politics*, 2d ed., London: Macmillan.

Heclo, Hugh (1978), 'Issue Networks and the Executive Establishment', in Anthony King (ed.), *The New American Political System*, Washington, D.C.: American Enterprise Institute, pp.87–124.

Hjern, Benny, and David O. Porter (1982), 'Implementation Structures: A New Unit for Administrative Analysis', *Organization Studies*, Vol. 2, pp.211–37.

Hufen, A.A.M., and A.B. Ringeling (eds) (1990), *Beleidsnetwerken*, The Hague: VUGA.

Jordan, Grant (1990), 'Sub-Governments, Policy Communities, and Networks: Refilling the Old Boots', *Journal of Theoretical Politics*, Vol. 2, pp.319–38.

Jordan, Grant, and Jeremy J. Richardson (1982), 'The British Policy Style or the Logic of Negotiation?' in Richardson (ed.), *Policy Styles in Western Europe*, London: Allen and Unwin, pp.80–110.

Jordan, Grant, and Klaus Schubert (1992), 'A Preliminary Ordering of Policy Network Labels', *European Journal of Political Research*, Vol. 21, Nos. 1–2 (February), pp.7–27.

Judge, David (1993), *The Parliamentary State*, London: Sage.

Kettl, Donald F. (1993), *Shared Power: Public Governance and Private Markets*, Washington, D.C.: The Brookings Institution.

Kingdon, John W. (1984), *Agendas, Alternatives, and Public Policies*, Boston: Little, Brown.

Lowi, Theodore J. (1979), *The End of Liberalism*, 2d ed., New York: Norton.

Luhmann, Niklas (1990), *Essays on Self-Reference*, New York: Columbia University Press.

Mandell, Myrna P. (1992), 'Managing Interdependencies through Program Structures: A Revised Paradigm'. Paper presented at Workshop on 'Management of Inter-organisational Networks', ECPR Joint Sessions, Limerick, Ireland: March 30–April 4.

Marsh, David, and R.A.W. Rhodes (1992), *Policy Networks in British Government*, Oxford: Clarendon Press.

Nystrom, Paul C., and William H. Starbuck (eds) (1981), *Handbook of Organizational Design*, Oxford: Oxford University Press.

O'Toole, Laurence J., Jr. (1986), 'Policy Recommendations for Multi-Actor Implementation: An Assessment of the Field', *Journal of Public Policy*, Vol. 6, No. 2 (April–June), pp.181–210.

O'Toole, Laurence J., Jr. (1988), 'Strategies for Intergovernmental Management: Implementing Programs in Interorganizational Networks', *International Journal of Public Administration*, Vol. 4, pp.417–441.

O'Toole, Laurence J., Jr. (1989), 'Alternative Mechanisms for Multiorganizational Implementation: The Case of Wastewater Management', *Administration and Society*, Vol. 21, No. 3 (November), pp.313–39.

O'Toole, Laurence J., Jr., and Robert S. Montjoy (1984), 'Interorganizational Policy Implementation: A Theoretical Perspective', *Public Administration Review*, Vol. 44, No. 6 (November/December), pp.491–503.

O'Toole, Laurence J., Jr., Peter L. Hupe, and Kenneth I. Hanf (1994), 'Managing Policy Implementation in Complex Networks in Walter Kickert, Joop Koppenjan, and Erik-Hans Klijn (eds), *Public Management and Complex Networks*, forthcoming.

Offe, Claus (1984), *Contradictions of the Welfare State*, edited by John Keane, London: Hutchinson.

Pappi, Franz Urban, David Knoke, and Susanne Bisson (1993), 'Information Exchange in Policy Networks'. In Fritz W. Scharpf (ed.), *Games in Hierarchies and Networks*, Boulder, CO: Westview, pp. 287–313.

Parks, Roger B. (1985), 'Metropolitan Structure and Systemic Performance: The Case of Police Service Delivery'. In Kenneth Hanf and Theo A.J. Toonen, eds, *Policy Implementation in Federal and Unitary Systems: Questions of Analysis and Design*, Dordrecht: Martinus Nijhoff, pp.161–91.

Rhodes, R.A.W. (1985), 'Power-Dependence, Policy Communities, and Intergovernmental Networks', *Public Administration, Bulletin*, 49 (April), pp.4–31.

Rhodes, R.A.W., and D. Marsh (1992), 'New Directions in the Study of Policy Networks', *European Journal of Political Research*, Vol. 21, No. 1, pp. 181–205.

Richardson, Jeremy J., and Grant Jordan (1979), *Governing under Pressure: The Policy Process in a Post-Parliamentary Democracy*, Oxford: Martin Robertson.

Sabatier, Paul A. (1986), 'Top-down and Bottom-up Approaches to Implementation Research: A Critical Analysis and Suggested Synthesis', *Journal of Public Policy*, Vol. 6, No. 1, pp.21–48.

Sabatier, Paul and Hank Jenkins-Smith (1993), *Policy Change and Learning: An Advocacy Coalition Approach*, Boulder CO.: Westview Press.

Scharpf, Fritz W. (1977), 'Public Organization and the Waning of the Welfare State: A Research Perspective', *European Journal of Political Research*, 5: 339–62.

Scharpf, Fritz W. (1978), 'Interorganizational Policy Studies: Issues, Concepts, and Perspectives', in Kenneth I. Hanf and Scharpf (eds), *Interorganizational Policymaking:*

Limits to Coordination and Central Control, London: Sage.

Scharpf, Fritz W. (1988), 'The Joint Decision Trap: Lessons from German Federalism and European Integration', *Public Administration*, 66, pp. 239–78.

Scharpf, Fritz W. (1993), 'Coordination in Hierarchies and Networks', in Scharpf (ed), *Games in Hierarchies and Networks: Analytical and Empirical Approaches to the Study of Governance Institutions*, Frankfurt am Main: Campus Verlag: 125–65.

Scharpf, Fritz W. (1994), 'Community and Autonomy. Multilevel Policy-Making in the European Union', *Journal of European Public Policy*, Vol. 1, No. 2.

Scharpf, Fritz W., Bernd Reissert, and Fritz Schnabel (1976), *Politikverflechtung*, Kronberg/Ts: Athenaum.

Schneider, Volker (1987), 'The Structure of Policy Networks', Paper presented at the ECPR Workshop, April.

Teubner, Gunther (1993), *Law as an Autopoietic System*, trans. Anne Bankowska and Ruth Adler, edited by Zenon Bankowski, Oxford: Blackwell.

Thompson, James D. (1967), *Organizations in Action*, New York: McGraw Hill.

Toonen, Theo A.J. (1987), 'The Netherlands: A Decentralized Unitary State in a Welfare Society', *Western European Politics*, Vol. 10 (October): 108–127.

Toonen, Theo A.J. (1990), 'The Unitary State as a System of Co-governance: The Case of The Netherlands', *Public Administration*, 68 (Autumn): 281–96.

van Waarden, Frans (1992), 'Dimensions and Types of Policy Networks', *European Journal of Political Research*, Vol. 21, Nos. 1–2 (February), pp.29–52.

Weissing, Franz, and Elinor Ostrom (1993), 'Irrigation Institutions and the Games Irrigators Play: Rule Enforcement on Government- and Farmer-Managed Systems', in Fritz W. Scharpf (ed), *Games in Hierarchies and Networks: Analytical and Empirical Approaches to the Study of Governance Institutions*, Frankfurt am Main: Campus Verlag, pp. 387–428.

Wilson, James Q. (1989), *Bureaucracy: What Government Agencies Do and Why They Do It*, New York: Basic Books.

Policy Networks in Dutch Water Policy

HANS T. A. BRESSERS, DAVE HUITEMA
and STEFAN M. M. KUKS

In addition to the well-known programme for flood protection, Dutch water policy consists of two main subsectors; water supply and ground water protection, and surface water quality management. In this contribution special attention is paid to the characterisation of these subsectors using two network variables; mutual commitment and interrelatedness. The dynamics of change of these features and their relation with policy opportunities are examined. The water supply sector was amalgated into larger companies and developed more cooperation as a result of the pressure of the environmental challenge, which made it impossible to continue pumping and billing. Though the sector in a sense became more integrated, this was accompanied by an increased need to do business with other interests, such as agriculture. The surface water quality subsector also moved from a very integrated community into a more open structure. This openness is, however, to a large extent organised by the sector itself, by incorporating other interests in their councils and committees. Both subsectors increasingly adopt a consensual approach in dealing with these other interests.

The most widely known water-management role of the Netherlands is surely the protection against flooding. Some other aspects of water management, however, have received more attention as a policy issue during recent decades. The history of water management in the Netherlands shows how the emphasis has shifted over the years and how this management has become more wide-ranging. In the course of time it has passed through four stages.

The first period is distinguished by protection against flooding from sea-water through the building of dikes. The main concern was keeping one's feet dry. This period started early in the Middle Ages. Safety has increased since then. In the second period protection against flooding remained a concern, but involvement in the control of the water level for the benefit of agriculture and

Hans Bressers is Professor of Policy Studies and Director of the Centre for Clean Technology and Environmental Policy at the University of Twente, The Netherlands; Dave Huitema is a Research Fellow, and Stefan M. M. Kuks is a Lecturer at the Centre. The data presented in this article are largely drawn from several previous studies conducted or supervised by the authors. Some additional information was gathered by selective interviewing of key participants, especially from organisations that provide a forum for the meeting of different interests, such as CUWVO.

shipping was added. In the third period the emphasis shifted to the protection of water quality.

Reconstruction and expansion of industry predominated after the Second World War. Agriculture was also swept along in this industrialisation process, leading to prosperity but also to a veritable surge of pollution. To combat this threat, the 1970 Pollution of Surface Water Act and the 1975 Pollution of Sea Water Act came into force. For a number of substances the result can be clearly shown.

The fourth period can be characterised as integrated care for the condition and use of water systems. This period started in 1985 with the memorandum 'Living with Water', in which the idea of integral water management based on an approach of water systems or water areas as a whole was introduced. Multifunctional and sustained use are prominent now. The question today is how these diverse interests can be reconciled.

The development of water management is analysed in these four periods, during which concern for water was repeatedly adapted to new social demands whilst retaining existing policy issues.

As suggested in the introduction of this volume, networks can be characterised on several dimensions [van Waarden, 1992]. In this article we concentrate on the dimension of *integration versus fragmentation*. At one end of this dimension networks are mere issue networks [*Rhodes and Marsh, 1992: 183*].

Kenis and Schneider [*1991: 40–42*] see networks as a specific class of policy-making structures beyond or between policy markets and characterised on the basis of three elements: actors involved, their linkages and the structure's boundary. In order to distinguish between policy communities and issue networks, Jordan [*1981: 46*] specifies these features of the following variables: the number of actors involved, the stability of the relations and the openness or closedness of the arena. Jordan and Schubert [*1992: 25*] combine the first and third variables and replace the second by the sectoral or transsectoral scope of the network. The background for this variable is that competing belief systems and interests hamper the networks' ability to act. Van Waarden [*1992: 46*] characterises issue networks, not only by their open boundaries and resulting high number of participants, but also by the difficulty in tracing the locus of decision-making and their diffuse dependencies and power relations as a principal characteristic.

In our view the number of participants as such is a risky variable to use in order to characterise a network. This variable depends heavily on the level of analysis, interpersonal or interstructural [*Rhodes and Marsh, 1992: 185*]. Only when a certain level of analysis is fixed can the number of participants be regarded as a relevant factor for the degree of fragmentation of decision-making. Van Waarden seems to imply that fragmentation of decision-making is a main characteristic of issue networks. Dietz and Ryecroft [*1987: 77–101*] characterise policy communities with the variables 'personal contacts' (outreach, prominence and the intensity of communication), 'personnel flows across organisations', 'legitimacy' (sympathy for a particular groups policy position) and 'power'. The last variable is in fact not being used separately but to measure whether the estimated power of the participants matches the distribution of sympathy. In total these variables seem to measure a metavariable which can be labelled as 'integration'. Kingdon [*1984: 123–125*] stresses the importance of the degree of fragmentation. His description of transportation and health communities shows that he does not regard the number of participants as a key factor, but rather the degree of interaction between them and the degree to which participants share the same understanding of what the sector is about. The number of actors is important only in so far as it changes the type of interaction within the network.

The variables used by Dietz and Ryecroft and by Kingdon reflect structural, cognitive and affective aspects of the dimension of integration versus fragmentation. The structural variable is the intensity and stability of mutual interaction. This interaction may consist of written and verbal communication, but also of exchange of personnel and the existence of formalised meeting groups and active intermediaries, which aim at an improvement of the contacts within the network. In an earlier paper we referred to this variable as 'interrelatedness' [*Bressers and Kuks, 1992: 10*]. The affective aspect of the dimension of integration versus fragmentation can be termed 'commitment': the extent to which individuals, groups and organisations within the network sympathise with each others' main objectives, as far as these objectives are relevant to the policy area [*Bressers and Kuks, 1992: 11*]. The cognitive aspect is not always easy to separate from the affective aspect and is for this reason excluded from the typology we introduce below. However it relates to the belief systems of the actors involved, and to the causal relationships they assume in the policy area.

The extent of interrelatedness and the extent of commitment can each be distinguished dichotomously, yielding a matrix with four cells. Of course we do not, by using these dichotomies, deny the fact that many institutions can be intermediate with respect to the distinguished variables. Policy communities are characterised by a combination of strong commitment and strong interrelatedness, issue networks by a combination of weak commitment and weak interrelatedness. Though both characteristics will tend to reinforce each other [*Kingdon, 1984: 126*], there is no reason to assume that the other two combinations will not occur.

What influences can we expect these different types of networks to have on policy formulation and policy implementation? Kenis and Schneider regard as one of the main applications of network analysis 'cross-network comparisons to develop (or test) hypotheses explaining the effect of aggregate characteristics of the policy network on specific interactions' [1991: 45]. Though the scope of this article does not allow testing hypotheses on these influences, some explicit expectations can serve as a useful backgrounds for the description in the following sections.

Our central hypothesis suggests that in the case of policy formulation the initial characteristics of the network will tend to reproduce themselves by means of the choice of goals and instruments [Luhmann, 1984; Mahoje, 1989: 116–144; Rhodes and Marsh, 1992: 198]. With respect to the policy objectives we simply assume that a strong commitment will result in a relatively strong resistance by policy-makers to objectives that require an extensive behavioural change of their target group. In this case the resistance is aimed at the outside world, which tries to force these objectives upon the network.

For policy networks with weak interrelatedness and a weak commitment (issue networks), we expect a preference for direct regulation. For the case of weak interrelatedness combined with strong commitment, we expect an emphasis on subsidies for investments and investigation and written information. A strong interrelatedness and a weak commitment will lead to an emphasis on responsibility (self-regulation) and the use of covenants and other negotiated instruments. A combination of strong interrelatedness and strong commitment (policy communities) will lead to a relatively pragmatic choice of instruments. Subsidies and personal information (education and advice) will be the most important instruments, although there also will be room for all other types of instruments when they seem to be necessary to restore 'law and order in our own house' [Bressers, 1993].

The relations between fragmentation in the network and *policy implementation* has been subject to extensive debate. Edwards views fragmentation as 'the dispersion of responsibilities for a policy among several organizational units' [1980: 134–141]. Though his conceptualisation of fragmentation is somewhat different from ours, the results of fragmentation he expects are nevertheless relevant: difficult coordination, duplication of services, agencies working at cross-purposes, functions that fall between the cracks, and agencies developing narrow *foci*, leading to inflexibility. Likewise, Mazmanian and Sabatier [1989: 11–12] use a concept of integration that is interesting for our purposes because they relate it to policy implementation. They operationalise integration in terms of, first, the number of veto/clearance points and, secondly, the extent to which supporters of statutory objectives are provided with power over those with a potential veto. Because the second is often absent, the first is extremely important in their view. They regard the difficulty of obtaining coordinated action as one of the best-documented findings in implementation literature. 'To the extent that the

TABLE 1
ACTORS INVOLVED IN GROUND WATER MANAGEMENT AND SURFACE
WATER MANAGEMENT AT THE NATIONAL, REGIONAL AND LOCAL LEVEL IN
THE NETHERLANDS

	Ground Water Management	Surface Water Management
Management at the National Level	Ministry for Public Works Public Works Agency Ministry for Environmental Protection	
Consultation at the National Level	Main participants: - Association of Dutch Water Supply Companies - Agricultural Board - Ministry for Environmental Protection - Ministry for Agriculture - Interprovincial Consultation	Main participants (by representation in the CUWVO): - Union of Waterboards - Interprovincial Consultation - Association of Dutch Municipalities - Public Works Agency - Ministry for Environmental Protection - Associations of Industries
Management at the Regional Level	Provinces (nationally represented by the Interprovincial Consultation)	
	Water Supply Companies (private companies, nationally represented by the Association of Dutch Water Supply Companies)	Water Boards (public agencies, nationally represented by the Union of Water Boards)
Consultation at the Regional Level	Main participants: - Provinces - Water Supply Companies - Farmers Associations	Main participants (by representation in Water Board): - Industries - Farmers - Municipalities
Management at the Local Level		Municipalities (responsible for sewerage system)
Production at the Local Level	Drinking Water Production Units (managed by the Water Supply companies)	Waster Water Treatment Works (managed by the Water Boards)

system is only loosely integrated, there will be considerable variation in the degree of behavioural compliance among implementing officials and target groups as each responds to the incentives for modification within their local setting' [*Mazmanian and Sabatier, 1989: 27*]. Both Edwards and Mazmanian and Sabatier seem to agree that lack of integration poses a major threat to successful implementation.

As a possible contribution to a strategy of handling lack of integration, Winter [*1990: 29–31*] refers to Bardach's idea of creating a 'fixer' as a structuring device. More fundamental are the questions posed by Goggin and others. They relate the essence of network analysis to the 'bottom up' perspective on implementation [*Goggin, Bowman, Lester and O'Toole, 1990a: 185*]. They regard the idea that a uniform and hierarchically well integrated administrative structure leads to a better implementation as a top down view. Several bottom up studies give examples of complicated structures actually encouraging success during implementation. They conclude that while simple and integrated structures are likely to produce a smooth process, it is important to keep in mind that prompt implementation does not always lead to optimal outputs and outcomes. Complicated and dynamic policy areas might benefit from complicated and dynamic implementation structures, not for realising planned action but for grasping any chance to enhance goal-attainment.

The way in which we operationalise the dimension of integration versus fragmentation, setting complexity aside and focusing on interaction and sympathy, links the concept to the notion that integration is good for implementation, including outputs. However, we also pay attention to complexity as a separate network characteristic.

This study concentrates on three sectors: surface water, groundwater and seawater. Seawater quality protection is partly dependent on surface water management. Another distinction is: legislation on quantity aspects, legislation on quality aspects and legislation on institutional aspects within each water sector. While quantity and quality are often integrated in the responsibilities of water management agencies, the division of surface water management and ground water management (including drinking water production) is reflected in the existence of separate agencies, with relatively few linkages. Water management in the Netherlands is therefore formulated and implemented in at least two separate policy networks. Table 1 gives an overview of the actors involved in groundwater management and surface water management at the national, regional and local level in the Netherlands

The next section of this study discusses groundwater protection and drinking water supply. The third section will focus on the policy network involved in surface water management. Both sections attempt to describe and characterise these networks in terms of complexity, commitment and inter-relatedness, give some of their history and assess their influence on relevant policy formulation and implementation processes and outputs. The conclusions compare networks both in relation to the theoretical concepts described in this section and in terms of the developments in their scope, approach and openness.

The Network of Organisations Involved in Groundwater Management

The Water Supply Sector Grows into a Policy Community

Environmental interests have only recently gained attention within Dutch groundwater management. Initially, groundwater was managed only for reasons of supplying drinking water and for related reasons of health care. For that purpose the Ministry of Health Care introduced the Water Supply Act in 1957, not only to make demands on the quality of piped drinking water, but also to institutionalise the organisation of the drinking water sector. This act formalised an already existing practice in which provinces could allow or forbid the establishment of new, or the extension of existing water supply companies.

Until the turn of the nineteenth century, most of the water supply companies were local and private initiatives. At the start of the twentieth century local companies were established, often with the participation of municipalities. Municipalities and private sector companies were not willing to cooperate in all cases, however. To guarantee the efficiency of waterworks all over the country, several provinces developed their own regulations for water supply, a practice later strengthened by the Water Supply Act.

Since 1975, most of the provinces have made plans for a further concentration of water supply companies. The number of companies was reduced from 102 in 1980 to 49 in 1990. But there are plans for a further reduction to about 30. The provinces and the drinking water sector itself, as represented by the VEWIN (the Union of Dutch Water Supply Companies), agreed that the structure of the drinking water sector in its present form does not fit the demands for securing clean water supplies in the future. They think that water supply companies can maintain their role only if they have a strong organisation, which implies sufficient technological know-how and financial capacity.

The supply companies that use surface water for the production of drinking water have more problems with guaranteeing good quality than those who use groundwater. The latter consider themselves to be relatively invulnerable, and that is why there is a lot of resistance among them to reorganisation plans. Their arguments are that they have never had problems with the supply of water, that it has always been of good quality, that their charges are reasonable and that their customers are still satisfied [van der Knaap, 1987]. The smaller companies especially – mostly without the participation of provincial authorities – try to maintain their autonomy. But they face the burden of demonstrating that they can still operate in an efficient way. The VEWIN is very cautious in taking a stand [VEWIN, 1989]. Actually, it supports the idea of developing more professionalism and efficiency in the drinking water sector. But the VEWIN tries to avoid confrontation with the smaller companies, since it wants to be an organisation that represents the entire drinking water sector.

We conclude that up to the 1950s the water supply sector may be seen as a rather fragmented network. Though the companies shared a common purpose, they acted separately. Water supply companies arose as local initiatives and for a long time they wanted to maintain their autonomy.

Even today, the smaller ones are still fighting against provinces in order to revise reorganisation plans. After 1957, the sector became more integrated because of two developments. First, reorganisations and mergers between companies created larger units in the sector and an increasing interrelatedness. Second, the interrelatedness and commitments within the sector increased because of the strengthening of organisations that were developed to support the collectivity of companies, like the VEWIN and the KIWA (a research institute for technological innovations in the water supply sector). The need for increasing efficiency in the sector encouraged a strong policy community with a technocratic approach to the problems that the sector was encountering. These institutional changes were thus generated from inside the policy community, based upon a common perception of the way forward.

The Water Supply Sector Encounters the Agricultural Sector in an Issue Network

A serious threat to drinking water supply is the presence of nitrates in groundwater. More than 50 per cent of Dutch groundwaters (especially in the east and south) are likely to become unsuitable as a drinking water source in the near future. They are situated in areas with a sandy soil and many intensive cattle breeding farms (which tend to spread more manure on the soil than is necessary). Although there were indications that excess manure was being produced in some regions in the Netherlands as early as the mid-1960s, it took until the 1980s – because of a struggle between the Ministry for Environmental Protection and the Ministry for Agriculture – before the government seriously began to deal with the manure problem. The Soil Protection Act, which came into effect in 1987, is the first Dutch legislation that aims at integrated protection of the soil and the underground water. It is primarily aimed at preventing excessive manuring, by regulating manure spreading on agricultural land. The Act contains a number of standards to fix the amount of manure which is allowed to be spread. These standards apply nationally.

The Soil Protection Act also provides additional protection for areas in which groundwater needs to be withdrawn for the supply of drinking water. Provinces are authorised to establish so-called groundwater protection areas and to enforce more restrictive manuring standards in these areas. The Act further provides that farmers within the protected area should be financially compensated for the losses (disposal costs for the surplus of manure) they suffer as compared to farmers outside the protected area. Requests by farmers for compensation will be dealt with by the provinces, which can collect funds for this by means of a charge paid by those who abstract groundwater (mainly the water supply companies). The levy is related to the amount of water abstracted. Water supply companies can charge the consumers of drinking water through a levy. In effect, the consumers of drinking water pay for the production of a collective good.

The reason for the compensation provision was to prevent protests from farmers in groundwater protection areas who encounter more restrictions than farmers outside those areas. Legislators feared that the more restrictive standards in ground water protection areas could not be enforced without compensation. The political parties on the left opened the discussion on a motion to reject the provision because it would implicitly admit a right to pollute. The provision was felt to contradict the polluter-pays principle. In the event, the equality principle took precedence. The consumers of drinking water seem to have had no voice in this political debate. They pick up the costs of pollution caused by farmers, as they do in other countries such as Britain and Germany.

The drinking water sector thus encounters a very strongly organised opponent from outside the sector, as far as the farmers are concerned. Although the agricultural sector only forms five per cent of the active working population in the Netherlands, it has considerable influence in Dutch politics. Since 1954 the agricultural sector has been nationally organised through the Agricultural Board. The agricultural lobby is very effective, which is, for example, reflected by the fact that it is usually consulted at a very early stage of policy-making. The Agricultural Board also has regional boards in each province that consult with the regional or local authorities, particularly about planning and land use. The regional boards play an important role in determining the manure policy for groundwater protection areas. They negotiate with the provincial authorities and with the water companies involved concerning the manure restrictions applicable in these areas over the disposal of the resulting manure surpluses, and how farmers are compensated for the losses they incur.

While the agricultural sector is strongly developed both at the national level and the regional and local level, the drinking water sector for many years was not. Traditionally, water supply companies are organisations that are proud of their autonomy, as described above. The VEWIN always played a modest political role, and at best it was only active in emergencies. Normally, the VEWIN mainly has a service function with respect to the drinking water sector. At the end of the 1980s, the VEWIN became more politically involved and responsive, although the political discussion over the Soil Protection Act had already been concluded. Also, because of a presidential change (the presidency of VEWIN was taken over by the governor of the province of Zuid-Holland), the VEWIN succeeded in moving the negotiations concerning the compensation in groundwater protection areas from the regional level (where one negotiator from the Agricultural Board representing the whole of the country negotiated with each water supply company

separately) to the national level. Since then, the framework for regional negotiations is at the state level.

We conclude that external interests and pressure on the water supply sector
in some sense strengthened the sector as a policy community. It became
a more tightly organised policy community, especially in terms of an
increasing commitment between the members of the community. Meanwhile,
however, the issue of agricultural pollution of groundwater confronted the
water supply community with another strong policy community, the agricultural sector. This sector is very experienced and has a long tradition of
lobbying and negotiating strategies. The agricultural sector as a network is
not only characterised by a strong commitment, but also by a strong interrelatedness. This strong interrelatedness forced the water supply sector to
participate in negotiations on a more aggregated (regional and national) level.
In fact, it strengthened the interrelatedness within the water supply sector.

*Consultations between Water Supply Companies and Farmer Organisations
as the Most Promising Strategy*

The discussion of the compensation provision shows that the regulatory
strength (control capacity) of the authorities is very limited in the case of
groundwater quality management. Although they try to regulate by means of
ordinances and prohibitions, the enforcement of these rules is difficult.
Therefore, a system has been chosen in which private organisations (water
supply companies) have to participate in the enforcement of the rules.

The drinking water sector is beginning to define its role, however. The
director of VEWIN, T. Martijn, states that:

> This is a considerable change for organisations which traditionally are
> engaged in pumping and presenting the bill. However, if you want to
> create groundwater protection areas, then others may have reduced
> opportunities to use the soil in these areas. If that is the case, ground-
> water protection can only be achieved by offering compensation to
> them. This is not a new phenomenon: the drinking water sector already
> contributes a third (about 20 million guilders) to the costs of the Rhine
> Salt Treaty. In the third National Water Management Directive this is
> called 'paying for quality' [*Jehae and van Soest, 1990*].

The compensation provision formally implies that farmers can claim their
losses against the province, which in its turn may charge the water supply
companies that abstract groundwater in that area. Water supply companies
prefer to settle the matter in a friendly atmosphere. They also want to control
the disposal costs of manure surpluses and to avoid unnecessarily high bills.
For both reasons, several water supply companies have become involved in

the disposal of manure surpluses. Also, an increasing number of companies are trying to buy out farmers in areas that are most vulnerable.

Although methods exist for the purification of groundwater in the case of pollution with nitrates, the drinking water sector strongly opposes this option as a long-term solution. The Director of VEWIN explains:

> If the water supply companies started with complete purification tomorrow, the polluters could no longer be forced to change their behaviour. We want to use the drinking water, and with that the consumer, as a crowbar for improving the environment [*Velema* et al., *1989*].

The strategy of consultation, chosen by the water supply companies to deal with agricultural pollution of groundwater, had already been tested by the companies needing to use surface water for their drinking water production. Those companies are mainly located in the western part of the Netherlands. They have huge problems with maintaining good water quality. A great part of the pollution in these rivers stems from foreign industries, which means that they are dealing with extra-territorial actors. The director of VEWIN indicated that VEWIN only reluctantly develops new techniques for analysing water for the purpose of tracing polluters. However, the data can often be used to exert pressure on polluting industries. For example, the City of Rotterdam has chosen to talk to polluting industries, even when they are abroad, rather than take judicial action. Mr F. Feith, of the City of Rotterdam, stated:

> We try to handle the collected data very carefully, just because we want to get in conference with the discharging industries. Negative publicity will be applied only when the polluter is really unwilling. However, threatening publicity has proved to be a very strong instrument [*Jehae and van Soest, 1990*]

This demonstrates that the drinking water sector realises that it has its own role in water management, and that it can often be more effective than other authorities. This seems to be true for the case of point source pollution. But is this also true for non-point source pollution? Consultation with polluters was seen to be the only solution to the problem, since the national and provincial authorities were unable to guarantee strict enforcement of regulations. However, the case of groundwater protection areas also demonstrates that the possibility of using a consultation strategy heavily depends on the extent to which non-point source polluters are organised. The agricultural industry is very well organised and that may be one of the reasons why it became the first target group addressed by the Soil Protection Act in 1987.

In practice, the approach seems to have been based largely on self-regulation. Thus, when the General Secretary of the Ministry for Agriculture signed an agreement with the Agriculture Board concerning the use of pesticides, he argued that for reduction in the use of pesticides by farmers, consultations with the target group should be held.

One can prohibit the use of pesticides, but the need for them will not disappear. Such a measure has hardly any effect, because the farmers would use other, even illegal, means which could be worse if used on a large scale. In practice, the reason for using too much pesticides today is that farmers have too little knowledge about how to use them and use excessive quantities 'just in case'. A more effective strategy might be to increase expertise within the agricultural sector itself.

However, it remains very difficult for authorities and water supply companies to address the problem of non-point source polluters who are not very well organised. One of the reasons why it is difficult to trace polluters is that pollution reaches the groundwater only after a long period. Even if farmers stopped all manure spreading, it would still take 15 to 30 years before the current nitrate pollution is extracted with groundwater used for the production of drinking water.

Finally, we may formulate some conclusions about the way in which the water supply community dealt with external threats. On the one hand, water supply companies reacted in a very technocratic way by searching for technological innovations to satisfy the demand for drinking water of an acceptable quality. On the other hand, they tried to oppose the Soil Protection Act which ignored the polluter-pays principle. They did not succeed in their opposition, although they were strongly supported by environmental groups. The water supply sector and the environmental groups have in common the fact that they support the polluter-pays principle. In this sense, the strong relations between the water supply sector and environmental groups can be conceived as the existence of a broader policy community. However, the interrelatedness in this community is weak: no strong or intensive interactions exist between both sets of actors. In the end, the polluter-pays principle was not applied, due to a successful lobby by the agricultural sector and the lack of political organisation and influence of drinking water consumers. The most feasible political outcome appeared to be to saddle customers with the costs of pollution prevention.

Another indication of the existence of interests that are common to the water supply sector and environmental groups is that they both stress the importance of strict rule enforcement. However, water supply companies do realise that it is very difficult to control the spreading of manure. The control capacity of the regulatory agencies (provinces) is limited with respect to this. That is why the water supply sector expects better results through direct negotiations with farmers' organisations. After the settlement of the compensation provision in the Soil Protection Act, consultation with target groups was left as the most promising strategy in the issue network in which the water supply sector and the agricultural sector both participate.

The Network of Organisations Involved in Surface Water Management

In this section we will focus on management of surface waters in the Netherlands. As described earlier, there are two aspects to this matter: quantity and quality. We shall focus mainly on the quality network in this section, with certain exceptions. However, since the two networks for water quality and quantity overlap, we also describe much of the quantity network.

First we describe the authorities in the surface water quality network. The governmental organisations in the network have a different relationship with the outside world when managing their two main tasks; collective wastewater treatment and reducing industrial emissions. Then we deal with some aspects of these 'extended networks'. All sections focus on the consequences of institutional and other network characteristics on interorganisational processes.

Water Quality Management Authorities

In 1970 the Pollution of Surface Waters Act (acronym in Dutch: WVO) came into force. The law was proposed in 1964 after serious deterioration of surface water quality in large parts of the Netherlands had emerged and after widespread recognition of the problem. However, the Act was not passed until 1969. It took so long because all kinds of government authorities lobbied to become the principal authority in this field: central government agencies, provinces, water boards and municipalities.

The law introduced the first general water quality regulations applicable to all surface waters in the Netherlands. The law distinguishes between national surface waters that are managed by the national government and other waters that are under the responsibility of other sub-national level governments. The national waters include the main rivers, the Waddensea and the North Sea. The water quality task of the national government consists of giving management directives, planning water management, granting permits to dischargers into state waters (including the discharges of effluent from treatment plants of adjacent water boards), collecting charges from the same category of dischargers, measuring surface water quality and subsidising abatement measures, typically the building of treatment plants by waterboards. The authorities responsible for regional waters have the same function, with the exception of subsidies, but with the important addition of building and operating water treatment plants [CUWVO, 1990].

The law assigns the responsibility for the regional waters to the provinces. However, the provinces are authorised to delegate these tasks to water boards or municipalities. This resulted in a delegation of the task by nine provinces to water boards. In 1993, however, one of the three remaining provinces delegated its task to a newly established water board and the other two are expected to follow soon. Nearly all treatment plants are managed by these provinces and water boards. Municipal treatment plants hardly exist and are regarded as an anachronism. The prime responsibility of municipalities in water quality management is the management of sewage systems, and to some extent, as we shall show later, pollution control of discharges into their sewage systems.

This complex configuration was a compromise in a long-running battle between provinces, water boards and municipalities over the issue. They were all eager to undertake this work. Not only the delegation arrangements, but also the relations between provinces and waterboards were subsequently influenced by the legal changes. Provinces have general tasks in supervising some of the policies of municipalities and water boards. The way they supervise the water policies of the water boards varies widely. In cases where the delegation was forced by the water boards rather than granted willingly by the provincial water agency, supervision is much more intense.

Since 1970, several extensive debates on the future of the Dutch water board system have taken place, in which not only the desirability of the water quality delegation was questioned, but also the existence of the water boards themselves. Organisations with wide powers, such as provinces and the Department for the Environment, challenged the assignment of these tasks to separate single-issue agencies, such as water boards. These discussions did lead to an extensive modernisation effort by the water boards, but not to a real weakening of their position. At the outset, it was a closed network of people with an interest in water quantity management. The water boards were considered a separate world, although they were formally government organisations. Also the scale on which they operated was very local. Because of their new tasks, water boards are now operating on a larger scale; many of them have merged. This means that water boards are now more like government organisations than previously. To a large extent, professionalisation has occurred, and more and more administrative and highly educated employees now work for water boards.

Also new interests are now represented in the councils of the water boards. These include renters of agricultural property, inhabitants of the area in which the water boards operate, domestic polluters, and industrial polluters. This, combined with a new policy planning structure, has led to a situation where water boards now have to consult and coordinate with others more intensively than previously. As the former chair of the Union of Waterboards put it:

> The water board organisation that existed not so long ago had, although
> it consisted of government organisations, few contacts with other
> administrative organisations. The water boards had their own problems,
> which created a strongly closed character. The others were not very
> interested ... it was considered to be the business of a limited group of
> interested parties ... This has changed as a result of the developments
> that the water boards have gone through. The water boards no longer
> stand alone, but are part of the Dutch administrative system, with all
> due consequences [*Kienhuis, 1987: 423–424*].

In addition to the challenge from other governmental organisations claiming parts of their tasks, the water boards were also forced to integrate in the
system and 'open up' to some extent. This was because of the features of
these new tasks themselves, demanding much more cooperation with others,
than had been the case with the older engineering tasks.

These changes did not decrease the overall importance of the 'Union of
Waterboards'. This is a private association which unites all Dutch water
boards in defence of their common interests and coordinates their policies on
a voluntary basis. The way in which the Dutch surface water management is
organised calls for much coordination. The association of water boards plays
an important role in this respect, without being dominant. A common sense
of togetherness is felt in the entire water management world against the threat
of a takeover of water quality responsibilities by the Ministry of Environmental Affairs. This is a threat to the water-oriented national level authorities
and agencies, to the provinces, to water boards, and even to environmental
departments at the provinces (and to public works departments of the same
provinces). There is very little animosity between water quality managers at
the national and the water board levels. A further binding mechanism is
cultural coordination, provided by a common education and training system.
These factors explain why there are coordination mechanisms with a high
degree of legitimacy in the eyes of individual water boards, which are consensus oriented, while having a broad array of participants. An example is the
Commission on the Implementation on the Pollution of Surface Waters Act
(CUWVO: see below).

Our conclusion is that the institutional and administrative structure of
surface water management in the Netherlands is very complex, but that
within the group of agencies directly involved there exist a common belief
system and a substantial degree of commitment and interrelatedness. This
concerns only the inner core of the administrative actors, however. To
characterise the broader network we should see it in action. Those actions
imply contacts with people and organisations outside the inner water community. The water community meets different groups of organisations under

different circumstances when carrying out its two main tasks: wastewater treatment and reducing industrial emissions. These fields will be discussed in separate sections below.

The Building of Wastewater Treatment Works

In this part of our text we focus on the network activity of building Wastewater Treatment Works (WTWs). The building process includes several stages, such as financing the project, designing the plant, siting and obtaining permits for the plant, and actual construction. Because construction and design of plants is not problematic administratively, this section focuses on financing, siting, and licensing of the plant, in that order. For analysis of the processes of acquiring the site, the licence and the planning permission, we conducted several interviews with representatives of municipalities, water boards and others.

One of the most distinctive features of Dutch water quality policy is the effluent charge which is used to finance nearly 100 per cent of expenditures, including the construction and operation of WTWs [Brown and Bressers, 1986]. The charge follows the rule that the polluter pays. The money raised by the charge has been used to build many WTWs.

In the Netherlands, WTW construction is typically a water board task. In some cases, national waters benefit from WTW construction, after which a subsidy from the Public Works Agency is available, but usually the water board pays all costs from the charge. For the water board, the charge system ensures that the costs of the treatment plant do not have to compete with other financial demands. On the other hand, those who pay are represented in the council of the water board. These representatives, although committed to the policy of their board, also consider it their task to avoid rapid increases in charges. Water board employees report that, because of the direct representation of groups with an interest who ultimately have to pay for the improvements, the water boards cannot freely tax and spend. This negative feedback mechanism is much weaker, though, than the constraints provided by the need to choose between a WTW and, for instance, a new leisure pool. Dutch practice has shown that municipalities invest too little in their sewage systems, and instead invest in visible projects like luxury swimming pools.

Two other aspects of WTW construction are the siting and the permitting procedures. Work by Bressers [1992: 160–161] indicates that these are the most problematic parts of WTW construction in the Netherlands in terms of delay involved. There are two aspects to siting: one is the actual acquisition of a site, and the other is the changing of the zoning ordinance that is necessary in most cases. The process of obtaining permits involves four separate permit procedures in the Netherlands. Let us start with the site.

Land-use regulations in the Netherlands are such that municipalities have to make land-use regulations for the non-urban areas. In most municipal zoning ordinances, the non-urban area is zoned as agricultural land, or as an industrial zone. WTWs are incompatible with almost any other use, except for industrial and public utilities or literally 'WTW'. WTWs are usually not built in industrial zones for several reasons. What this means is that the proposed site is usually in an agricultural zone, and that the existing zoning ordinance has to be amended in most cases. The procedure for amendment is the same as the procedure for an original zoning ordinance. In fact, the amendment is considered to be a zoning ordinance itself. The procedure for the enactment of a zoning ordinance by municipalities is generally considered to be very difficult and time-consuming. The planning regulations still reflect the post-1960s 'participation in planning' fashion, although several amendments were made in the 1980s. The procedures involve consultation with organisations, firms, and individuals. It also involves public hearings, and consultation periods for the public. Once the city council has taken a final decision on the ordinance, the ordinance has to be approved by the province. People who objected at the city council stage can also object at this earlier stage. The province also hears the provincial planning commission, which has representatives of several governments, agencies, and interest groups as its members. After this, people with objections can file them with the minister of planning, and after that with the highest administrative court. The procedure, if followed all the way, may take five years or more.

Acquisition of the land is usually less problematic. The sound financial position of water boards usually enables them to meet the demands of landowners (costs of land acquisition are small as compared to the costs of WTW construction). Water boards usually ask a member of their council who lives in the neighbourhood of the proposed site to negotiate with the landowner. Many council members are farmers themselves, so they know the value of the property, and they can communicate with the landowners very effectively. This mechanism also plays a role in objections or appeals against zoning ordinances and permits. A member of the council goes and talks with the objectors or plaintiffs. In some cases water boards hire a negotiator who assesses the value of the land, and does the negotiating; the water board informs the appraiser of its own price limits.

The process of acquiring a licence involves several procedures. Depending on the type of water that the WTW will be discharging into (national or regional) waters, a water quality manager will have either to issue a discharge permit to the WTW itself or apply for a permit with the Public Works Agency. Also, a building permit has to be issued by municipalities, a nuisance permit is required (a nuisance permit states limits to noise and odour levels at certain reference points), and a groundwater abstraction permit has to be issued by the province.

In most procedures the network of participants is potentially wide. This is a consequence of the philosophy of the Dutch government in the 1970s, which favoured public participation. In practice we found that the number of third parties actually participating in the process is small, and is largely determined by personal interests. Interestingly, our data indicated that the length of the licensing and siting processes for WTWs was determined not so much by citizen participation as by the need to gather information and to communicate this information to the agencies granting the permissions, and by the lack of (skilled) personnel at the agencies [*See Huitema, 1993*]. The Dutch government is currently revising many of these procedures, based on the assumption that citizen participation is too great a burden.

It appears that there is considerable interaction between the water boards and municipalities. Water boards and municipalities interact when zoning ordinances are drafted, and on the issue of the sewage system that is operated by the cities. These interactions may have a high frequency, but their goal is usually only consultation. One water board went so far as to meet the municipalities on a regular basis in order to keep all of them informed of each others' plans. The relation between municipalities and water boards has been described by several interviewees as one of mutual dependence; water boards need municipalities for the siting of their WTWs (and for several permits); but municipalities, which have become increasingly environmentally conscious, have to have their wastewater treated, and in most cases this is exclusively a task of water boards. On the other hand, municipalities often oppose concrete suggestions for sites because they want to protect neighbouring citizens from nuisance or want to use the site or its immediate surroundings for housing development.

There is a difference between financing, on the one hand, and granting the different permissions, on the other. The financing of WTW construction is an issue that is determined by the water authorities themselves, and requires little external interaction, except when subsidies from the Public Works Agency can be obtained. Thus it is an example of integrated policy-making. The other two issues, licensing and siting, require coordination with other actors. On the other hand, issuing a permit and finding a site are by definition temporary and local issues. The actors involved are geographically confined and once the licence has been issued, and a site has been found for a WTW, the interactions cease. It is therefore debatable whether we can speak of a network that is involved in allowing WTWs to go ahead, or whether we should analyse each building process as a separate *ad hoc* network. Nevertheless, in so far as these networks share common characteristics, we can speak about the treatment plant building networks in general.

Licensing and siting are not especially complex as tasks, yet the distribution of responsibilities and stakes among the participants involved is often restricted to a specific case, and cannot be regarded as interrelated in general. The degree of commitment, both general (sympathy with each others' main objectives) and specific (commitment to the job), varies considerably from case to case. On this basis, most of these *ad hoc* networks can be labelled as issue networks rather than policy communities.

Reducing Industrial Wastewater Emissions

One of the main threats to surface water quality is the discharge of pollutants in industrial wastewater. We have already shown that for the main rivers, the coastal seas and the main waterways, the national government has the responsibility for water quality policies and their implementation. All other waters are under the responsibility of regional water managers (the provinces or the water boards to which most provinces delegated their tasks). It is obvious that in the implementation process these organisations are not alone. There is a web of evolving interactions, which is often – and rightly – seen as the essence of the process. This section describes some aspects of these relationships.

In the case of state waters, the national government is the responsible actor. This responsibility is mandated to the Public Works Agency. This agency has a decentralised structure. It consists of a central directorate, an important research institution (RIZA), some service departments and regional directorates. They coordinate in an informal working group called FWVO, although this coordination is regarded as unsatisfactory [*Algemene Rekenkamer, 1987: 11*]. The existence of regional directorates means that the regional water authorities of a province often interact with a sub-agency of the Public Works Agency covering the same territory as the province.

When granting and enforcing permits the Public Works Agency and its sub-agencies deal with the industries that discharge into their waters, as do the required water boards. There are some differences, however. One difference is that generally the direct dischargers into state waters are much larger companies than the dischargers into regional waters. Many of the country's largest industries are direct dischargers into state waters, especially the river Rhine and its various estuaries. The second difference is that the sub-agencies lose the responsibility for indirect dischargers (into sewage systems that discharge into state waters) once a treatment plant has been built. That is because only the regional boards are entitled to build sewage treatment plants. Consequently these regional water boards themselves become dischargers into state waters with the effluent of their treatment plants, and are subject to permit granting from the Public Works Agency. Another consequence is that the permitting of some categories of indirect discharge becomes the responsibility of the regional water boards instead of the Public Works Agency.

This complex constellation of actors calls for strong coordination. By 1973 the Committee on the Implementation of the Pollution of Surface Waters Act (in Dutch: CUWVO) was established by the Minister of Traffic and Public Works, which has the responsibility for water policies and whose ministry includes the Public Works Agency (RWS). This committee developed into 'the common consultation organ of all parties involved in water quality management' [CUWVO, 1990]. The CUWVO currently has three functions: coordination, guiding research and giving advice on subjects such as administrative and judicial matters, implementation aspects of collecting effluent charges, the measurement of water quality and emission standards. It no longer confines itself to the water quality aspects which are regulated by the WVO. Other topics such as river beds and the finance of water quality management, unrelated to abstraction point sources, are now viewed as issues the CUWVO may address.

The CUWVO has three layers. These are the committee itself, its working groups and their subgroups. The committee consists of two members each for the Union of Water Boards, the Public Works Agency and the Interprovincial Consultation (the association of Dutch provinces), and one member each for the Association of Dutch Municipalities and the Ministry for Environmental Protection.

From a policy network point of view Working Group VI and its subgroups are the most interesting. They consist not only of governmental organisations but also of representatives of the target groups: representatives of branches of industry and chambers of commerce. The working group has prepared by far the largest number of recommendations. They are named reports, but are referred to by many water quality members and others as policies, even in written documents [Dommel, 1992: 49] or guidelines [Algemene Reken-kamer, 1987: 16], and even sometimes by the CUWVO itself [CUWVO, 1992: 2]. Working Group VI is one of the most important sources of new emission-oriented water quality policies. This means that Group VI is the main platform for the development of new water quality policy. Due to its leading position it has been thought sensible to refer issues as general as enforcement of permits to Group VI. Working Group VI consists not only of representatives of governmental organisations, but also of representatives of trade associations. In the subgroups, the representatives of the relevant governmental organisations and representatives of firms of branch organisations of the industry involved, meet and negotiate emission standard-guidelines, schedules for compliance, and so on. The secretary general of the CUWVO, Eric Kraaij, stated in an interview with us that he did not want to hide the fact that the different interests involved mean that often firm negotiations are inevitable. But with a good dose of common sense it is often possible to come to an agreement. In practice, problems are solved rather effectively. When it proves to be impossible to reach full agreement in the subgroup, the issue is taken to the working group level, wherein representatives of industries play a part. In the working group the remaining questions are solved 99 per cent of the time.

This decision-making style of the working group resembles much of the target group consultation that the Ministry for Environmental Protection organised in implementing the National Environmental Policy Plan for 1989/ 1990. The Secretary General of the CUWVO stated that he often comments to public officials of Environmental Protection, who have just discovered this strategy, as follows: 'Very good that you have started to extend to all other sectors of the environment the approach we have been using for a long time in the water sector. It works!'.

That it works is certainly true in terms of its effects on the policies of provinces and water boards. The reports are accepted by the water quality managers and the latter hardly ever deviate from them [*Strikker, 1988: 40, 48–49*]. Firms of the same branch all over the country generally face the same demands, regardless of the water quality manager involved. Furthermore it is difficult for these firms to reject those demands as unreasonable, simply because their representatives in the subgroup agreed to them. According to the CUWVO Secretary General, there is even a growing case law on this matter. Judges point to the reports in their verdicts. The firm has to have a really strong case before being allowed dispensation. On the other hand, it is more difficult for water quality managers to demand more than the CUWVO agreement. They too will win the case in court only if it is a very convincing one.

In practice, the CUWVO provides a very important arena for the Dutch surface water quality network in which almost all network organisations participate in consensus building. The consensus building orientation in the formulation of policies reflects a pre-existing orientation in daily implementation. An important background for this is the Dutch effluent charge system (see for example Brown and Bressers [*1986*]). Here, we limit ourselves to some implications of the charge system for interorganisational relationships. A very important aspect of the charge system is that it directs the nature of the interactions into a much more constructive form of consultation because it lets pollution prevention pay. Furthermore, it provided the water boards with an *entrée* to the firms, even when permit-granting responsibilities did not provide that in the numerous cases of firms discharging to a municipal sewage system.

The position of indirect dischargers leads us to the relationship between water managers (both regional and national) and municipalities. The water manager originally only had an indirect relationship with the industries that discharge into a sewage system. They granted permits to the municipalities who discharge their sewage into the surface water and had, of course, the opportunity to formulate conditions. But it was unclear how far they could go in their requirements.

This was not so much a problem in relation to the oxygen-demanding pollutants. From early on it was decided that the effluent charge, which has this type of pollution as its main basis, could be levied directly by the water managers in the firms (and households). That not only implied that these firms had a strong incentive to decrease their discharge of organic pollutants, but also that water board officials had an *entrée* into those companies with indirect discharges. They could legitimately discuss with these firms the organic pollution of their wastewater and the possibilities of decreasing it. Because this also offered firms the possibility of reducing their charges (through reducing their discharges), this facilitated the consultation process. On that basis, water board officials also often tried to discuss pollution from heavy metals and other pollutants. Indeed, they often claimed that certain discharges would not be allowed in the near future. Legally they had no basis for such statements. The water boards also introduced an effluent charge on heavy metals on the basis of the extra costs of operating treatment plants. Heavy metals polluted the remaining sludge of the plants which often has to be treated as chemical waste instead of being sold as fertiliser. Although these activities, including the assessment of the charge, did succeed in approximately halving the heavy metal content of industrial wastewater, the situation was still considered unsatisfactory.

For this reason the Pollution of Surface Waters Act was changed in 1981 in order to give the water managers direct responsibility over a number of substances or categories of firms that were to be listed in a governmental decree. This was again some sort of victory over the municipalities for the water boards which had always wanted that responsibility. Apart from the difficulties mentioned above, international agreements and treaties, for instance on grey list and black list substances, made such a change inevitable. For practical reasons it was decided to list not substances, but categories of firms, as the new responsibility of the regional water boards. The CUWVO played an important role in selecting the branches of industry that were to be subject to the new regulations.

Strikker [*1988*] concluded that some confusion remained regarding the selection of firms that should be included in the categories. Water boards often tried to interpret the categories as broadly as possible in order to expand their jurisdiction. Stikker also found that while for black list substances zero discharges were the official goal, in practice this was translated into 'best available means' – which more often than not was further eroded into 'best practicable means'. One has to remember that it was originally a deliberate choice not to use the latter criterion for black list substances.

The negotiation-oriented approach of the water managers should not be seen as a cultural phenomenon only, but also as a rational use of scarce powers [Bressers, 1992: 173–174]. Respondents of Strikker [1988] claimed that a stricter interpretation would not lead to a better environment, but only to more violations of requirements. Such a claim rests on a judgement of the possibilities of enforcing the regulations. While the opportunity for enforcement by the water manager was greatly improved by the shift in responsibilities from municipalities to water managers, in practice they are still weak. This is due to the dependence on other actors such as judges and public prosecutors – a feature that remained largely intact.

In order to reduce these dependencies, policy documents of water managers state that they prefer to use the option of administrative sanctions wherever possible instead of opting for penal sanctions, which are also possible under the law [Groningen, 1990]. In practice they try to avoid imposing sanctions altogether. Whenever they can they try to reach the goal of compliance by issuing exhortations or, as a respondent in the Bressers 1983 study put it, by 'talking, talking, talking'. Illustrative of this is the recent CUWVO report [1992] on enforcement. This report is a sort of instruction guide organised around a flow chart. Starting with an observed offence, few paths lead to actual sanctions. The text contains many warnings about the difficulties that occur when following these paths. This approach can lead to a decision to issue only a warning, to legalise or even to tolerate illegal action. In essence, the emphasis is on bargaining, not on compulsion.

In terms of the characteristics of this broader network in action we conclude that its complexity has not led to fragmentation. Although the degree of commitment is limited, due to the natural tension between the polluters and the surface water quality managers, there is a rather high degree of interrelatedness. The polluters are represented on the board of the water authority, the actors involved participate in well-developed negotiation platforms, and the implementation process involves regular contacts between authorities and industries, partly guaranteed by the existence of the effluent charge system.

Conclusions

In this study we have considered the role of policy networks in Dutch water policy. In the Netherlands two rather separate networks of water institutions can be identified: one for soil protection and the provision of drinking water (the groundwater network); and one for the treatment and discharge of wastewater (the surface water network). Before we compare these networks in terms of the concepts presented at the outset, we shall use this concluding section to compare the developments in the scope, the general approach and the openness of both networks.

Scope

The surface water network originated from the need for protection against flooding and the need to create an adequate system of waterways for draining. Later (since 1970) the tasks of the existing organisations (water boards) were extended to surface water quality management, because they already had knowledge of surface water. In other words, the network had to broaden its scope to include also the quality of the input of water into surface water systems, and – in order to do that properly – to include also aspects of the consumption of drinking water (to affect the amount and composition of polluted wastewater).

The groundwater network started with the production and supply of drinking water by water supply companies. These companies were increasingly confronted with the limitations of the amount of groundwater that can be abstracted without encountering other interest groups. Therefore they became involved in the protection of the quality of groundwater. The drinking water companies also had to broaden their scope to include several aspects of soil pollution. It is interesting to see that for both networks, environmental quality issues were the main factors causing the extension of the scope of the network.

Approach

The networks are also similar in their dominant engineering approach to water problems. The surface water network started with the establishment of a body that could undertake the building activities necessary for the protection against flooding and the development of waterways. There was no need for a behavioural change of target groups at that time. However, the task of water boards extended to the management of water quality. It was the Pollution of Surface Waters Act that created the possibility of stimulating polluters to meet the policy standards through behavioural changes by means of permit giving. It took some time before the water boards used this policy option with the same energy as they exerted on the 'technological' approach. As far as industries as target groups are concerned, the water boards are making more and more efforts to legitimise their goals through consultations with branch organisations.

A similar development can be seen in groundwater management. Initially, water supply companies tried to satisfy the need for drinking water through technical measures. Later on, however, they encountered the limits of growth because of other interests involved (especially agriculture). The agricultural pollution of groundwater through fertilisers and pesticides became a major concern. In the end, it would be possible to provide enough drinking water only through expensive technical measures such as purification. To protect the quality of groundwater for drinking water production, financial compensation for farmers and consultation with farmers are the main policy instruments. This turned out to be a considerable change for organisations which traditionally were engaged in pumping and presenting the bill.

Openness

The overall view in both networks today is that a greater openness can be perceived: the traditional organisations are incorporating or developing more expertise in consultation with other interest groups on which they depend. Although initially the dominant engineering approach was the main source of stability in both networks, instability arose because of the confrontation with interests of environmental protection and agricultural production. This caused a shift towards an approach in water management that is more directed at influencing the behaviour of other interest groups involved.

Also, a tendency can be perceived towards an aggregation of interests on a more central (national) level. In the surface water network, the Union of Water Boards tried mediation with representatives of industries within the national Commission on the Implementation of the Pollution of Surface Waters Act. In the groundwater network the Union of Dutch Water Supply Companies tries to mediate with the Agricultural Board which is the main national representative of farmers in the Netherlands.

Besides the developments described, two other factors are accelerating the opening up of both networks. One factor is the initiative of the national authority – begun in 1985 – to enforce integration in Dutch water policy. Water institutions are pressed to consider the relationship of their activities with other sectors of water management and even with other policy sectors (especially environmental protection, nature conservation and urban and rural planning). Another factor is the general tendency – stimulated by provincial authorities – to increase the efficiency of water boards and water supply companies. In both networks, mergers and reorganisations are very common.

Commitment and Interrelatedness

The water policy networks described above have complexity in common. Nevertheless the inner cores of the networks combine a high degree of commitment with a high degree of interrelatedness. In the surface water policy community this tightness has a long history. In the case of the drinking water sector the character of the policy community developed more recently. However, these linked communities encounter other interests whenever they start to act. The networks described incorporate these other interests in very different ways.

The surface water network is fragmented into rather separate issue networks when building treatment plants. The complex division of responsibilities is reflected in often difficult administrative processes. Though the building of treatment plants as such is a more or less straightforward task, these processes can take many years. Perhaps this kind of task would benefit from a simpler network structure, as evidence from the privatised facilities in the US seems to indicate [*Heilman and Johnson, 1992*].

In the case of the efforts to decrease industrial wastewater pollution the surface water network managed to remain intact to a greater degree. The centrifugal influence of complexity is counteracted by all sorts of centripetal mechanisms that foster regular interaction and consensus building. The case shows that complexity does not always lead to fragmentation: a type of network emerged that had weak commitment and strong interrelatedness. The high degree of interrelatedness in the policy formulation stage leads to a relatively smooth implementation process, actually showing the expected emphasis on responsibility and the use of negotiated instruments, rather than relying on a strict judicial enforcement of regulations. Viewed against the background of the enormous variety and complexity of the changes in industrial production processes involved – when decreasing the pollution of industrial wastewater with a variety of substances – and also compared to the environmental policy sectors of air pollution and waste prevention, the surface water sector produced very positive outcomes.

In these observations we see support for our view that the integration *versus* fragmentation dimension should not be based on mere complexity variables; and support also for the view of Goggin *et al.*, that complex tasks may be better off with complex network structures.

The drinking water network presents yet another situation. Its core became integrated more recently and developed into an even tighter community under outside pressure. The background to this is that the participants in their activities were not only confronted with various outside actors, but with another, strong and long established policy community: the agricultural network. Though the various negotiation processes involved can be viewed as *ad hoc* issue networks, the opponents (the farmers) were supported by their general network relationships. This forced the drinking water companies to seek similar support in their own community, thus strengthening their union, even though this union supports strong reforms in the sector's structure. A coalition with the environmental groups is based more on commitment than on interrelatedness and is still too weak to be considered as a part of the 'network' in the proper sense of the term.

REFERENCES

Algemene Rekenkamer (1987), *Milieubeleid oppervlaktewateren* (Environmental Policy on Surface Waters), The Hague: Tweede Kamer der Staten Generaal (Second Chamber of Parliament), vergaderjaar 1987–1988, No. 20020.

Brauw, W. M. de, and H. J. M. Naaijkens (1989), *Grondwaterbeheer* (Groundwater Management), Zwolle.

Breejen, E. K den (1991), 'Een Bedrijfstak in de Zorgen; het Tienjarenplan van de VEWIN', *Milieu en recht* (Environment and Law), No. 3, pp. 142–50.

Bressers, Hans T. A. (1993), 'Beleidsnetwerken en instrumentenkeuze' (Policy Networks and the Choice of Instruments), *Beleidswetenschap,* Vol 7, No. 4.

Bressers, Hans T. A. (1992), 'The Cleaning-up Period in Dutch Water Quality Management: Policy Instruments Assessed', in Hans T. A. Bressers and Laurence J. O'Toole (eds) *International Comparative Policy Research* (Enschede: University of Twente Press), pp.155–74.

Bressers, Hans T. A., and Mac Honigh (1986), 'A Comparative Approach to the Explanation of Policy Effects', *International Social Science Journal*, Vol 38, No. 2, pp.267–88.

Bressers, Hans T. A., and Pieter Jan Klok (1988), 'Fundamentals for a Theory of Policy Instruments', *International Journal of Social Economics*, Vol 15, Nos. 3/4, pp.22–41.

Bressers, Hans T. A., and Stefan M. M. Kuks (1992), *'The Agricultural Policy-network and Environmental Policy'*, paper presented at the European Group of Public Administration Conference 1992, Pisa, 48 pp.

Bressers, Hans Th. A., and Laurence J. O'Toole, Jr. (eds.) (1992), *International Comparative Policy Research*, Enschede: University of Twente Press.

Brown Jr., Gardner, and Hans Bressers (1986), *Evidence Supporting Effluent Charges*, US National Science Foundation Report.

CUWVO (1990), *Functie, werkwijze, en samenstelling* (Function, Operation, and Composition), The Hague: CUWVO.

CUWVO (1992), *Handhaven is doen* (Enforcement is Action), The Hague: CUWVO.

Dietz, Thomas, and Robert W. Ryecroft (1987), *The Risk Professional,* New York: Russell Sage Foundation.

Edwards, George C. (1980), *Implementing Public Policy,* Washington: Congressional Quarterly Press.

Glasbergen, P., M. C. Groenenberg, and F. A. Roorda (1989), *Naar een Strategisch Grondvaferbeheer* (Towards a Strategic Groundwater Management), Den Haag: Vuga.

Goggin, Malcolm L., Ann O'M. Bowman, James P. Lester and Laurence J. O'Toole, Jr. (1990a), 'Studying the Dynamics of Public Policy Implementation: A Third Generation Approach', Palumbo D.J. and D.J. Calista (eds), *Implementation and the Policy Process: Opening up the Black Box* (New York: Greenwood Press), pp.181–98.

Goggin, Malcom L., Ann O'M. Bowman, James P. Lester and Laurence J.O'Toole, Jr. (1990b), *Implementation Theory and Practice: Toward a Third Generation,* Glenview: Scott, Foresman and Company.

Groningen, Province of (1990), *Draaiboek Handhaving Milieurecht voor de Provincie Groningen* (Guidelines for the Enforcement of Environmental Policies in the Province of Groningen), Groningen.

Heide, O. van der, 'De Wetgeving met Betrekking tot Waterschappen', *Tijdschrift voor Openbaar Bestuur* (Journal of Public Administration), Vol 13, No. 20, pp.436–43.

Heilman, John G., and Gerald W. Johnson (1992), *The Politics and Economics of Privatization,* Tuscaloosa: University of Alabama Press.

Huitema, Dave (1993), *Any Objections? Permitting and Siting of Wasterwater Treatment Works in the Netherlands and Alabama,* Enschede: Masters Thesis, University of Twente.

Jehae, Michael, and Jan Paul van Soest (1990), 'Stratego in Waterland; Bestuurlijke Mogelijkheden voor Drinkwaterbeleid Berperkt', *Nieuwe Beta* (New Beta), No. 4, pp. 8–9.

Jordan, A. Grant (1981), 'Iron Triangles, Woolly Corporatism and Elastic Nets: Images of the

Policy Process', *Journal of Public Policy*, Vol 1, No 1, pp.95– 123.

Jordan, Grant, and Klaus Schubert (1992), 'A Preliminary Ordering of Policy Network Labels, *Policy Sciences*, pp. 7–27.

Kenis, Patrick, and Volker Schneider (1991), 'Policy Networks and Policy Analysis: Scrutinising a New Analytical Toolbox', Marin B., and R Mayntz (eds), *Policy Networks: Empirical Evidence and Theoretical Considerations*, Frankfurt/Boulder: Campus Verlag/Westview Press, pp. 25–59.

Kienhuis, J. H M., 'Het Waterschap in Perspectief', *Tijdschrift voor Openbaar Bestuur* (Journal of Public Administration), Vol. 13, No. 20, pp.416–23.

Kingdon, John W. (1984), *Agendas, Alternatives, and Public Policies*, Boston: Little Brown.

Knaap, J.W.M. van der (1987), Provinciale Invloed Boven Water; Ervaringen met de Water-leidingwet in de Provincies Utrecllt, *Bestuur* (Administration), Nr 10, pp 300–05.

Kuks, S. M. M. (1988), *Mestbeleid in Grondwaterbeschermingsgebied* (Manure Policy in Groundwater Protection Areas), Enschede.

Luhmann, N. (1984), *Soziale Systeme: Grundriss Einer Allgemeinen Theorie*, Frankfurt am Main.

Majone, Giandomenico (1989), Evidence, Argument and Persuasion in the Policy Process, New Haven: Yale University Press.

Marin, Bemd, and Renate Mayntz (eds) (1991), *Policy Networks: Empirical Evidence and Theoretical Considerations*, Frankfurt/Boulder: Campus Verlag/Westview Press.

Mazmanian, Daniel A., and Paul A. Sabatier (1989), *Implementation and Public Policy*, Lanham, MD: University Press of America.

Meijden, D. van der (1988), 'De Bescherming van het Grondwater', *Milieu en recht* (Environment and Law), No. 2, pp.46–58.

Michaels, Sarah (1992), 'Issue Networks and Activism', *Policy Studies Review*, Vol 11, Nos. 3/4, pp.241–258.

Palumbo, Dennis J., and Donald J. Calista (eds) (1990), *Implementation and the Policy Process: Opening up the Black Box*, New York: Greenwood Press.

Rhodes, R A. W. and David Marsh (1992), 'New Directions in the Study of Policy Networks', *Policy Sciences*, pp .181–205.

Sabatier, Paul A., and Daniel A. Mazmanian (1981), 'The Implementation of Public Policy: A Framework for Analysis', in Mazmanian D.A. and P. A. Sabatier (eds), *Effective Policy Implementation*, Lexington: Heath and Company, pp.3–35.

Strikker, M. (1988), *Evaluatie van het Beleid met Betrekking tot Lozingen op Rioleringen Afkomstig van Bedrijven* (Evaluation of Policies on Industrial Discharges into Sewage Systems), Enschede: Master Thesis, University of Twente.

Verburg, J. J. I., 'Waterbeheer 2000; Ontwikkelingen en Verwachtingen met Betrekking tot Organisatie en Instrumentarium', *Tijdschrift voor Openbaar bestuur* (Journal of Public Administration), Vol 16, No. 2, pp.536–41.

Velema, W., F. Boer, T. Verheul (1989), 'Aardappel; en Koken in Spa Blauw', *Intermediaire* (Intermedia), 24 February.

VEWIN, (1989), *Hoofdrapport Tienjarenplan 1989* (Main Report on the Ten Year Plan), Rijswijk: VEWIN.

VEWIN (1991), *De openbare watervoorziening in feiten en cijfers* (Public Water Supply in Facts and Figures), Rijswijk: VEWIN.

Waarden, Frans van (1992), 'Dimensions and Types of Policy Networks', *Policy Sciences*, pp.29– 52.

Waterschap de Dommel (1992), *Voorontwerp Waterbeheersplan Maas- en Diezepolders* (Pre-design Surface Water Plan Maas- en Diezepolders), Nieuw-Kuijk.

Winter, Søren (1990), Integrating Implementation Research, in Palumbo D. J. and D. J. Calista (eds), *Implementation and the Policy Process: Opening up the Black Box* (New York: Greenwood Press), pp.l9–38.

Zeeuw, F. de, and H. B. Gels (1990), 'Rioolwaterbeheer en Drinkwatervoorziening in een Hand?', *Bestuur* (Administration), No. 7, pp. l91–94.

Zevenbergen, P., 'Gemeente en Waterschap', *Tijdschrift voor Openbaar Bestuur* (Journal of Public Administration), Vol 13, No. 20, pp.433–36.

Networks of Cooperation:
Water Policy in Germany

WOLFGANG RÜDIG and R. ANDREAS KRAEMER

German water policy-making defies easy categorisation. Policy processes are highly complex, fragmented, and diverse. Concentrating on the areas of drinking water supply and water pollution, the most important feature is the enormous importance of regional government in both the formulation and implementation of policy. The role of local government, and of municipal water utilities, is also crucial. The various forms of horizontal cooperation between individual municipalities and between the *Länder* are important, the latter having become particularly important as the *Länder* try to preserve their strong influence in the face of increasing policy activism by the EU. Historically, cooperative solutions have dominated much of policy development since the nineteenth century. In the face of powerful agricultural and industrial interests, the creation of networks of cooperation is still at the heart of policy, but the state relies less on authority or common interest than on exchange, with financial policy instruments coming to dominate. While water policy has been thoroughly reframed as part of environmental policy, environmental groups have played a relatively marginal role, although conflicts conceived in terms of local versus centralised water supply have gained some prominence in particular regions.

Introduction

The 'cooperation principle' is one of the three guiding principles of German environmental policy laid down in the environmental programme of 1971. While the 'polluter-pays principle' and the 'precautionary principle' have received exhaustive attention, the cooperation principle is comparatively unknown. In a governmental system that has been described as 'cooperative federalism', the importance given to the principle of cooperation may not surprise. In its original formulation, the cooperation principle mainly alluded to the desire to involve all social forces, including environmental groups, in the decision-making process. More recently, the cooperation principle is cited in

We gratefully acknowledge the financial support of the Anglo-German Foundation for the Study of Industrial Society. The project was codirected by Professor M. Jänicke, Dr L. Mez, Professor J. J. Richardson and Dr W. Rüdig. We thank the editors of this special issue for their extensive comments on previous versions of this paper.

the context of informal arrangements about environmental measures between the state and industry [*Rengeling, 1986; Lübbe-Wolf, 1992*]. Whatever its exact interpretation, the cooperation principle highlights a very important feature of German policy-making: the large number and variety of governmental and non-governmental political actors, and the necessity to formulate and implement policy through interaction between these actors.

The water sector is a good case in point. German water policy displays a wide variety of organisations, rules, networks and policy contents. Mostly, water policy is not a federal matter but is the subject of policy processes at the sub-national level. Consequently, there is no one integrated national water policy, nor a set of national actors which might form a singular water policy network.

Furthermore, for various reasons the idea of regarding 'water' as one big policy area, functionally organised around the water cycle, has not come to dominate the institutional structure of water-related policy areas. While the reason for this absence is itself an important research question, the reality of water-related political processes in Germany we have to deal with consists of a highly complex, fragmented, diverse system which defies easy categorisation. It is the nature of this policy area which makes the seemingly simple task of describing policy networks in the water policy area in Germany a rather formidable enterprise.

Our aims in this paper are modest. We try to give an overview of the actors involved in water policy-making,[1] and try to characterise their interrelationship. In the absence of detailed case studies of German water policy-making, many of our statements will have to be tentative and merely serve to identify areas for further empirical research. There is practically no political science literature on German water policy.[2] A substantial body of literature exists which is addressed to the water law and water engineering communities. This literature was analysed to the extent it had a bearing on the questions addressed in this paper. Our understanding of policy processes in the water sector has also been enhanced by interviews with decision-makers and policy experts.

The nature of policy actors and their interrelationship in a particular national setting is likely to be influenced by two types of factors: specifically national patterns of policy-making, and particular sectoral conditions of the policy field. In the following section, we draw attention to the specifically German aspects of policy-making which are important for our understanding of German water policy. We then go on to try to explain the genesis of water policy actors in an historical analysis. We argue that all the major national actors in water policy-making today have their origin in developments of the late nineteenth and early twentieth centuries. After emphasising the high degree of continuity in German water policy-making, we then look at the

modern challenges to the water policy network, in particular the influence of
the environmental movement. We conclude with a brief discussion of the
nature and impact of policy networks in German water policy-making.

The Character of Policy Networks: National and Sectoral Dimensions

There has been a long-standing debate about the relative weight of national
and sectoral factors in explanations of policy processes in an internationally
comparative context (cf. Rüdig [1988]). While some doubt has been shed
on the notion that policy-making predominantly reflects national styles or
cultures, the move to focus on the comparison of policy sectors across nations
has not obviated the need to consider the specifically national features under
which policy-making is conducted. The specific uses of the 'policy network'
concept as the most fashionable analytical tool of the international policy
literature cannot be separated from particular national developments [van
Waarden, 1992].

German water policy-making is strongly influenced by specific national
factors. The basic tenets of German policy-making have been analysed on
numerous occasions (cf. Dyson [1982]; von Beyme, [1985]; Katzenstein,
[1987]). While all these analyses do not see one single 'policy style' at work
and detect a growing 'sectorisation' of policy-making, there are nevertheless
a number of distinctive features which are common to policy-making in
Germany.

The first 'iron' principle of German policy-making is its legalism. Over
the years, an enormous body of laws, rules and regulation has been built up
relating to water. A collection of only the most important legal texts relating
to water easily fills six large loose-leaf binders [Wüsthoff and Kumpf, 1958-
1994]. German legalism does not simply mean that water policy has to be
formulated and implemented within a relatively tight legal framework, in
which the operation of actors and their interrelationship is governed by laws
or other binding and legally enforceable rules. The principle of the Rechts-
staat also establishes the need for a complex system of legal rules with a high
degree of internal consistency [Dyson, 1980]. Any new policy measure has to
conform to this system, and new policies frequently fail in the policy formulation stage not because they are politically unacceptable or do not pass an
economic cost-benefit test, but because they are incompatible with established legal structures.

A second 'key' feature of German policy-making is its federal structure.
The German 'states', the Länder, are involved in policy formulation through
the upper house of parliament, the Federal Council (Bundesrat), which consists of representatives of Land governments. In many areas of water policy,
federal legislation can only be 'framework' legislation, and each Land has the

right to pass its own water legislation within that framework. Furthermore, the implementation of federal legislation is normally a matter for the *Länder*, and regulations governing the implementation of federal legislation require the consent of the *Bundesrat*. Policy-making in Germany has been described as highly fragmented and intertwined, with new initiatives from the federal level facing numerous obstacles in policy formulation and implementation (cf. Scharpf *et al.* [*1976*]; Katzenstein [*1987*]).

In addition the principle of municipal autonomy, of local self-government, is enshrined in the constitution. Partly as a result of a long tradition of jealously guarded municipal autonomy, partly because German central government has been comparatively weak, local authorities have retained a range of services in the energy and water supply fields which in many other countries have been taken over by other state or private bodies [*Braun and Jacobi, 1990*].

We are thus suggesting that the principles of legalism, federalism and municipal autonomy are features of the German political system which may have some important bearing on decision-making processes in the water area. However, German policy-making cannot simply be understood in terms of a simple addition, or combination, of these constitutional principles. In fact, the recent political science literature on German policy-making is full of references to counter-tendencies undermining these principles: the 'legalisation' (*Verrechtlichung*) of policy-making has been the subject of some criticism [*Voigt, 1983*], and informal aspects of policy-making are attracting increasing attention [*Hartwich and Wewer, 1991; Benz and Seibel, 1992*]; German federalism and municipal autonomy are seen to be undermined by the centralisation of financial control and by the operation of the federal political parties [*Abromeit, 1992*].

Within international comparison, these 'counter-tendencies' obviously have to be seen within their specific national context. While the orthodoxies of constitutional textbooks may have to be modified in any analysis of 'real' German politics, this does not completely invalidate the continued importance of the basic features of the German constitutional set-up. However, these debates introduce a series of important questions, and, as we shall see, the water sector is one policy sector which appears particularly suitable to analyse these questions. The degree of legalisation, and the importance of federal, *Land*, and local government are to be seen as variable between one policy sector and another. Of particular importance for water policy-making, as we shall see, are forms of horizontal cooperation, between different *Länder* and between local authorities. These can take a number of different forms and involve highly legalistic as well as completely informal processes.

In this context the notion of networks blends in extremely well. In fact, some of the German network literature specifically emphasises the usefulness of that concept in terms of analysing 'informal' policy processes. Here, the notion of a 'political network' is intrinsically linked to a development of a polity which has moved away from policies being formulated and implemented within a hierarchically structured state apparatus governed by tight legal rules. The network notion only comes into its own for these authors once policy-making is determined, or least influenced, by a wider range of semi-autonomous bodies whose relationship to each other is not formalised [*Kenis and Schneider, 1991; Mayntz, 1993; Scharpf, 1993*]. Within a comparative framework, such a specifically German concept of a political network as distinct from legalistically operating administrative hierarchies may make little sense. But it raises important empirical questions on the nature of German networks.

The historical development of the basic features of the German water policy sector can best be mapped in terms of challenges to be met, some related to specific water-related developments, some arising from more general political changes. The basic structure of the water policy sector was the result of the challenges of the nineteenth and early twentieth centuries which were associated with agricultural change, industrialisation and urbanisation processes. Essentially, the main tenets of water policy were in place by the 1920s, and further legal and organisational development culminated in the 1950s.

Since then, the most important challenge German water policy has faced emerged with the new environmental agenda. Unlike many other areas of environmental policy-making where new legislation, new organisations, and environmental administrations were essentially created from scratch, in the water sector there was a very elaborate set-up of policy actors already *in situ*. In the following section, we look at the genesis of these institutions which could claim to have been engaged in environmental management for many years.

Agricultural Development, Industrialisation and Urbanisation

The agriculture-water interaction, with people either claiming agricultural land from water or bringing water to areas to allow cultivation, has given rise to specific water management organisations for many centuries. Organisations in charge of flood protection and the draining of wetlands go back to the Middle Ages. By the nineteenth century, more advanced technology became available to allow for more large scale drainage and river control projects, and a major era of water construction projects was started [*Abel, 1967; Haushofer, 1963*].

Central to the traditional water management tasks had been local forms of cooperation. The first cooperative societies (*Genossenschaften*) concerned with irrigation date back to the fourteenth century, whilst cooperatives to look after coastal dams have an even longer history. While these co-operatives at first were purely private enterprises, the increasing use of irrigation and drainage in agriculture in the early nineteenth century created the need to give these organisations a legal basis. With the involvement of the state, however, these cooperative societies were increasingly made not just the subject but also the agent of public policies. The Prussian law of 1843 created the possibility for the authorities to initiate such cooperative ventures and force everybody affected to become a member. While the operation of the cooperative societies was governed by formal rules set by the state, the societies essentially managed themselves, usually financed by contributions from their members. The law of such cooperative societies for water and soil (*Wasser- und Bodenverbände*) was developed further over the years and, increasingly, such cooperative societies became instruments of government policies to deal with major water problems. This organisational form has maintained its importance very well: by the mid-1960s, more than 16,000 such societies were in existence in West Germany [*Dornheim, 1980*]. With a new federal law on *Wasser- und Bodenverbände* passed in 1991, envisaging such societies to be active in a wide variety of water management tasks, the continued commitment to this organisational form is not in question [*Deutscher Verband für Wasserbau und Kulturforschung, 1991*].

While *Wasser- und Bodenverbände* became the dominant form of water management in Northern Germany, other states followed a more traditional, hierarchical model of policy-making. Bavaria, for example, had a long tradition as a unitary state with a strong central administration [*Bosl, 1965*], and Bavarian water management reflects that tradition. Also, the authorities had to tackle a wide variety of water engineering tasks, particularly in the Alpine region, with a strong emphasis on hydro-power. In 1830, the *Oberste Baubehörde* (Highest Construction Agency) had been created as an extension of the State Ministry of the Interior and was empowered by King Ludwig I with the control of all public construction. The agency remained the highest water management authority in Bavaria for more than 160 years into the 1990s [*Strobel, 1988*].

While the evolution of water organisations was influenced by specific state cultures and by the nature of the water management problems to be dealt with, the nineteenth century saw the evolution of water administrations as part of the state apparatus, regulating various aspects of the water cycle. While Bavaria was again a front-runner with a comprehensive water law passed in 1852, other states had comprehensive water laws in place in the early twentieth century. The first comprehensive federal German water legislation, the *Wasserhaushaltsgesetz* (Water Management Law) of 1957, was the culmination of this development. It placed all 'flowing' waters (streams, rivers), coastal waters, and ground water under public control, with any 'use' of these waters, such as abstraction or discharge of waste water, needing approval of the water authorities [*Giesecke* et al., *1989*]. The exact nature of the water administration remained a matter for the *Länder*. A three-tier system is usually employed: the highest water authority is usually vested in a *Land* Ministry, there is an intermediate water administration at the regional level, with the lowest water offices at the local level. Importantly, as water management historically emerged from the needs of agricultural development, the water administrations were usually part of the agricultural policy domain, and were controlled by *Land* agriculture ministries.

Water management for agricultural purposes did not remain unchallenged. Germany saw a rapid industrialisation process towards the end of the nineteenth century. The new industrial concerns had a variety of interests in the water domain. First, industry needed substantial amounts of water for its production processes. Second, many industries depended on using water for the disposal of waste products of the production process. And third, industry needed large workforces to be settled in towns which in turn needed access to water for drinking and other domestic purposes.

Organisationally, solutions to many of these problems followed the pattern adopted for agricultural development and a wide variety of other economic activities [*Dyson, 1992*]. Tasks were placed in the hands of organisations in which actors benefiting from the resolution of the problem cooperated with each other, either voluntarily or, if necessary, as a result of state compulsion. While the state created the legal framework for these organisations, their day-to-day running was left to themselves, following the principle of self-administration. In the case of coping with the water-related problems of rapid industrialisation and urbanisation, the application of this model was limited to the area where the problems were most urgent – the Ruhr area.

The solution to the water problems of the Ruhr area involved two parts: first, one river, the Emscher, was exclusively reserved for the discharge of waste water; second, the major river, the Ruhr, was developed into the major source of water supply for domestic and industrial purposes. With the beginning of urbanisation and industrialisation, the Emscher had become a convenient dumping ground for urban and industrial waste water. This became a major health hazard, and to alleviate these problems, it was necessary to improve its flow and allow the waste water to run off without delay. For that purpose, a special cooperative society, the *Emschergenossenschaft,* was formed in 1904, incorporating all public bodies and private companies (in particular mines and steel mills) emitting waste water into the river. The public investment was to be funded by charges levied on the members [*Ramshorn, 1957*].

For the Ruhr, a similar model was adopted. As the major source of water for the region, the Ruhr simply did not carry enough water. This could be alleviated through the construction of a series of dams regulating the river's flow. Private companies had formed the *Ruhrtalsperrenverein* (Ruhr Dam Society) in 1899, but the state intervened to transform the status of the society along the lines of the *Emschergenossenschaft*, to force all those benefiting to join up and mobilise more resources for the construction effort. Apart from regulating river flow, the use of the Ruhr as a source of drinking water also required the effluents directed into the river to be cleaned. For that purpose, a separate cooperative society, the *Ruhrverband* (Ruhr Association), was formed based on the same organisational principles [*Ruhrverband and Ruhrtalsperrenverein, 1988*].

These cooperative societies are generally seen to have been successful in reaching their stated aims (see for example Kneese and Bower [*1968*]; Bower *et al.*, 1981]. The state created an effective network by ensuring that the private interests of network actors were identical with the public interest to be achieved [*Schleicher, 1986*]. Major advances in waste water treatment technology originated in these societies, with their professionals taking a leading role in their emerging disciplines. With this success, similar cooperative associations were formed for other river systems in the region [*Imhoff, 1992; Imhoff and Albrecht, 1993*]. But there were also losers. The Emscher river was condemned to the state of a waste water canal. The *Emschergenossenschaft* was very successful in that respect but its members were reluctant to take on the costs of comprehensive waste water treatment. For many years, the polluted Emscher water flowed into the river Rhine without any treatment, and it was only as a result of pressure from the state that investment in that area started to be made. Economically, the main losers of the increase in industrial water pollution were the fishermen of the Rhine and the other major rivers. They lodged frequent protests against pollution, but within a few decades, their trade was to vanish [*Wey, 1982; Brüggemeier and Rommelspacher, 1990; Dominick, 1992*].

In terms of the creation of actors and networks, the challenge of industrial pollution created new institutions where the interests of industry itself required them. The model of the Ruhr associations for large-scale, regional water management remained popular in North Rhine-Westphalia, but was not taken up elsewhere in Germany. Public waterways were largely seen as a 'free good' by industry, and effective regulation of emissions was successfully resisted. Industrial pollution was also seen as essentially 'harmless', and the great rivers like the Rhine were ascribed great natural cleaning powers. While such views look naive now, they had a basis in the specific 'threat' experiences of the time: the main danger for urban dwellers in fact did not come from industrial pollution but from the organic waste products which found their way into the water cycle and provided a major threat to public health.

The rapid industrialisation and urbanisation process created a major demand for the large-scale supply of water. Water supply in Germany had been fairly rudimentary, mainly relying on the use of local wells [*Garbrecht, 1985*]. The systematic adoption of centralised systems of supplying drinking water only slowly developed in Germany during the nineteenth century, and only quickened in pace when the industrialisation and urbanisation process accelerated substantially towards the end of the century. At that time, local authorities were the most active player, building up a whole new range of infrastructure services: gas, electricity, and water [*Ambrosius, 1987; Brown, 1988, 1989; Braun and Jacobi, 1990*]. While private companies were initially involved,[3] the solution which became most commonly adopted was the formation of general municipal supply companies, the *Stadtwerke*, which came to dominate gas, electricity and water supply in most major towns and which have maintained their position to the present day. These *Stadtwerke* have a fairly high level of expertise, and they are usually of some, but not necessarily major, economic importance for the municipal budget. A very important aspect of their continuing strength is their relative financial independence: Local water utilities are relatively free to set water charges to drinking water consumers, but these charges have to reflect the necessities of running and maintaining adequate drinking water supply [*Kraemer, 1994a*]. The setting of these water charges is controlled by higher administrative bodies within each *Land*, but conflicts about the setting of these charges are virtually unknown.

Local utilities can, however, be too small for major tasks, particularly if they only serve small communities in rural areas. But this has been no hindrance to authorities. They frequently joined forces to form municipal organisations designed to deal with a specific, common task. The so-called *Zweckverband*, unlike the *Wasser- und Bodenverband*, involves cooperation only between local authorities. The legal basis for *Zweckverbände* was a special national law of 1937 regulating this form of cooperation, supplemented by *Land* laws on municipal cooperation. Despite later reforms of the structure of local authorities which abolished many of the smaller authorities, the *Zweckverband* has remained a highly popular and flexible form of horizontal cooperation, particularly in regions where local authorities have traditionally been very strong. The *Zweckverband* model has also been adopted by many authorities for sewerage services [*Schauwecker, 1988; Deutscher Verband für Wasserwirtschaft und Kulturbau, 1991*].

Even where conditions required the build-up of regional water supply systems, these often remained under the control of local authorities. For example, one major regional water supply network in Baden-Württemberg in south-western Germany was set up by the main local authorities in the region, using the *Zweckverband* formula. The other main regional supplier was originally set up by the state of Baden-Württemberg but was then also given the form of a *Zweckverband* in 1965, an indication of the strength of local authorities in that particular part of Germany [*Schauwecker, 1988*].

A range of new and old German water institutions thus were successfully employed to ensure a satisfactory level of supply to industrial and domestic consumers. But two further major water-related public health problems had to be addressed: the disposal of domestic waste water, and the bacteriological contamination of drinking water supplies. In the nineteenth century, the link between public health and urban waste had been established, and the introduction of the water closet linked to a public sewer in England, hailed as a major contribution to public health, was soon introduced in Germany. The operation of such sewerage systems was and remains purely a matter of local administration. It is seen as a *Hoheitsaufgabe*, a sovereign function, and, importantly, not as a public enterprise such as the *Stadtwerke*. The operation of sewerage systems is financed by the local authorities who are entitled to collect a charge from local residents and businesses to cover the costs of the service. Water supply on the one hand and sewerage services on the other have remained strictly separate in most cases, with the different legal form of these services being one formal obstacle to their integration [*Jacobi, 1988; Kraemer, 1994b*].

While the construction of sewerage systems solved one public health problem, the large-scale dumping of sewage in rivers created another. In many towns, sewage ran off into the same river that served as the source of local drinking water. After a major debate about the possible adverse impact of such a practice among bacteriologists, the Hamburg cholera epidemic of 1892 established beyond doubt that the bacteriological contamination of drinking water from sewage was a major public health risk. This stood at the beginning of the development of water treatment and drinking water regulation in Germany. Since 1900, all drinking water had to be the subject of inspections by health professionals to check for bacteriological contamination. The health administration in Germany was characterised by a decentralised system of local *Gesundheitsämter* (Health Offices) which were generally in charge of public health matters in their locality (cf. Labisch [*1986*]). The *Gesundheitsamt* had to control the quality of drinking water and had the powers to close down supplies if they constituted a health hazard. While there were no binding guidelines, there was broad consensus amongst health professionals on what constituted such a health hazard. Legislation introduced in the 1960s and, finally, the passing of a *Trinkwasserverordnung* (Drinking Water Ordinance) in 1976, specifying maximum permissible concentrations, essentially codified what had already been practised before [*Schumacher, 1991*].

While health policy was a matter for federal legislation, the implementation of that legislation was in the hands of the *Länder*. There was thus an administrative structure completely separate from the water administration, from the federal to the *Land* to the local level, which was in charge of drinking water regulation. In terms of its own standards, drinking water regulation was generally extremely effective. Bacteriological contamination of drinking water had virtually been eradicated by the 1960s. But the separation between the health and water administration proved to become more problematic once drinking water had come to be politicised with a broader water policy framework.

Post-War Water Policy in the Pre-Environmental Era

The immediate post-war need to boost food production led to vigorous water construction efforts to increase agricultural productivity. But the 'economic miracle' of the 1950s also led to rising demand for water, and there was the perceived need for a national policy on water. In particular the German Employers Federation, the *Bund der Deutschen Industrie* (BDI) became very active in lobbying for a federal water law. Renewed attempts to make water management a federal matter failed as the *Länder* vigorously defended their rights. The Federal Water Management Law of 1957 was thus only framework legislation leaving many of the real decisions to the *Länder*, but for the first time created a federal legal basis for water decision-making [*Weßels, 1989*].

The 1950s and 1960s saw a major expansion of water supply activities. Regional supply networks, for example those in Baden-Württemberg, were installed. Overall, the existing institutions coped well with the new demands, and new institutions following previous patterns were created where necessary. While agricultural and industrial interests had clashed quite openly on a number of occasions in the early period, water policy in the 1950s and 1960s was not a matter of 'high politics'.[4] A broad social consensus on the role of economic development spurred on by technological progress dominated, and at least some water pollution appears to have been acceptable to most of the public as an undesirable if unavoidable result of 'civilisation'.

The decision to leave major responsibility with the *Länder* has had major repercussions up to the present day. On the administrative side, the most notable innovation of this period was the formation of the *Länderarbeitsgemeinschaft Wasser* (Land Working Group Water, LAWA) in 1956. The LAWA is, in legalistic terms, a purely informal coordination body for *Land* civil servants to come together, but it quickly became one of the most important actors in water policy-making. LAWA is the embodiment of water as a policy area of national importance which is controlled by the coordination of actors at sub-national level.[5]

The recognition of water as a policy area of national importance also stimulated the organisation of other water interests at the national level. Outside the political and administrative system, it is professional and industrial interests that play an important role. In a highly technical policy area such as water, the influence of technical expertise is obviously crucial. Leading in this field are three national associations concerned with different aspects of water management.

For the water supply services, the *Deutsche Vereinigung des Gas- und Wasserfaches* (German Association of Gas and Water Experts, DVGW), whose origins go back to 1859, is the most influential professional body. In the waste water area, there is the *Abwassertechnische Vereinigung* (Association for Waste Water Technology, ATV) formed in 1948. The various professions involved in the mainly agricultural aspects of water management found their way into a broad variety of organisations. It was only in 1978-79 that the most important of those merged in the *Deutscher Verband für Wasserwirtschaft und Kulturbau* (German Association for Water Resources and Land Improvement, DVWK) [*Rümelin, 1991; van Riesen and Kieslinger, 1988*].

These three associations are recognised as the main professional organisations in their field.[6] They have a special status because they are the 'rule'-giving professional associations. Legally, the technical norms developed by the associations have no standing *per se*, but they define proper technical practice which is used for guidance by decision makers. Legislators have increasingly inserted so-called indeterminate legal terms such as 'generally recognised technical rules' or 'state of the art technology' into environmental legislation including water legislation (cf. Giesecke *et al.* [*1989*]; Breuer [*1987*]). This puts a particular requirement on those implementing such legislation – that is, *Land* governments – to rely on technical expertise to interpret such terms and translate them into practical decisions. The technical rules of the professional organisations can provide such guidance.

Apart from *Land* administrations as main agents of policy-making and implementation, and the professional and technical associations, the water policy sector included the water industry as a major player. The industrial peak association of the water industry, both private and public, is the *Bundesverband der Gas- und Wasserwirtschaft* (Federal Association of Gas and Water Industries, BGW). The first association of the German water industry was formed in 1892. The BGW is the main lobbying organisation of the German water supply utilities; it cooperates closely with the professional organisations. There are a number of other organisations which represent water interests under certain circumstances. In particular, the *Verband Kommunaler Unternehmen* (Association of Municipal Enterprises, VKU) includes the majority of *Stadtwerke* and lobbies on their behalf. The VKU is particularly vociferous in maintaining the independence of municipal suppliers. Given the organisational nature of sewerage services, there was never any 'industrial' association to represent what would be the industrial equivalent to the BGW. The interests of municipal sewerage services were thus in the hands of the peak associations of local authorities.

We have no detailed studies of the history of LAWA, the professional water organisations and the other actors to allow us an insight into their operation. Various bodies have been formed over the years to coordinate the activities of the professional groups, but none of these umbrella bodies appears to have any substantive independent role in the policy-making process. Nevertheless, it looks fairly clear that the entire water 'community' in the 1950s and 1960s shared a certain view of the development of the water sector. The water cycle was to be managed to serve a growing, increasingly urbanised and industrialised, economy. And the only way that appeared to be possible was with an increasing reliance on 'large' technical solutions. At the same time, the basic organisational, political and administrative framework was largely accepted, and water actors worked within that system.

The Environmental Challenge: The Reframing of Water Policy

In the 1970s, water has come to be redefined within the environmental policy sector. This 'reframing' process was gradual, but it started within the framework of the environmental policy activism of the early 1970s. The sources of policy initiative in this area remained diverse, and even in the 1970s and 1980s, the 'politicisation' of water in terms of media attention, public protest, and party political campaigning was minuscule in comparison with the energy sector. After the first reforms were carried out, the environmental challenge encountered more serious problems over the regulation of drinking water quality in relation to agricultural pollution.

In 1969, the Social-Democrat/Liberal reform government identified 'the environment' as a major new policy area, and a new policy initiative was set in motion which created an essentially new framework for a range of activities under the policy heading 'environmental policy'. This started a process which eventually saw 'water policy' become a sub-sector of environmental rather than primarily agricultural policy-making.

The environmental policy initiative was not driven primarily by public concern. While the 1960s had seen a variety of environmental issues come to the fore, the inclusion of the environment in its comprehensive reform programme was much influenced by recent developments in US policy. Furthermore, the environment was seen by the government parties as a new issue which was 'neutral' in party political terms. The Liberals (FDP), in particular, perceived the environmental programme as a chance to raise their profile, and most environmental functions were transferred to the Interior Ministry under Hans-Dietrich Genscher [*Küppers* et al., *1976; Müller, 1986; Weßels, 1988*]. At *Land* level, separate environment ministries were slowly emerging. At federal level, that only happened in 1986 [*Weale* et al., *1991*]. This period of environmental activism created some new environmental actors, such as the *Umweltbundesamt* (Environmental Protection Agency, UBA) and the *Rat der Sachverständigen für Umweltfragen* (Expert Council for Environmental Questions) but they mainly had purely advisory functions with little direct impact on the water policy-making process. More important was the *Umweltministerkonferenz* (Conference of Environmental Ministers) which included all *Land* and Federal ministers concerned with the environment. It has been meeting regularly since 1972, and provided a forum for both vertical and horizontal policy coordination [*Müller, 1986*].

Legislative activism in the early 1970s was mainly concerned with air pollution. Apart from another – failed – attempt to wrest legislative control in water management matters from the *Länder* [*Roth, 1988*], the major water-related action was the initiation of a major investment programme in new waste water treatment plants [*Müller, 1986*]. That was a measure that could be quickly implemented without requiring new legislation and was also highly effective in terms of demonstrating that something was done.

After the arrival of Chancellor Helmut Schmidt and the recession induced by the oil crisis, the climate for environmental policy became more difficult. Nevertheless, the Federal Water Management Law was finally amended in 1976. Of the many individual changes, the introduction of new guiding norms for water management which sought to redefine the tasks of water regulation within an environmental framework was of some importance as a legal step signalling the reframing of water management as part of environmental policy. The 1976 amendment also set in place a range of new planning functions, and envisaged development of detailed plans for whole river systems as well as the integration of general economic and land use planning processes with water-related concerns.

While the government's intention to place water within an explicitly environmental political arena was clear (cf. Müller [*1986*]), the effects of the amendment on water administration practice have probably been minimal (cf. Breuer [*1987*]; Gieseke, *et al.* [*1989*]). Studies of the implementation of water law in the mid-1970s highlighted major problems. Water administrations were reluctant to mobilise even the pre-1976 regulatory instruments against water polluters because they had to balance water pollution considerations with other aims such as employment and economic development. Administrators often sought to come to informal arrangements. As water pollution was often less visible than other forms of pollution, the role of environmental protest was of little importance for the administrative process

[*Winter, 1975; Mayntz* et al., *1978*]. These findings of the 1970s also appear to be typical of administrative practices in later years [*Lübbe-Wolf, 1992*]. In view of this regulatory failure, the use of economic incentives became an important topic of policy debate in the water sector in the 1970s.

The first concrete result of that debate materialised, in fact, also in 1976: the *Abwasserabgabengesetz* (Wastewater Charges Law). The idea behind it was rather novel, at least in the German context: to encourage industry and municipalities discharging waste water into rivers to install or improve their treatment plants by imposing a charge based on the polluting content of the discharge. This idea had taken a major legal hurdle in 1972 when Germany's most eminent water law expert declared it legally feasible, but it encountered major opposition from industrial interests. As a result, it was watered down considerably, and its provisions were only fully implemented in 1981. The size of the charge was considered far too small by environmentalists and other observers to have a major effect [*Mayer-Tasch, 1978; Wey, 1982; Breuer, 1987*]. Nevertheless, a principle was established which contributed to the start of a much wider debate about environmental charges, and later, environmental taxation (cf. Wicke [*1993*]).

Water policy in the 1970s was thus touched by the new environmental wave, but it really remained a marginal issue in terms of environmental politics. The period of governmental activism until 1974 was replaced by a period of citizen activism in the rest of the decade. But water related issues hardly played a role as citizen initiatives of the early 1970s mobilised protests against issues such as road planning and the siting of industrial facilities. By the mid-1970s, protests against energy projects, in particular nuclear energy, had clearly become dominant in terms of public mobilisation [*Rüdig, 1980*]. As the water industry successfully met the quantitative demands for water supply, and major public investment removed the most obvious problems of water pollution, it was a new range of water issues in the 1980s that led to a politicisation of water.

Politicisation: Drinking Water and Agricultural Pollution

In the late 1970s and early 1980s, environmental policy became thoroughly politicised.[7] New environmental actors emerged in force, confronting governments at all levels. The electoral success of the newly formed Green Party heightened the concern of the established parties for environmental issues. These developments had a major impact on the environmental agenda. Governments moved to meet these concerns, while established economic interests became increasingly alarmed at the cost of environmental measures. With the European Union (EU) emerging as a major environmental player, environmental policy became an ever more complex, multi-layered domain.

While water-related issues were still not very prominent the heightened general politicisation had meant that environmental groups had firmly become associated with an 'anti-establishment' position. When a few young scientists challenged the practices of a water utility in Bremen, the whole industry was united in its condemnation of the protesters [*Lahl and Zeschmar, 1982*]. The relationship between the major industrial and professional interests, government, and various 'polluters' could generally be described as cosy before the 1980s (cf. *Grant*, et al. *1988*]). The post-war consensus about a growth-oriented and technology-led social and economic development placed environmentalists and Greens on the outside, as challengers to the 'system'. But as environmentalism made further inroads, either directly or indirectly, that cosiness was breaking up, and a number of fault-lines appeared which made water policy-making rather more complex and politically controversial.

Ideologically, there was a conflict between two different views of water. On the one hand, a holistic environmentalist view of the water cycle envisaged a return of all waterways as closely as possible to their natural state and a reliance primarily on a local supply of drinking water [*Lahl and Zeschmar, 1982; Greenpeace, 1989*]. On the other hand, the high-technology view of water development relied primarily on advances in sewage disposal and water treatment technologies and the construction of large, regional water supply systems, involving the transport of water over long distances, either from reservoirs or ground-water resources. This fundamental conflict was, however, rarely politicised in such a simple way. Historically, the richness of ground-water resources, and the relatively strong position of local water suppliers, had ensured that regional, long-distance water supply had never become very important. In 1987, the share of drinking water supplied from reservoirs was only seven per cent [*Stadtfeld, 1989*]. Legislators in the 1980s were even more determined than in the 1970s to place water management in an environmental context. Apart from such declarations of intent and preferences, specific conflicts erupted when vested economic interests clashed with the new environmental policy initiatives.

These conflicts emerged around two problem areas: environment vs. industry, and environment vs. agriculture. Overall, the clash between industrial and environmental interests has attracted less attention. The major efforts made in the past in conjunction with highly advantageous geological conditions prevented industrial water pollution from constituting a risk to drinking water supplies.[8] Cases of industrial water pollution, such as the spill of a cocktail of chemicals into the Rhine at the Sandoz chemical plant in Switzerland in November 1986, or the detection of old industrial dumping grounds threatening ground water supplies, occasionally made the headlines, but they were not a major target for sustained environmental campaigning.

With the increasing run-down of the coal and steel industries, much of the traditional water pollution is, in fact, disappearing. This facilitated the move to start the reconversion of rivers that had been little more than sewers into their original state. The most prominent case is the renaturation programme for the river Emscher which is vigorously pursued by the *Land* government as part of a programme to clean up the image of the *Ruhrgebiet* and attract new industries [*Jahresbericht der Wasserwirtschaft, 1994: 82-83*].

Central to water-related environmental debates in Germany was the question of agricultural pollution, focusing on the issues of nitrates and pesticides. The ball was set rolling by a European directive adopted by the Council of Ministers in 1980, after five years of debate in Brussels, to little public acclaim at the time. The directive about the quality of water for human consumption [*80/778/EEC*] specified maximum permissible concentrations for a wide variety of substances. The maximum values for nitrate, set at 50 mg/l, and for pesticides, set at 0.1 µg/l for each individual pesticide and at 0.5 µg/l for all pesticides together, had not caused substantial discussion at the time [*Kromarek, 1986*]. In fact, the policy-makers were largely unaware of the problems countries would face in implementing this directive. The reason was the intensification and industrialisation of agriculture which was pushed forward by another arm of European polity in the form of the Common Agricultural Policy, leading to increasing use of nitrate-based fertilisers and of pesticides.

The scale of the problem only became clear when systematic monitoring of drinking water and ground water commenced in the early 1980s. The EU drinking water directive was formally implemented in Germany in 1986 with the amendment of the Drinking Water Ordinance, but the pesticide standards were only made compulsory from 1 October 1989 to allow for the development of the necessary measuring techniques. The federal government's decision to delay the implementation of the pesticide aspects of the Drinking Water Ordinance raised public attention, and environmental groups started to campaign on the issue (cf. Greenpeace [*1989*]; *Süddeutsche Zeitung*, 11 August 1989). The European Commission also complained that the ordinance did not properly implement the directive. A further revision of the German Drinking Water Ordinance was passed by the *Bundesrat* in October 1990 to meet these concerns (cf. Hallauer [*1991*]).[9]

In order to meet new drinking water standards, water utilities sometimes faced difficult choices: local wells either had to be closed down with water supply being taken over by regional networks, or a major effort had to be made to remove the polluting substances, either by the installation of expensive de-nitrification equipment or the removal of the source of the pollution problem by regulating the use of fertilisers and pesticides. In the environmentalist 1980s, there was considerable political pressure to move from a purely technical fix to policies limiting the use of fertilisers and pesticides and thus clear up ground water pollution. In practice, utilities were often able to comply by blending water from different sources. A major crisis was thus averted, and immediate compliance problems were limited to few cases, mainly small water utilities in rural areas.

For the medium and long term, there was, nevertheless, a broad consensus in the environmental policy domain that the nitrate and pesticide problem had to be tackled at its source. Such demands were not only made by environmentalists, but also the water supply industry wanted more effective measures to limit the pollution of ground water used for drinking water purposes [*Pluge, 1989*]. But any such attempt had to contend with the interest of the farmers, who were forcefully represented not only by their own associations, but also by federal and *Land* agriculture ministries who opposed any compulsory limits on the use of fertilisers.

The formulation to the political solution of this problem started with a suggestion from the federal Agriculture Minister made in 1984: if farmers had to limit their use of fertilisers, then they had to be compensated financially for their loss. This solution was heavily opposed by several interests, amongst them environmentalists and the water supply industry. They argued that compensation would violate the 'polluter-pays' principle, paying the polluter for not polluting rather than the other way round (cf. Conrad [*1988*]). Politically, it was clear, however, that no government was prepared to engage in a major conflict with agricultural interests. As a result, the fifth amendment to the Water Management Act passed in 1986 allowed the payment of compensation to farmers [*Conrad, 1990a*].

This was a major new step in environmental policy: it was recognised that the usual regulatory system based on licences and permits was administratively ineffective and politically unfeasible. Apart from the representation of agricultural interests in the political process, the water administrations charged with implementing water laws originated, as we saw, as service providers for the agricultural sector. The federal decision to allow compensation avoided these pitfalls; what remained less clear is how effective such a scheme could be in combating agricultural water pollution. With such a politically controversial issue, the federal level was probably not too unhappy that the details of the scheme had to be worked out by the *Länder*. Indeed, the attempt to formulate a common technical framework for water protection zones by a DVGW/LAWA committee turned out to be fraught with difficulties as agricultural and environmental concerns clashed [*Conrad, 1990a*]. The initiative was thus firmly in the court of individual *Land* governments.

A range of models has been developed (cf. Bruckmeier and Teherani-Krönner [*1992*]; Baldock and Bennett [*1991*]; Kraemer and Warnke [*1992*]), but, basically, one can distinguish between two types of policies: one relies mainly on information of farmers, cooperation between farmers and water utilities, and other voluntary measures. Compensation can be paid to farmers, but this is a matter between the utilities and farmers, and the *Land* government is not directly involved in any major resource transfer. The role of the government is limited to education, persuasion, and advice about environmentally sustainable farming methods. Essentially, the state here creates the general framework for 'networking' between the various actors, but does not force any actor to engage in any particular 'exchange' relationship. On the contrary, it sees the policy problem less in terms of 'exchange' than in creating a new consensus about agricultural practices. This is a model adopted, for example, in North Rhine-Westphalia and Bavaria.

The second solution was pioneered in Baden-Württemberg and essentially meant that actors were forced to enter an exchange relationship. Compensation is paid to farmers directly by the state in exchange for reducing their use of nitrates and pesticides. In order to generate the funds to pay compensation, the scheme involved the imposition of a so-called *Wasserpfennig* (water penny), a charge levied for abstracting water from ground or surface sources. The measure was heavily opposed by industrial water users who argued that the charge was not related to any service rendered by the *Land*, and thus illegally imposed a new tax burden on industry. But water abstraction charges have since become highly popular and have been introduced in a number of other *Länder*. The legal debate about the constitutionality of such a charge continues, however, and a ruling of the Federal Constitutional Court on the *Wasserpfennig* is pending.

The direct effects of the various schemes to limit nitrate pollution on the technical compliance with the provisions of the drinking water directive have probably been very minor. Most measures to reduce the pollution of ground water by agricultural activities have a medium to long time-scale. This leads to tricky administrative and political problems. The *Länder* have generally granted derogations to water utilities where ground water pollution abatement programmes have been put in place, allowing them to maintain water supplies from these wells while measures are taken to reduce their nitrate content. However, there are cases where the ground water supply is so contaminated that the *Land* is unwilling to sustain a recovery programme and would like the local utilities to link up to a regional supply network. Local environmental groups, however, in some cases opposed such a connection. Once the need to clean local ground water resources is removed by the link-up to the central supplier, so they argue, local environmental policy will suffer as water protection zones will be abolished and the land is used for commercial purposes. In Baden-Württemberg, local citizens have the right to organise local referenda to challenge decisions made by their local administration. In one celebrated case, a local referendum against the connection to the long-distance water supply was successful in the town of Wertheim. Environmentalists have accused *Länder* like Baden-Württemberg and Bavaria of furthering the interests of the centralised water industry. In these cases, the nitrate debate thus has been linked to a broader debate over the centralised vs. decentralised nature of the water industry [*Roling, 1992; Weinzierl, 1991*].

In their efforts to combat ground water pollution, *Land* governments thus face contradictory demands: environmental groups campaign for the preservation of local wells while the EU has criticised *Länder* for granting derogations too liberally. To complicate matters further, formal implementation of the EU drinking water directive and the environmental programmes to clean up ground water are administratively separated. The standards of the EU drinking water directive, as embodied in the German Drinking Water Ordinance, are implemented by the health authorities. As already explained, drinking water is formally part of health policy, and a hierarchy of administrative units, ranging from the federal Department of Health to *Land* health ministries down to local *Gesundheitsämter,* have the task of regulating it. The policy sector has its own source of technical expertise and also its horizontal forms of co-operation between *Land* health ministries to coordinate implementation measures. However, the health administration has no direct responsibilities for regulating water pollution which is creating the problems for drinking water supplies. Coordination between the two separate administrative hierarchies involved is thus vital. It is prominently at sub-*Land* level, in the development and implementation of specific programmes to combine the clean-up of ground water resources and the maintenance of drinking water supply within legal limits, that coordination between the water administration, the health authorities, the water utilities and farming interests have been developed. However, Conrad's [*1990a*] exhaustive study of local programmes to combat nitrate ground water pollution revealed no common pattern: the degree of involvement of each type of actor appears to differ from case to case. But clearly, a policy development model based on co-operation, rather than enforcement, appears to gain ground, even in those *Länder* that have introduced direct compensation payments to farmers [*Kraemer and Warnke, 1992; Jahresbericht der Wasserwirtschaft, 1994*].

The environmental challenge has thus led to a wide range of new political initiatives, actors, and processes. If we look at the actors involved in modern water policy, we see a very broad range: local citizen initiatives, national environmental groups, agricultural and industrial interests contest the policy field, but are rarely an integral part of the policy-making process. Governmental actors at all levels are involved, most prominently the environmental and health administrations, supported by the professional organisations and the water supply industry. While there is clearly no one group of actors determining policy throughout the sector, the *Land* governments clearly emerge as the most important actors, not just in the implementation but also the initiation of policies. The increasing importance of EU environmental policies has been one challenge to the predominance of their role, but they have successfully protected their position. Following Maastricht, the *Länder* formalised their right to play a full part in the development of EU policies. In the water sector, it is through the LAWA that the interests of the *Länder* are represented. European integration thus appears to have strengthened the role of LAWA even further. While individual *Länder* will always seek to go their separate ways where it suits them, the LAWA provides a vehicle for new policy ideas to be raised, facilitating a political process originating at the *Land* rather than federal level.

Conclusions

What is the role of networks in German water policy-making, and what difference have they made? Our overview of the historical development and analysis of some current patterns of policy-making demonstrates the high importance of cooperation between a wide range of public and private actors. All three forms of inducements to cooperate, namely 'authority, common interests, and exchange' [*O'Toole, 1988: 425*], can be found. The first cooperative ventures, originating in the Middle Ages, were based on the perception of common interest, but already by the mid-nineteenth century, the state became involved, and cooperative associations began to include an element of force. Importantly, the state limited its involvement to the creation of the legal framework, leaving the members themselves in control of the day-to-day running of these ventures including the mobilisation of resources. As such cooperative solutions had a long tradition and proved effective, such policy instruments had a high level of legitimacy. Cooperative arrangements continued to be a favourite policy instrument in the latter half of the twentieth century.

One of the most striking features of the German water policy sector is the central role of horizontal cooperation. At the local level, important water-related services are provided by municipal authorities teaming up with each other. At *Land* level, coordination between different governmental actors has been an important feature. While individual *Länder* pursue their own policies where appropriate, the development of a federal framework of water law, and, more recently, the emergence of a large body of EU water legislation, creates a strong self-interest for the *Länder* to engage in cooperation with each other and develop a common *Land*-perspective in negotiations with the federal and EU levels. Appropriately, the LAWA has thus become a central player in German water policy-making. These findings suggest that horizontal cooperation between *Länder* is a very important feature of policy-making in Germany which is hardly recognised in the political science literature on German policy-making.[10]

Horizontal forms of cooperation owe much of their stability to a constitutional framework which provides *Länder* and municipalities with a fairly effective defence against centralisation attempts. Also, the fact that water was such a long-standing policy domain within *Land* control made it difficult to overcome *Länder* resistance to increased federal influences. Another, and perhaps the most important, defence has been success: local authorities and the *Länder*, either on their own or in horizontal coordination, have generally delivered the goods. This inherent stability has made it possible that new challenges of the late 1980s and 1990s, in particular privatisation and unification, had no profound impact on the structure of the German water policy sector.[11]

While common interest has been by far the most important incentive for cooperation between governmental actors, the relationship between the state and, respectively, industrial and agricultural interests has also been characterised mainly by informal cooperation rather than force. State authority was invoked in specific circumstances at the beginning of modern agricultural and industrial development, but in more recent years agricultural and industrial interests have normally been too strong, contributing to an implementation deficit in water policy. In the main water-related conflict area of environment vs. agriculture, policy makers are increasingly turning to exchange models of inducing cooperation. The increasing introduction of charges for water-related services, and the development of compensation schemes, give monetary exchanges an increasingly important place within the range of environmental policy instruments. The relative effectiveness of such policy instruments still remains to be evaluated.

How do we place German water policy in terms of the 'policy community – issue network' dimension? It is easy to describe a core group of actors which would be involved in any major decision and which is likely to share a joint vision about the development of policy. But it would be misleading to describe it in terms of a national 'policy community' because key decisions are rarely made at federal level. Where major conflicts are involved, the federal level is usually only too happy to leave the most difficult decisions to the *Länder*. Policy evolves out of the interaction of a complex web of actors located at federal, *Land*, and local level, with horizontal cooperation at *Land* and local level being of particular importance. Overall, the 'coordination principle' is thus alive and well in German water policy-making.

Coordination plays less of a role for environmental groups. While the context for water policy has certainly changed profoundly in the last twenty years as a result of the rise of environmentalism, environmental groups have not become 'insiders'. A consensus in the 'closed' communities of technical and legal water experts may be achieved on an individual issue, but this is often not the end, only the beginning, of the political process. Policies can often be effectively challenged through the parties, the courts, through government at all its levels. The role of Greens in local and *Land* government has also produced a new actor at the heart of policy-making that is more likely to respond to such 'outsider' demands. The complexity and fragmentation of German water policy-making thus makes is impossible to associate it with a fixed location on a 'policy community – issue network' continuum. There are policy formulation processes which fit the 'policy community' model quite well, for example where a broad consensus between *Land* and federal governments and professional organisations is achieved and no outside interests are sufficiently affected to mobilise against it. But there are policy processes, for example the case of nitrate policy in Baden-Württemberg, where there is no such consensus and where a wide variety of interests, environmental, agricultural, and industrial, seek to maximise their impact through various channels, from lobbying *Land* government to local referenda and proceedings in the courts.

The history of German water policy-making has been characterised by the employment of a wide variety of policy processes and instruments. While this variety is perpetuated in the present, some common trends are apparent: networks of horizontal cooperation remain or even increase in importance for governmental actors; and monetary exchange becomes a major policy instrument to deal with agricultural and industrial interests, supplementing informal cooperation. However, with water demand continuing on a downward trend and major investments to deal with remaining water pollution problems, particularly in East Germany, having been made [*Jahresbericht der Wasserwirtschaft, 1994*], it looks unlikely that the German water management system will be faced with new major water-related challenges in the near to medium term. Incremental changes of the present system in a routine, 'low politics' environment, protecting German structures against various EU harmonisation trends [*Kraemer and Warnke, 1992*], looks like the most likely scenario for the future.

NOTES

1. We concentrate on parts of the water cycle related to water pollution and drinking water supply. Many other water-related issues, for example the use of waterways for transport, are only briefly mentioned or not covered at all.
2. The only major exceptions are the implementation studies of the 1970s (cf. Mayntz *et al.* [*1978*])and the case studies of agricultural water pollution, in particular nitrate policy (cf. Conrad [*1988, 1990a,b*]).
3. Only few private water suppliers survived: West Germany's largest single water supplier,

Gelsenwasser, was formed in 1887 as a private company to supply water to the growing mining industry. It grew to become a major water supplier, delivering drinking water to industry and local authorities in the Ruhr area [*Scherer, 1987, 1992*].

4. One exception of only episodic importance was nuclear energy. The water administrations resisted plans to construct a number of nuclear power stations along Germany's main rivers, using large amounts of surface water for cooling purposes. In 1958, water management was made the responsibility of the new Federal Ministry of Atomic Affairs, apparently in an attempt to stifle the anti-nuclear resistance of the water administration. Water was transferred to the Health Ministry in 1963 [*Radkau, 1983*].

5. There are numerous other organisations involving the cooperation of *Länder*, between *Länder* and the Federal Government, as well as international and transnational organisations concerning the management of specific water management problems. For example, in the case of the Rhine, the International Commission for the Protection of the Rhine Against Pollution (ICPR), formed in 1950, provides a forum for international negotiations [*Dupont, 1993*]. Water utilities along the Rhine also organise themselves in a transnational working group. Within Germany, the *Länder* concerned formed a working group for the protection of the Rhine, and there is also a commission to link the *Land* and federal levels and to provide an input into the international arena.

6. There are, however, numerous other organisations representing different aspects of professional interests in the water industry. A detailed description is beyond the scope of this paper (cf. Rümelin [*1991*]).

7. For general accounts of the background of German environmental policy-making in the 1980s, see Grant, *et al.* [*1988*]; Paterson, [*1989*]; Boehmer-Christiansen and, Skea [*1991*]; Weale *et al.* [*1991*]; Weale [*1992*].

8. It is in no small part for this reason that major organisational changes, for example, the integration of water supply and sewage disposal, have never seriously been on the political agenda. While there are legal and economic obstacles [*Jacobi, 1988*], these may have been overcome but there was no specific 'problem pressure' to contemplate such reorganisations on a large scale.

9. In July 1990, the Commission had taken Germany to the European Court of Justice over this issue. In its judgement of November 1992, the European Court of Justice upheld the Commission's complaint about the shortcomings of the 1986 ordinance. However, the Commission had already conceded that the 1990 amendments of the drinking water ordinance fully met the formal legal requirements of implementing the directive, but claimed that German authorities were not implementing the directive in practice. The court refused to admit that argument on procedural grounds [cf. reports on the judgement in *Europäische Zeitschrift für Wirtschaftsrecht*, Vol. 4, No. 3, February 1993, pp. 99-101; *Neue Zeitschrift für Verwaltungsrecht*, No. 3, 1993, pp. 257-258]. While the Court thus did not rule directly on German administrative practices, it firmly rejected the view of some German water law experts that it would be legal not to meet EU-standards for drinking water if this would involve excessive costs incommensurate with the risks to the population (cf. Kolkmann [*1991*]).

10. Despite the long-standing nature of these cooperation arrangements, horizontal cooperation between Länder has only recently emerged as a research topic in the German political science literature (cf. Scharpf [*1989*]; Benz *et al.* [*1992*]).

11. While politically-motivated privatisation initiatives had a marginal impact on the water sector, the process of unification essentially saw the reproduction of West German organisational forms within an East German setting, adapted to the specific local and regional conditions. Unfortunately, the detailed discussion of these developments is not possible within the confines of this article [cf. Kraemer [*1990, 1992*]; van der Wall and Kraemer [*1993*]; Kraemer [*1994b*]; Kraemer and Warnk, [*1992*]).

REFERENCES

Abel, W. (1967), *Geschichte der deutschen Landwirtschaft vom frühen Mittelalter bis zum 19. Jahrhundert*, 2nd. ed. Stuttgart: Verlag Eugen Ulmer.
Abromeit, H. (1992), *Der verkappte Einheitsstaat*, Opladen: Leske + Budrich.
Ambrosius, G. (1987), 'Die wirtschaftliche Entwicklung von Gas-, Wasser- und Elektrizitätswerken ab ca. 1850 bis zur Gegenwart' in Pohl, P. and Treue, W. (eds), *Kommunale Unternehmen: Geschichte und Gegenwart*, Wiesbaden: Steiner, pp. 125-153.
Aurand, K., Hässelbarth, U. Lange-Asschenfeldt, H. and W. Steuer, (eds) (1991), *Die Trinkwasserverordnung: Einführung und Erläuterungen für Wasserversorgungsunternehmen und Überwachungsbehörden* 3rd ed. Berlin: Erich Schmidt Verlag.
Baldock, D. and G. Bennett (1991), *Agriculture and the Polluter Pays Principle*, London: Institute for European Environmental Policy.
Benz, A. and W. Seibel, (eds) (1992), *Zwischen Kooperation und Korruption: Abweichendes Verhalten in der Verwaltung*, Baden Baden: Nomos.
Benz, A., Scharpf, F.W., and R. Zintl (1992), *Horizontale Politikverflechtung: Zur Theorie von Verhandlungssystemen*, Frankfurt am Main: Campus.
Boehmer-Christiansen, S. and J. Skea (1991), *Acid Politics: Environmental and Energy Policies in Britain and Germany*, London: Belhaven Press.
Bosl, K. (1965a), 'Die historische Staatlichkeit der bayrischen Lande', in Bosl, K. (ed.), *Zur Geschichte der Bayern*, Darmstadt: Wissenschaftliche Buchgesellschaft, pp. 644-664.
Bower, B.T., Barré, R., Kühner J. and C.S. Russell (1981), *Incentives in Water Quality Management: France and the Ruhr Area*, Washington, D.C.: Resources for the Future.
Braun, G. E. and Jacobi, K.-O. (1990), *Die Geschichte des Querverbundes in der kommunalen Versorgungswirtschaft*, Cologne: Sigillum Verlag.
Breuer, R. (1987), *Öffentliches und privates Wasserrecht*, 2nd. ed., Munich: Beck.
Brown, J. C. (1988), 'Coping with crisis? The diffusion of waterworks in late nineteenth-century German towns', *Journal of Economic History*, Vol. 48, pp. 307-318.
Brown, J. C. (1989), 'Public reform for private gain? The case of investment in sanitary infrastructure: Germany, 1880-1887', *Urban Studies*, Vol. 26, pp. 2-12.
Bruckmeier, K. and P. Teherani-Krönner (1992), 'Farmers and Environmental Regulation: Experiences in the Federal Republic of Germany', *Sociologia Ruralis*, Vol. 32, pp. 66-81.
Brüggemeier, F.-J. and T. Rommelspacher (1990), 'Umwelt', in Köllmann, W., Korte, H., Petzina, D. and W. Weber, (eds), *Das Ruhrgebiet im Industriezeitalter, Geschichte und Entwicklung*, Düsseldorf: Schwann im Patmos Verlag, Vol. 2, pp. 509-559.
Conrad, J. (ed.) (1988), *Wassergefährdung durch die Landwirtschaft: Die Nitratbelastung des Trinkwassers als Problem praktischer Politik*, Berlin: edition sigma.
Conrad, J. (1990a), *Nitratdiskussion und Nitratpolitik in der Bundesrepublik Deutschland*, Berlin: edition sigma.
Conrad, J. (1990b), *Nitrate Pollution and Politics: Great Britain, the Federal Republic of Germany and the Netherlands*, Aldershot: Avebury.
Deutscher Verband für Wasserwirtschaft und Kulturbau (ed.) (1991), *Seminar Organisationsformen der Wasserwirtschaft*, Bonn: Deutscher Verband für Wasserwirtschaft und Kulturbau.
Dominick, R.H. III (1992), *The Environmental Movement in Germany: Prophets and Pioneers, 1871-1971*, Bloomington: Indiana University Press.
Dornheim, C. (1980), *Das Recht der Wasser- und Bodenverbände*, Berlin: Erich Schmidt Verlag.
Dupont, C. (1993), 'The Rhine: a study of inland water negotiations', in Sjöstedt, G. (ed.), *International Environmental Negotiation*, Newbury Park, CA.: Sage, pp. 135-148.
Dyson, K. (1980), *The State Tradition in Western Europe*, Oxford: Martin Robertson.
Dyson, K. (1982), 'West Germany: The search for a rationalist consensus', in Richardson, J. (ed.), *Policy Styles in Western Europe*, London: George Allen & Unwin, pp. 17-46.
Dyson, K. (ed.) (1992), *The Politics of German Regulation*, Aldershot: Dartmouth.
Garbrecht, G. (ed.) (1985), *Wasser: Vorrat, Bedarf und Nutzung in Geschichte und Gegenwart*, Reinbek: Rowohlt.
Giesecke, P., Wiedemann, W. and M. Czychowski (1989), *Wasserhaushaltsgesetz unter Berück-*

sichtigung der Landeswassergesetze und des Wasserstrafrechts, Kommentar, 5th ed. Munich: Beck.

Grant, W., W. Paterson and C. Whitston (1988), *Government and the Chemical Industry: A Comparative Study of Britain and West Germany*, Oxford: Clarendon Press.

Greenpeace (1989), *Wasser ist Leben: Trübe Aussichten für's kostbarste Nass*, Hamburg: Greenpeace.

Hallauer, J.F. (1991), 'Neue Rechtsnormen für Trinkwasser', in Aurand *et al.*, pp. 24-32.

Hartwich, H.-H. and G. Wewer, (eds) (1991), *Regieren in der Bundesrepublik II: Formale und informale Komponenten des Regierens in den Bereichen Führung, Entscheidung, Personal und Organisation*, Opladen: Leske & Budrich.

Haushofer, H. (1963), *Die deutsche Landwirtschaft im technischen Zeitalter*, Stuttgart: Verlag Eugen Ulmer.

Imhoff, K. R. (1992), 'Wasserwirtschaftliche Erfolge im Abflußgebiet der Ruhr', *Korrespondenz Abwasser*, Vol. 39, pp. 321-329.

Imhoff, K. R and D.R. Albrecht (1993), 'Water resources management in the Ruhr river basin', *European Water Pollution Control*, Vol. 3, pp. 44-48.

Jacobi, K.-O. (1988), 'Grenzen und Möglichkeiten der Zusammenfassung von Wasser und Abwasser in der Kommunalwirtschaft', *Zeitschrift für öffentliche und gemeinwirtschaftliche Unternehmen*, Vol. 11, pp. 250-265.

Jahresbericht der Wasserwirtschaft (1994), 'Gemeinsamer Bericht der mit der Wasserwirtschaft befaßten Bundesministerien – Haushaltsjahr 1993; Länderarbeitsgemeinschaft Wasser (LAWA) Jahresbericht 1993; Jahresberichte der Wasserwirtschaft: Berichte der Bundesländer 1993', *Wasser & Boden*, Vol. 46, No. 7 (July).

Katzenstein, P. (1987), *Policy and Politics in West Germany: The Growth of the Semi-Sovereign State*, Philadelphia: Temple University Press.

Kenis, P. and V. Schneider (1991), 'Policy networks and policy analysis: scrutinizing a new analytical toolbox', in Marin, B. and Mayntz, R. (eds), *Policy Networks: Empirical Evidence and Theoretical Considerations*, Frankfurt am Main/Boulder, CO.: Campus/Westview Press, pp. 25-59.

Kneese, A. V. and B.T. Bower (1968), *Managing Water Quality: Economics, Technology, Institutions*, Baltimore: John Hopkins Press.

Kolkmann, J. (1991), *Die EG-Trinkwasserrichtlinie: Die Nitrat- und Pestizidgrenzwerte und ihre Umsetzung im deutschen Umweltrecht*, Berlin: Erich Schmidt Verlag.

Kraemer, R.A. (1990), *The Privatisation of Water Services in Germany*, Berlin: Forschungsstelle für Umweltpolitik, Free University Berlin.

Kraemer, R. A. (1992), 'An east-west tug of water: water services in united Germany' in: Bressers, H.Th. A. and O'Toole, L.J. (eds), *International Comparative Policy Research*, Enschede: Twente University Press, pp. 101-126..

Kraemer, R. A. (1994a), 'Paying for water and sewerage in Germany', Paper presented at the Conference *Hydrotop '94*, Marseilles, 12-15 April.

Kraemer, R. A. (1994b), 'Restructuring water institutions in Germany', Paper presented at the Conference *Hydrotop '94*, Marseilles, 12-15 April.

Kraemer, R.A. and A. Wafnke (1992), *Zukunftsperspektiven der Trinkwasserversorgung*, Bonn: Büro für Technikfolgenabschätzung des Deutschen Bundestages.

Kromarek, P. (1986), *Die Trinkwasserrichtlinie der EG und die Nitratwerte*, Berlin: Wissenschaftszentrum Berlin für Sozialforschung.

Küppers, G., Lundgreen, P. and P. Weingart (1978), *Umweltforschung – die gesteuerte Wissenschaft?*, Frankfurt am Main: Suhrkamp.

Labisch, A. (1986), 'Gemeinde und Gesundheit: Zur historischen Soziologie des kommunalen Gesundheitswesens', in Blanke, B. Evers, A. and H. Wollmann (eds), *Die Zeite Stadt*, Opladen: Westdeutscher Verlag, pp. 275-305.

Lahl, U. and B. Zeschmar (1982), *Wie krank ist unser Wasser? Die Gefährdung des Trinkwassers: Sachstand und Gegenstrategien*, 3rd. ed., Freiburg: Dreisam Verlag.

Lübbe-Wolf, G. (1992), 'Das Kooperationsprinzip im Umweltrecht – Rechtsgrundsatz oder Deckmantel des Vollzugsdefizits?', in Benz and Seibel, pp. 209-232.

Mayer-Tasch, P.C. (1978), *Umweltrecht im Wandel*, Opladen: Westdeutscher Verlag.

78 NETWORKS FOR WATER POLICY

Mayntz, R. (1993), 'Policy-Netzwerke und die Logik von Verhandlungssystemen', in Héretier, A. (ed.), *Policy-Analyse: Kritik und Neuorientierung,* Opladen: Westdeutscher Verlag, pp. 39-56.

Mayntz, R., Derlien, H.-U., Bohne, E., Hesse, B., Hucke, J. and A. Müller (1978), *Vollzugsprobleme der Umweltpolitik: Empirische Untersuchung der Implementation von Gesetzen im Bereich der Luftreinhaltung und des Gewässerschutzes,* Stuttgart: Kohlhammer.

Müller, E. (1986), *Innenwelt der Umweltpolitik: Sozial-liberale Umweltpolitik – Ohnmacht durch Organisation?,* Opladen: Westdeutscher Verlag.

O'Toole, L.J. (1988), 'Strategies for intergovernmental management: implementing programs in interorganizational networks', *International Journal of Public Administration,* Vol. 11, pp. 417-441.

Paterson, W.E. (1989), 'Environmental politics', in Smith, G., Paterson, W.E. and P. H. Merkl, (eds), *Developments in West German Politics,* London: Macmillan, pp. 267-288.

Pluge, W. (1989), 'Sicherung der Wasserversorgung durch Vorsorge', *BWK Intern* (Wasser & Boden), No. 1, pp. 1-5.

Radkau, J. (1983), *Aufstieg und Krise der deutschen Atomwirtschaft, 1945-1975,* Reinbek, Rowohlt.

Ramshorn, A. (ed.) (1957), *Fünfzig Jahre Emschergenossenschaft, 1906-1956,* Essen: Emschergenossenschaft.

Rengeling, H.-W. (1986), 'Das Kooperationsprinzip', in Kimminich, O., von Lernsner, H. Freiherr and P.-C. Storm (eds), *Handwörterbuch des Umweltrechts,* Berlin: Erich Schmidt Verlag, Vol. 1, pp. 935-941.

Roling, B. (1992), 'Der Wertheimer Wasser-Fall', in Landeszentrale für politische Bildung Baden-Württemberg (ed.), *Kommunale Umweltpolitik,* Stuttgart: Kohlhammer, pp. 56-68.

Roth, H. (1988), 'Recht der Wasserwirtschaft', in Wüsthoff *et al.* , Vol. 1, Part C9, pp. 1-28.

Rüdig, W. (1980), 'Bürgerinitiativen im Umweltschutz: Eine Bestandsaufnahme der empirischen Befunde', in Rammstedt, O. (ed.), *Bürgerinitiativen in der Gesellschaft,* Villingen: Neckar Verlag, pp. 119-184.

Rüdig, W. (1988), 'Outcomes of nuclear technology policy: do varying political styles make a difference?', *Journal of Public Policy,* Vol. 7, pp. 389-430.

Rümelin, B. (1991), 'Chronik: 100 Jahre deutsche Verbände der Wasserwirtschaft', in Deutscher Verband für Wasserwirtschaft und Kulturbau (ed.), *Wasserwirtschaft im Wandel der Zeiten. 100 Jahre Deutsche Verbände der Wasserwirtschaft 1891-1991,* Bonn: Deutscher Verband für Wasserwirtschaft und Kulturbau, pp. 46-85.

Ruhrverband und Ruhrtalsperrenverein (ed.)(1988). *1913-1988: 75 Jahre, Im Dienst für die Ruhr* Essen: Ruhrverband und Ruhrtalsperrenverein.

Scharpf, F.W. (1989), 'Der Bundesrat und die Kooperation auf der "dritten" Ebene', in Bundesrat (ed.), *Vierzig Jahre Bundesrat,* Baden Baden: Nomos, pp. 121-162.

Scharpf, F.W (1993), 'Positive und negative Kooperation in Verhandlungssytemen', in Héretier, A. (ed.), *Policy-Analyse: Kritik und Neuorientierung,* Opladen: Westdeutscher Verlag, pp. 57-83.

Scharpf, F.W., Reissert, B. and F. Schnabel (1976), *Politikverflechtung: Theorie und Empirie des kooperativen Föderalismus in der Bundesrepublik,* Königstein/Ts.: Scriptor.

Schauwecker, H. (1988), *Bodensee-Wasserversorgung: Zweckverband und Gemeinschaftsunternehmen,* Stuttgart: Konrad Theiss Verlag.

Scherer, P. (1987), '100 Jahre Wasserversorgung im Ruhrrevier', *gwf-Wasser/Abwasser ,* Vol. 128, p. 2.

Scherer, P. (1992), 'Regionale Wasserversorgung im Wandel am Beispiel der Gelsenwasser AG', *Korrespondenz Abwasser,* Vol. 39, pp. 315-320.

Schleicher, H. (1986), 'Building coordination structures', in Kaufmann, F.-X., Majone, G. and V. Ostrom (eds), *Guidance, Control and Evaluation in the Public Sector,* Berlin, de Gruyter, pp. 511-530.

Schumacher, W. (1991), 'Entwicklung der Rechtsnormen für Trinkwasser', in Aurand *et al.,* pp. 13-23.

Stadtfeld, R. (1989), 'Die Entwicklung der öffentlichen Wasserversorgung, 1970-1987', *gwf-Wasser/Abwasser,* Vol. 130, pp. 33-40.

Strobel, L. (1988), *Wasserwirtschaft in Bayern als Zukunftsauftrag und Herausforderung* Munich: Bayrisches Landesamt für Wasserwirtschaft.

van der Wall, H. and R.A. Kraemer (1993), *Die Wasserwirtschaft in der DDR,* Bonn: Wirtschafts- und Verlagsgesellschaft Gas und Wasser.

van Riesen, S. and R.M. Kieslinger (1988), '40 Jahre Abwassertechnische Vereinigung', *Korrespondenz Abwasser* , Vol. 35, pp. 743-749.

van Waarden, F. (1992), 'The historical institutionalization of typical patterns in policy networks between state and industry: A comparison of the USA and the Netherlands', *European Journal of Political Research,* Vol. 21, pp. 131-162.

von Beyme, K. (1985), 'Policy-making in the Federal Republic of Germany: a systematic introduction', in von Beyme, K. and M. Schmidt (eds), *Policy and Politics in the Federal Republic of Germany,* Aldershot: Gower, pp. 1-26.

Voigt, R. (ed.) (1983), *Abschied vom Recht?,* Frankfurt am Main: Suhrkamp.

Weale, A. (1992), 'Vorsprung durch Technik? The politics of German environmental regulation', in Dyson, pp. 159-183.

Weale, A., O'Riordan, T. and L. Kramme (1991), *Controlling Pollution in the Round: Change and Choice in Environmental Regulation in Britain and Germany,* London: Anglo-German Foundation for the Study of Industrial Society.

Weinzierl, H. (1991), *Ökologische Offensive: Umweltpolitik in den 90er Jahren,* Munich: Heyne.

Weßels, B. (1989), 'Politik, Industrie und Umweltschutz in der Bundesrepublik: Konsens und Konflikt in einem Politikfeld 1960-1986', in Herzog, D. and B. Weßels (eds), *Konfliktpotentiale und Konsensstrategien: Beiträge zur politischen Soziologie der Bundesrepublik,* Opladen: Westdeutscher Verlag, pp. 269-306.

Wey, K.-G. (1982), *Umweltpolitik in Deutschland: Kurze Geschichte des Umweltschutzes in Deutschland seit 1900,* Opladen: Westdeutscher Verlag.

Wicke, L. (1993), *Umweltökonomie,* 4th ed. Munich: Vahlen.

Winter, G. (1975), *Das Vollzugsdefizit im Wasserrecht: Ein Beitrag zur Soziologie des öffentlichen Rechts,* Berlin: Erich Schmidt Verlag.

Wüsthoff, A. and Kumpf, W. (founders), von Lersner, H. Freiherr and H. Roth (eds) (1958-1994), *Handbuch des Deutschen Wasserrechts, Neues Recht des Bundes und der Länder, Loseblatt-Textsammlung und Kommentare,* 6 Vols, Berlin: Erich Schmidt Verlag.

Water Policy Networks in the United States

JOHN G. HEILMAN, GERALD W. JOHNSON, JOHN
C. MORRIS and LAURENCE J. O'TOOLE, JR

Evidence suggests that the US water sector is characterised by multiple arrays but not an overarching sector-wide arrangement encompassing all the major decision-making participants. The water policy field is marked by considerable fragmentation in structure, as well as by largely-uncoordinated policy. Several forces – including 'metapolicy' shifts, professionalism and alterations in professional dominance, and the tension between advocates of more integrated water policy-making (on the one hand) and interests favouring the *status quo* (on the other) – have influenced the dynamics of network changes over time. Evidence also suggests that the structure of network organisation in the water sector has impacts on policy outputs. The network idea adds to the understanding of policy change in the US case, but there are also reasons to expect network-based investigations to face limitations in explanatory power in the field of comparative policy.

The objectives of this article are threefold: to provide a descriptive overview of water policy networks in the United States; to offer some explanation for how the networks have evolved over time, especially the last couple of decades; and to suggest, more tentatively, some conclusions regarding what differences these networks make for policy processes and outputs. This last issue in particular is a matter of importance in the comparative study of policy networks, and it is one addressed more fully in the concluding essay of this collection.

The three issues are treated here in order. Following a descriptive characterisation, which includes the use of several analytical dimensions helpful in comparative portrayal, the article turns to some important themes in the development of American water policy networks. The essay then deals with the significance of network structure and dynamics for questions of policy.

John Heilman and Gerald Johnson are Professors of Political Science at Auburn University, John Morris is Assistant Professor of Political Science at Mississippi State University, and Laurence O'Toole is Professor of Political Science at the University of Georgia, USA.

Two research assistants aided in the work reported here. Gloria Burch of Auburn University helped to refine and conduct the survey and to assemble an earlier version of the manuscript. Letha Strothers of the University of Georgia aided in the review of previously-published research. Their contributions are gratefully acknowledged. The authors are also appreciative of the comments and suggestions of two American water policy scholars, William Blomquist and Helen Ingram, who reviewed a draft of the article. Needless to say, none of these individuals should be held responsible for any errors of fact or interpretation that may remain.

How Water Policy Networks in the United States Appear – Plural, Complex, and Fragmented

Water policy in the US is developed and executed in many networks rather than one or two tightly-integrated clusters. Depicting these arrays is a daunting task. For reasons of space and emphasis, the coverage here is general. We provide an account of the structure of the water policy sector overall and the networks within it, rather than a comprehensive and detailed treatment of each network and all the links among them (see the Appendix for an overview of formal institutions and major policies).

Terms of Discourse

As explained in the introduction to this collection, policy network refers here to 'clusters of relatively autonomous but interdependent actors that are incorporated into the process of public policy making' [*Schneider, 1992: 19*]. Our interest is focused on networks as persistent multi-actor patterns of relationship in the American water policy sector. They are defined by the set of relevant actors and their patterns of relation. The number of actors and the configuration of their relationships in the network may vary along a number of dimensions, several of which are summarised in the introductory essay of this collection. Rhodes and Marsh [*1992*] suggest that patterns of dependencies in networks vary along four dimensions. Van Waarden [*1992*] develops a more complex set of distinctions and thus implies a great variety of types. And there is the more precise and narrow literature derived from sociometric analysis (for prime examples, see Knoke and Kuklinski [*1982*]; Laumann and Knoke [*1987*]; and Pappi, Knoke, and Bisson [*1993*]).

Some of these treatments are framed in broad, suggestive terms, while others address a level of conceptual and empirical detail that goes beyond the objectives of the present effort. Here we first address the structure of the US water policy networks by considering 'sectoral structure', by which we mean the full set of actors and the structure of their relationships in the field of water policy. We then consider the same territory using the concept of 'network', by which we mean patterns of regular relationships in the water policy sector. Therefore, network is used as a generic label embracing different types of arrays [*Schubert and Jordan, 1992: 1*], including but not limited to arrangements as various as policy communities and issue networks [*Rhodes and Marsh, 1992; Judge, 1993*]. We characterise both significant portions of the policy sector, water quantity and water quality, at two important policy stages, formation and implementation. The extent of integration across segments of the sector and parts of the policy process are questions addressed here as well.

To describe the water policy sectoral structure, we apply three of Jordan and Schubert's network dimensions: number of participants, scope of issue (for instance, sectoral or transsectoral), and level of institutionalisation (stable to *ad hoc*). In addition, we include tentatively four features of network structure commonly employed in network analysis: overlap (both within and among sector and subsectors), dominance (within and among networks), coordination (consciously linked behaviour within or among networks), and openness (accessibility to network membership by those interested in participating).

One point to note in this characterisation, however, is that the extant research literature on networks does not do full justice to the subtleties of interdependence in the US water policy setting. As the depiction below suggests, some of the patterning in this sector can be observed only sporadically. A number of actors organise with each other to respond to issues as they arise but maintain no regular or formal links. They may be aware of the potential for organisation, but this awareness does not translate into an ongoing structure with a specific focus on water issues. A snapshot and exclusively-behavioural view of the sector's structure is likely to miss this dimension. Modifying Heclo's well-known treatment of issue networks [*1978*], we designate these aspects of sectoral structure as *latent policy networks*. The concept may seem nearly as troublesome, and difficult to confirm or disconfirm in empirical terms, as the 'nondecisions' of the community power debate [*Bachrach and Baratz, 1963; Polsby, 1980*]. However, the pervasiveness of these arrangements suggests they should be taken into account in initial efforts to understand the ways that networks influence policy – in this sector at least. Accordingly, we explain some of the evidence below and suggest implications in the third section of the study. We have elected to use the phrase latent 'policy' rather than 'issue' networks because the latter phrasing would imply Heclo's full characterisation of not only the structure but also the dynamics of these multi-actor constellations, and his portrayal is focused in particular on policy formation rather than other parts of the process as well. The term 'latent' itself is meant to indicate more than a mere hypothetical; such constellations do indeed emerge at intervals in the water sector.

Sectoral Structure

A review of previously-conducted empirical research and the survey data gathered for this article both support the generalisation that the US water policy sector is currently characterised by a high degree of pluralism.[1] The population of the sector can perhaps best be described as a dynamic collage: water policy in the US involves many actors – public and private individuals, groups, organisations, and associations – which interact in various ways on multiple levels of government and industry. These actors form hundreds, even thousands, of both stable and unstable and also open and closed networks – depending on the issue, the geographic location, and a set of economic and political factors. There is no single US water policy network. Rather, multiple networks can be found at the sectoral, subsectoral, and issue levels for both policy formation and implementation. These arrangements differ on all seven dimensions identified earlier.

The present structure in the water sector is a product of changes over decades that have involved shifts from some relatively closed, limited, and formal arrangements to the more complex and somewhat more open patterns of recent years. This section sketches some features of the current arrays; the following one treats the dynamics of network change.

In US water policy networks today, some actors deal with one another in relatively stable network relationships. These operate in a continually shifting, less fixed context of intermittent participation by, and shifting coalitions among, a broad range of actors. In these cases the structure thus consists of multiple, relatively stable network cores, surrounded by larger latent policy network-like arrays. Some of the more important units represented by actors in these cores are reviewed later in the article. The broader arrangements are clearly visible only at those intermittent times when issues are being actively considered. Actions in the latent policy networks have multiple causes and effects. They take place in the context of subtle relationships that can be characterised in very different fashions, depending on one's vantage point and perspective, with actors connected in only partially-observable ways. Nevertheless, sufficient order is evident in the setting to allow for the conduct of some systematic analysis. It is to this task that we now turn.

Policy Formation and Implementation for Water Quality and Quantity

While the structure of the water policy sector does not cluster neatly based on the distinction between water quality and quantity, nor around abrupt boundaries between formation and implementation, the sectoral structure is shaped to some degree by these distinctions. Both network membership and network structure vary, depending on water cycle and policy cycle phases. The following discussion identifies major sectoral actors and develops the arguments that, first, the actors and structures of relationships for water quality differ somewhat from those in water quantity and, secondly, there are substantial differences between structures and network members for policy formation and those for implementation. In very general terms, policy formation is more centralised and organised at the national level for water quality than for quantity, with Congress and the Environmental Protection Agency (EPA) heavily involved (see below). Water quantity networks and processes, on the other hand, depend heavily on widely-varying regional, state, or even local conditions.

Water Policy Sector

Quantity	Quality

	Quantity	Quality

Formation	Government/ Executive, Legislative, & Judicial
	  US Congress
	  Army Corps of Engineers
	  Bureau of Reclamation
	  USEPA
	  Regional, State, and Local Actors
	
	Environmental Groups
	
	Impacted Groups
	  National League of Cities
	  National Association of Water Customers
	
	Professional Associations
	  American Water Works Association (40%)
	  Association of Metropolitan Water Agencies
	  National Water Resources Association
		Government/ Executive, Legislative, & Judicial
		  US Congress
		  USEPA
		  Regional, State, and Local Actors
		
		Environmental Groups
		  Sierra Club
		  Water Environmental Federation
		  Clean Water Coalition
		  National Wildlife Federation
		  Natural Resources Defence Council
		
		Impacted Groups
		  Chemical Manufacturers Association
		  Water Industry Coordinating Council
		  American Water Works Association
		  (60%)
		  National Rural Water Association
		  National Association of Water Customers
		  Natural Water Resources Association
		
		Professional Associations
		  Association of Metropolitan Sewerage
		  Agencies
		  Association of State and Interstate Water
		  Pollution Control Administrators
		
		Scientific and Health Groups
		  American Public Health Association
		  EPA Science Advisory Board

Implementation	Government/ Executive, Legislative, & Judicial
	  USEPA
	  US Congress
	  Army Corps of Engineers (East)
	  Bureau of Reclamation (West)
	  Federal Energy Regulatory Commission (East)
	  Regional, State, and Local Actors
	
	Environmental Groups
	
	Impacted Groups
	  Power Companies (East)
	
	Professional Associations
	  National League of Cities
		Government/ Executive, Legislative, & Judicial
		  US Congress
		  USEPA
		  Regional, State, and Local Actors
		  State Environmental Agencies
		
		Environmental Groups
		  Sierra Club
		  National Wildlife Federation
		  Natural Resources Defence Council
		  Water Environmental Federation
		
		Impacted Groups
		  Municipalities
		  Industrial firms
		  Farmers and agribusiness
		
		Professional Associations
		  Association of State and Interstate Water
		  Pollution Control Administrators

Policy Stage

FIGURE 1

ILLUSTRATIVE ACTORS IN WATER POLICY BY SECTOR AND STAGE

The literature and much of the survey data support the assessments that the water policy sector is decentralised and that the separation of water quality and water quantity issues is deeply rooted (see, for example, Rosenbaum [1985: *41–51 passim, 150, and 168*]; Rabe [*1986: 12, 24–25, 125*]; Smith [*1992: 111*]; and material cited by Kenski [*1990: 60*]). A senior staff member of the US Senate Public Works Committee articulated the sense of many respondents when he observed that the distinction between quantity and quality is the only difference of any significance in the water policy sector. He argued that the separation of these issues is both mandated by Section 101 of the National Clean Water Act and honoured in jurisdictional responsibilities of different Congressional committees and staffers, despite the urgings of various water policy reform groups.

These overall tendencies do not capture all the current structural arrangements in the sector, since some interesting shifts in recent years have linked certain actors in common policy development efforts across quantity and quality and through certain core administrative units [*McCool, 1992*]. Both the Corps of Engineers and the Bureau of Reclamation have expanded their set of projects into water quality efforts. Accordingly, their Congressional authorisation processes have brought an unusually large and diverse set of participants into bargaining efforts: urbanites, environmentalists, fish and wildlife preservationists, along with the more familiar water supply project advocates. Results in policy formation have included legislation addressing both quality and quantity issues within single statutes (see, for instance, the 1992 Omnibus Act for the Bureau of Reclamation). These emerging processes may be fueled in part by the reduced role of the EPA in water quality infrastructure development (see below). In any event, the selectively more-integrated arrays do not translate into anything approaching coordinated water policy. The overall importance of the subsectoral networks, which dominate much of the policy formation and implementation action in the field of water and have been persistently important for decades, is accordingly the focus of coverage here.

An Overview of Actors in the Waterscape

Figure 1 displays some of the more permanent actors by policy stage and water policy phase. In three cells, these are organised into four major groups: governmental actors, environmental groups, economically-impacted groups, and professional associations. For water quality formation, a category for science and health groups has also been added, since these actors along with certain individual experts can play important roles on some issues. Some actors operate in more than one cell. There is, however, significant specialisation of effort. The Water Environmental Federation, for instance, is a major professional association interested in water quality, while the American

Water Works Association (AWWA) formally serves that role for water quantity.[2] The Bureau of Reclamation and the Army Corps of Engineers are major federal agencies historically involved in quantity but only recently seeking broader roles; their function has been especially important for flood control, development, and irrigation projects. The specialisation is more finely developed, in a geographic sense: the Bureau is most active in the West, the Corps in the East.

As already noted with respect to the broad arrangement of the sector, the structures of actors and networks involved in water quantity are more decentralised than for quality. Further, implementation in both portions of the sector is more decentralised than is formation. The water quality policy formation cell, then, is characterised by the highest levels of centralisation and coordination of the four, although it too is populated with a substantial number of actors.

For instance, the EPA Science Advisory Board serves as a potential co-ordinating point for scientific and public health experts' influence on water quality policy development in Congress or via EPA regulations, despite the fact that thus far it has not operated very actively or in a coordinated fashion. Its influence has been limited and its advice ignored, although some expect the role to expand in the future.

A degree of coordinated, even community-like subsectoral operation for water quality policy formation can be seen in the case of wastewater treatment. As Rosenbaum concluded with respect to this subject, which involved until recently the most costly federal water policy programme:

> Like most other major federal grant programs, the waste treatment program also nurtured a well organized, vigorous coalition of interests with a stake in the program and a zeal to keep it growing. This large, diverse aggregation included the Association of Metropolitan Sewage Agencies, the National Utility Contractors Association, the Association of State and Interstate Water Pollution Control Administrators, and many potential contractors for facility materials. This coalition of professional waste treatment officials, facility contractors, equipment manufacturers, professional engineers (often the consultants in designing the facilities), and others became part of the program's permanent political infrastructure [1985: 168].

The characterisation of the full water policy sector offered earlier applies as well to the major portions of the sector and also to specific water policy subsectors within each portion. For example, a recent report of a labour-management group 'noted the lack of coordination between water-quantity and water-quality programs and the failure of water agencies to deal with the interdependence between surface water and groundwater at various governmental levels' (cited in Kenski [*1990: 60*]).

Subsectoral Networks

A review of the evidence at the subsectoral level suggests two conclusions. First, stable networks organised around regularly-important phases of the water cycle or significant geographically-specific locales for water issues are apparent. A Congressional staffer characterised water policy networks at the subsectoral level as having some relatively stable memberships drawn from the larger water policy sector and some issue-specific though regular members drawn from a wide range of organisations. The dominance by organisational actors within these networks varies greatly by issue. For instance, in the network arrayed around questions of nonpoint source pollution control, business actors are largely nonparticipants while agricultural interests are heavily involved. In the 'toxics' network, by contrast, cities are absent but business interests are major participants. Secondly, subsectoral networks can themselves sometimes be decentralised and diffuse. For example, 'policy formation and implementation of groundwater is constrained by multiple actors and a diffusion of responsibility. The result has been considerable fragmentation and a lack of coherence and unity in groundwater protection policy' [*Kenski, 1990: 60*].

Indeed, further differentiation within specialised arenas may also be developing, at least at the national level. As Rabe observes, 'the dominant trend in the formation and implementation of federal environmental policy has continued to subdivide the system into specialised and autonomous components' [*1986: 12*]. Survey data collected for the present study suggest that these 'specialised and autonomous' components come together in varying configurations to form arrangements of sufficient diffuseness and intermittency to merit designation as latent policy networks, a term introduced above.

For instance, a federal wetlands official reported that wetlands policy attracts involvement by private property groups ranging from land use planners to home builders to other propertied interests with special advocates operating from the White House during recent administrations. These actors are largely absent in all other subsectors of American water policy and are mobilised into interactive relationships only on those relatively isolated occasions when their interests are directly at stake.

It is clear, then, that a plethora of networks operates in the US water policy sector. An important question is the extent to which the networks are themselves 'networked', or significantly linked into larger patterns, perhaps even a coordinated network or array of networks at the sectoral level and for broad portions of water policy.[3] As the discussion to this point has implied, there is relatively little clear evidence of overarching networking. Some recent shifts linking certain water quality and quantity processes are referred to above; but these do not include all major sectoral actors, nor do they link decisions coherently. Accordingly, an analysis that places subsectoral networks in the broader policy framework may provide some insight. The overall structure provides multiple points of access to influence. As Rosenbaum observes with respect to one important formal decision forum – the Congress – the 'divided jurisdictions ... provide different interest groups with some point of committee access during ... policy formation, and consequently these groups resist efforts to reduce the number of committees with overlapping jurisdictions' [1985: 42].

The same observation may well apply to the sector itself: participants in subsectoral networks currently operating may see advantage in this pattern and thus resist integration. In a similar manner, the multiplicity of subsectoral network interests may tend to constrain the emergence of broader coordination or meta-networking.

Network and Community: A Note on Conceptual Clarity

The discussion in this article has emphasised structural features. In addressing the prominence of the many subsectoral arrays, the treatment has highlighted the number of actors and multi-unit arrangements. Still, some observers of the US water scene note certain broad cognitive and normative similarities shared by many actors on water matters. These have included a well-understood technical vocabulary, the treatment of an engineering perspective as central to decision-making (though this feature may be shifting under the dynamics of networks' change, as explained later), and implicit utilitarian assumptions concerning water as a resource. Although membership in subsectoral networks is diverse on many dimensions, the conflicts among participants quite real, and the arrays unquestionably fragmented across the sector, the commonalities may point to a conceptual ambiguity in the scholarly coverage of policy networks and communities.

The US case, these observations suggest, is an instance in which subsectoral 'networks' operate but certain limited 'community'-like features obtain across much of the sector. The structural issue (the network question) for the sector is largely answered here in the negative: the array of actors is not linked into an integrated pattern. Yet some common perspectives persist across structural divides. These shared views are themselves reminiscent of certain characteristics often asserted about policy communities.

The treatment of the 'community' notion in scholarship on policy arrangements may conflate two analytically distinguishable features: structures of interdependence, or networks, and shared knowledge and perspectives across actors, or presence of certain 'communitarian' attributes. The implication has typically been that structural integration into tight networks is empirically associated with shared normative and cognitive orientations. (The hypothesised cause-effect chain might work in both directions.) The conceptual fuzziness becomes noticeable in the US water sector, with structural complexity coexisting with some commonalities of perspective.

It is likely that further conceptual clarification regarding policy networks and policy communities is a necessary requisite for the development of useful empirical theory. In particular, distinctions among structural, normative, and cognitive, dimensions would seem to be essential.

The Array of Networks: Characteristics

Earlier studies as well as the present investigation support the conclusion that empirically-identifiable networks can be found for the water policy sector in the US. The networks constitute, however, complex and subtle sets of relationships among many actors operating in multiple subsectors, at several levels of public decision, and with sporadic but complicated links to related policy sectors such as agriculture, natural resources, and economic development. It is clear that detailed mapping would reveal complex constellations of primary, secondary, and tertiary relationships. For present purposes, sketching some summary characteristics of the array of networks in the sector can suffice. In this regard, the analytical dimensions identified earlier can each now be revisited.

Number of Groups. The US water policy subsectoral networks are multiple. Congress operates through scores of water policy committees that function with a fair degree of independence from each other, and each contributes to the formation of policy in association with various constellations of other interested actors. Sixteen major pieces of national legislation are currently in force on groundwater alone, and 11 agencies at the federal level are responsible for their implementation. Each of the states has jurisdiction to create substantial additional water legislation, and most operate multiple regulatory permit programmes. Four major federal water planning agencies currently function, and a different set of agencies can be identified for more specialised water policy functions. While certain actors participate with some regularity in a number of the arrays (see below), hundreds of other environmental, industry, and professional organisations and associations collaborate and (more often) compete or ignore each other in their efforts at influencing diverse parts of the sector. Many more are involved indirectly or intermittently, depending on the issue.

Scope of Issue. Scope of issue refers to whether networks operate across the water policy sector, a major portion thereof, within a subsector, or trans-sectorally. Networks of varying scope operate in the US. Water policy issues cross sectors, and so do some networks – even though there may be formal barriers to integration. The AWWA and the Water Environmental Federation (this latter unit is the major professional association for water quality) further report that their memberships are in large part overlapping, despite their differences in organisational structure, leadership, and objectives. Thus, the same actors may be members of multiple networks, and members of these networks can be found to join networks in other sectors, depending on the issue.

Level of Institutionalisation.   Some US water policy networks are stable, others unstable. Or, perhaps more accurately stated, their membership and members' levels of activity may vary over time. While there are clearly 'permanent' and regularly-active members at the core of some networks – for instance the Bureau of Reclamation and the Corps of Engineers – others intermittently but predictably coalesce around the more permanent members in accordance with the consideration of specific issues as does, for instance, the Home Builders Association on issues of wetlands policy. This broader pattern, clearly less institutionalised than water networks in many national settings, has been designated here as latent policy networks.

Overlap, Dominance, and Coordination.   The data show that within and among water policy networks various degrees of overlap, dominance, and coordination can be documented. There have been multiple efforts, with limited success, to organise various portions and subsectors of water policy. The Federal Water Pollution Control Act, with its national standards and permit programme, represents an example of an attempt to coordinate water policy implementation. For drinking water matters, to cite another instance, a Water Industry Coordinating Committee composed of five major professional associations (the AWWA, the National Rural Water Association, the Association of Metropolitan Water Agencies, the private-sector National Association of Water Companies, and the National Water Resources Association) has been established to concert efforts in this subsector. Similarly, a number of environmental associations have come to designate the National Wildlife Federation as their lead agency for water quality issues. The EPA has recently established a formal Management Advisory Group which attempts to coordinate water policy among federal agencies. Coordination and integration are themes of some note, then, within and among American water policy subsectors and networks. Nevertheless, the degree of such coordination at all levels has thus far been more hope (on the part of some of the actors) than reality. No networks of significance approach the substantive characterisation found in the literature on policy communities.

The history of American water policy is replete with federal initiatives to coordinate [*Light and Wodraska, 1990*] (see also Foster and Rogers [*1988*]). However, water policy networks are at most instrumentally·coordinated for the attainment of specific, time-bound, and limited objectives. And within the patterns of interdependence, the characteristically fluid sets of relationships offer only limited evidence of dominance. For example, in the West the Bureau of Reclamation is a lead, if not dominant, actor for water supply. Yet there are also very powerful regional and state actors who vie for leadership with the Bureau. The same basic observation – great variability, but generally limited overlap, dominance, and especially coordination – can be made for the full range of water policy networks. This conclusion stands despite the observable commonalities in perspective, mentioned earlier, shared among many of the most regular participants in water policy formation and implementation.

Openness.   Given the fluidity of network structure as described here, and although there is variation as well in network openness – ease or accessibility to network membership – it is not surprising that US networks are in many instances relatively open. However this generalisation does not always hold. For example, the national wetlands policy network is open at some stages and for some issues, but closed for others. Participation in the process of regulatory review is formally open and is, in fact, mandated by law to be accessible. On issues that bear on programme structure or control, such as policy deliberations on allowable methods of mitigating wetlands' destruction or creating new wetlands, the network is open only to selected actors. On this dimension, then, and for some subsectoral networks, certain features common in the scholarly characterisation of policy communities are visible in the US setting.

How It Got This Way: History, Evolution, and Dynamics of Water Policy Networks in the US

An examination of shifts in water network structures in the US reveals official, authoritative formal control giving way to somewhat more participatory, less structured network arrangements over the course of the twentieth century. There is evidence of a secular trend from the involvement of a limited number of official actors to more, including more informally-networked actors and larger numbers of networks over time. The numbers of actors per network, of specialisations, and of types of interests represented have also grown. The range of variation in characteristics across these networks at any given time has also risen steadily.

Nevertheless, as the networks have evolved, efforts have been apparent, involving official and some non-official actors, to integrate decision-making on water. The objectives have been varied: some efforts have aimed to move more policy to the national level, some to centralise in the hands of fewer actors, and some to tie subsectoral deliberations together ('horizontal' integration within watershed boundaries, for example). These initiatives have seen uneven success, as evidenced by a succession of commissions and boards addressing these questions throughout the twentieth century. There have been and remain persistent factors contributing to dispersion of influence within and among the networks: the scale of the nation (diversity of conditions, water basins, agendas), the well-known American preference for division of official authority among national units and intergovernmentally, and the efforts of some interests who are served by such arrangements to resist more cohesive structuring. The dispersion is aided, as well, by a fact of life regarding water policy in the US: water issues have rarely occupied a central place on the policy agenda, or been highly salient during implementation. Consequently, water policy matters *per se* have been handled largely as instrumental to other broad policy questions (for instance, development or economic recovery). These forces contribute to dispersion within several networks, splintering across subsectors, and diachronic instability.

Yet some stability – and some degree of integrative capacity – is fostered amidst the broader constellation by the persistent presence of the same actors, mostly professionals and highly-professionalised organisations – who have been involved both across subsectors and over time. These actors seem more important than ever, because of the trends toward more complex network constellations; but they come nowhere near being able to 'steer' policy formation or implementation, except, perhaps, at the subsectoral level.

The underlying premise of this section is that networks may be treated as a dependent variable for analysis; that is, network development, membership, and configuration is dependent on external or contextual factors, including changes in broad policy goals. Therefore, following a brief historical review of US national water policy, subsequent sections address the dynamics of change and development of water policy networks in the US by organising the discussion around three broad, highly interrelated explanations for changes in network structures and configurations: changes in what we term 'metapolicy' in the public policy context; professionalisation of the water policy networks; and shifting politics and the struggle between dispersion and centralised coordination.

History and Evolution of Water Policy Networks

The development of water policy networks in the US has followed an unplanned and unsystematic path. Early attempts at water policy were directed toward inter-state dispute resolution, and typically involved

Congress, the courts, state actors, and the Corps of Engineers [*Foster and Rogers, 1988: 15*]. As westward expansion continued in the eighteenth century, irrigation, flood control, and transportation issues became more important. While it is unclear to what degree these early configurations can be termed 'policy networks', three broad conclusions may be drawn from the available data. First, the number of players active in water policy was small, for both policy formation and implementation. Second, during most of the period prior to the twentieth century, water policy in the US was dominated by formally authoritative actors, principally federal regulatory agents. Third, the authoritative actors, especially Congress, were reluctant to allow new parties, even other formal federal ones, to play roles in water policy. For example, the Reclamation Act of 1902 marked the first time Congress allowed substantial delegation of programme authority to an executive agency, in this case the Department of Interior.

The early twentieth century was marked by a gradual increase in the number of authoritative actors clearly influential in water policy. The Federal Power Commission (FPC), for example, was created in 1920 as an interagency unit responsible, in part, for the first true federal attempt at water resources planning [*Foster and Rogers, 1988: 17*]. Composed primarily of federal government actors from the departments of War, Interior, and Agriculture, the FPC, with its multi-unit character and its emphasis on combining and regularising like functions, formed the nucleus for later efforts to increase the number of actors active in formation and implementation.

The 1940s saw the creation of voluntary organisations for water policy arranged around natural river basins and watersheds. An interesting feature of these organisations was a strong emphasis on the inclusion of state and regional agencies. Congress proved quite ambivalent about the problems of water policy and programme coordination during this period [*Foster and Rogers 1988: 21*]. Although laws designed to improve interagency coordination were enacted, incentives abounded for Congress to divide authority. As late as 1946, Congress maintained three distinct committees for water projects, each tied to one of the three major federal construction agencies. Water policy actors were therefore faced with conflicting incentives. On the one hand, the voluntary nature of these configurations allowed for flexibility, meaningful interaction, and pragmatic approaches to policy. On the other, alliance with a congressional committee under a formalised structure allowed for regularised organisational behaviours, maintenance of congressional patrons, and the ready political support of allied interest groups.

The postwar period was marked by efforts to centralise and coordinate US water resource policy at the national level. An array of commissions issued reports calling for the creation of executive boards, formal river basin commissions, and greater congressional oversight and planning [*Foster and Rogers, 1988: 23–*31].

The increased importance of environmental concerns in the late 1960s and 1970s led to another shift in network structure and membership. Environmental groups moved from low-key, peripheral roles in water policy and sought positions of influence. As a respondent from the Sierra Club said:

> until the 1960s we were thought of as a bunch of tree-hugging nature freaks. But when the environmental movement really took hold, all of a sudden we were important. Other organisations began to seek us out, ask our opinion, and include us in the policy discussion. They could no longer ignore us.

Significant growth in membership during this period also bolstered policy influence.

Kenis and Schneider [*1992: 27*] have suggested that 'policies are formulated to an increasing degree in informal political infrastructures outside conventional channels such as legislative, executive, and administrative organizations'. The development of water policy networks in the US fits this pattern, as more actors outside the formal framework became active. Indeed, Kenis and Schneider's contention that policy networks have emerged recently in response to a dispersion of capacity for action throughout the social matrix seems, at first glance, warranted in the US case.

It must be noted, however, that the US Constitution specifically defines an institutional structure that disperses capacity for action, both horizontally and vertically. Therefore, it is unclear how 'recent' this dispersion is in the US case. The implications of this setting are developed more fully in the last section of the article. We now turn to three themes that illuminate the development of US water policy networks.

Theme 1: Metapolicy Shifts and the Impact on Water Policy Networks

The development of water policy networks in the US can be understood in part through an examination of metapolicy[4] changes, or shifts in broad national political goals. The point here is that very general changes in national policy – metapolicy shifts – cause alterations in network structure and participation, and the modifications in network pattern and membership in turn catalyse changes in policy process and output. In this manner metapolicy shifts have a direct impact on policy, plus an indirect effect mediated through network transformations. Metapolicy shifts can change networks, and networks affect major features of policy, as a case example developed below demonstrates. Foster and Rogers [*1988: 37*] point out that until the last 20 years water policy in the US has served simply as a means to achieve other social goals. As the nation grew in the late eighteenth century and early part of the nineteenth century, water policy involved mainly the construction and maintenance of waterways and canals to aid transportation. To the extent that it existed as a discernible entity, water policy was simply an instrument to facilitate attainment of the larger goal of infrastructure construction to aid economic development.

The westward expansion of the nineteenth century prompted adaptations in water policy to help develop the west. Because much of the western lands was not arable without substantial irrigation efforts, congressional action led to the development and execution of irrigation projects [*Foster and Rogers, 1988: 15–16*]. During the Great Depression of the 1930s water policy came to the forefront of the economic development policy agenda. Once again the policy activity was not the result of a perceived need to address water issues, but rather to find gainful employment for thousands of citizens, facilitate social and economic development, and aid in the growth of economic infrastructure. Water policy therefore revolved around the construction of huge public works projects – dams, reservoirs, hydroelectric plants, and aqueducts. The Tennessee Valley Authority (TVA), for example, not only provided employment for thousands of workers, but also rendered a tremendous stimulus to the economically stagnant South. TVA projects provided both transportation networks and electricity to a part of the nation which until this time had little of either.

The growing concern for environmental protection in the 1960s changed the character and objectives of national water policy and supported changes in both the relevant policy networks and the manner in which they exerted political influence. Environmental groups took advantage of the increased salience of the issue in the broader polity and began to play a meaningful role in policy networks, though not without antagonism from more well-established actors. Not infrequently the newer groups relied on public demonstrations to publicise their objectives; when their efforts met with success, the result stemmed from the broader legitimacy of the policy issues they raised.

The effects of changes in political agendas and metapolicies on policy networks can perhaps be best illustrated by changes in water quality structures. As noted above, the increased emphasis on environmental quality in the late 1960s and early 1970s generated new national policies and provided opportunities for altered membership in networks. However, in spite of the federal attempts to address water quality matters, it became clear by the late 1970s that needs continued to increase [*EPA, 1984*]. The Construction Grants programme created by the Clean Water Act of 1972 was being used not as a supplement but rather as a replacement for state funds. With the election of Ronald Reagan in 1980, the political and economic moods shifted as well. Reagan's 'New Federalism' brought a decreased role for the federal government.

Partly in response to growing needs, the Reagan Administration began to push for private sector involvement in water quality. Legislation passed early in Reagan's first term provided inducements for private involvement by offering tax incentives for investment in infrastructure projects. While some privatised arrangements were developed, by the mid-1980s most of the tax incentives were eliminated. The result was a further adaptation of water policy and restructuring of subsectoral networks. The Water Quality Act of 1987 brought policy nearly full circle by returning administrative and funding responsibility to the states and communities. The Act allowed for the creation of 'state revolving funds' (SRFs), a mechanism through which states could supposedly become self-sufficient in water quality infrastructure funding through implementation of a perpetual fund scheme. SRF introduced a new set of actors into water quality, thus changing network structure fundamentally. Traditional network players at the state level (state bureaucracies, local governments, local bond attorneys – attorneys specialising in local governments' issuance of debt to finance capital improvements) have been moved toward the periphery. The more central roles have been occupied by professional investment bankers, finance companies, and private financial consultants. Thus, the network for implementing water quality policy has seen changes in the membership in the core of the structure, as a consequence of shifts in the broader policy context.

In sum, change in water policy and water policy networks has been driven by shifts in metapolicy on subjects ostensibly unrelated to water. The 'garbage can' dynamic (see Cohen *et al.* [*1972*]) evident in this observation has implications for how one conceives of 'policy networks' in the world of water. While there may be a 'core' of actors in a particular water subsector, it may also be useful to conceive of some water policy activity as taking place at the interstices of other sectors or other (non-water) networks.

Theme 2: Professionalisation of Water Policy Networks

Water policy over the long term has seen a gradual movement toward greater professionalisation. In the early years of the nation, the Corps of Engineers (formed by George Washington in 1795 at the US Military Academy at West Point) was the sole source of trained engineers in the country, and the Corps was often called upon to address public works needs in the states [*Foster and Rogers, 1988: 13*–15]. The Corps' virtual monopoly guaranteed them a pre-eminent role in water policy until the advent of the Bureau of Reclamation in the early 1900s. The Bureau, too, emphasised engineering in its treatment of water issues. As Congress began to take a more proactive role in water policy, network membership began to broaden, although similar professional groups and perspectives played very central roles in both water policy formation and implementation. The broadening of memberships in the 1960s and

1970s challenged the authority and influence of water professionals, but did not displace them from their central positions. As a respondent from the AWWA suggested, 'when all the debate about what to do is over, somebody still has to tell these people how to build it, how much it will cost, and how long it will take [to build]'.

As the above discussion of metapolicy suggests, changes in water quality policy have added a new set of professionals to the network, with some consequential shifts in influence and basic assumptions. The recent entrance into water quality policy networks of such newer professions as bond financing and investment banking has introduced expertise in and advocacy for not only different technologies, but also alternative policy premises: for financial soundness, for instance, a standard that can be in tension with more traditional 'water' criteria on such issues as infrastructure priorities. While the roles of these newer professionals vary from state to state (see Heilman and Johnson [*1991*]), and while such changes do not signal a professionalised representation of all the interests that can be at stake, shifts such as this one are both observable and significant.

The theme of professionalisation, then, encompasses motifs of both stability and change. The former derives from the long-term roles played by both water engineers and authoritative governmental actors. Furthermore, there is some evidence (presented earlier) that these parties interact with one another across policy subsectors. The AWWA, for example, is active in both water quality and water quantity issues, as are the EPA, environmental groups, more recently the Corps and Bureau of Reclamation, and of course the Congress. A core group of professionals thus contributes to networks' stability. The motif of change stems from the broader set of policy issues that have dominated the water policy arena (note the SRF example).

Theme 3: Politics and the Tension Between Dispersion and Centralised Coordination

The history of US water policy has been marked by a tension between dispersion and centralised coordination of policy; incentives for each have ebbed and flowed over time. It should be noted that in some of this discussion the term 'dispersion' refers to the policy process overall, rather than to the network-like arrangements through which actors may participate in that process. This theme has three interrelated dimensions: shifts from decentralisation to centralisation (and back again); tensions between national versus regional/state/local control of water policy; and dominance of sectoral versus subsectoral arrays. Rather than trying to treat these themes *seriatim*, we consider them together in historical perspective.

Early water policy was notable for the relatively peaceful coexistence of central and local authority within the sector. The federal government settled water disputes through implementation of the 'consent provision' of the US Constitution [*Foster and Rogers, 1988: 13*], while most other aspects of water supply were in the hands of individual states. As the westward movement continued, regional organisations structured around natural river basins or watersheds became more prominent.

The net effect was movement toward centralisation of some water policy at the federal level. Beginning in 1920, a series of commissions and advisory boards recommended an increased federal role in water policy to coordinate diverse interests and needs [*Foster and Rogers, 1988: 19–28*]. Water quality policy is again illustrative. Responsibility for this issue through the 1960s was primarily in state hands. The federal government's role was small, and networks were organised nationwide into state-level arrays. With the renewed activism of the federal government in the 1970s, and with an increased awareness of environmental protection at the national level, national authorities began to play a more active role. The legislative adoption of national quality standards and funding mechanisms (the Construction Grants programme) administered by EPA are indicative of the increased federal presence. The change in scope and activity of the associated networks is evidenced by the renewed prominence of federal actors, especially congressional committees and national agencies. A survey respondent from EPA noted:

> we [the EPA] were created in order to centralise federal efforts in environmental protection. We had the political mandate, the expertise, and organisational clout to make a difference. Our efforts have been designed to make us a leader in environmental protection, not a follower of others.

The metapolicy shifts discussed above also affected the efforts at centralised coordination. During the Reagan years, efforts were made in a variety of policy fields to reduce federal involvement and return authority to the states, local governments, and the private sector. The actions of the 1980s had the effect of trimming the federal role in water quality policy. Although Washington often retained control over water quality standards within EPA,[5] the shift was clear – the federal government would be more passive.

The balance between dispersion and centralised coordination has thus come nearly full circle. Early US water policy activity was conducted in a decentralised fashion. Geophysically-based structures developed around natural watershed boundaries, prompting the emergence of regional network structures. The movement toward federal coordination and centralised network structures reached its zenith in the late 1970s, only to be supplanted by a return to state and regional networks in the 1980s and 1990s. Stephen Born has concluded that 'the states are now the driving force in water resources innovation with the federal government floundering to define its mission and role' (quoted in Light and Wodraska [*1990: 597*]). In short, subnational sectorally more integrated network arrangements may be developing; but this dynamic comes in tandem with a weakening of national-level coordination overall. Fragmentation remains a dominant characteristic of the American setting, but its forms – and the *loci* of sectoral dominance – may be shifting.

Based partly on metapolicy changes (in this instance, reduced federal activity, an increased role for the private sector, and the rise of the environmental movement), partly on an ongoing struggle between centralised coordination and dispersion, and partly on a change in professionalisation (from engineering to finance) at the network 'core', the result at present is a water policy sector marked by numerous networks with stable cores of professionals, as discussed earlier, surrounded by many additional actors arrayed in the constellations we have called latent networks.

So What? Conclusions on Policy Networks and the Policy Process, US-Style

In this concluding section we consider why networks might matter in the policy process. We close with some observations about the contributions that the network concept may make to the study of public policy.

The most promising avenue for exploring network impacts involves attention to policy content. This emphasis fits relatively cleanly into the empirical and conceptual context already established in this article. The second section not only identifies metapolicy content and the status of the federal-local ebb and flow as useful explanatory tools in the examination of networks, but also provides an empirical example of how policy affects network structure *and how the network in turn affects policy outcomes*.

We now, therefore, revisit the example treated earlier and consider its implications for an understanding of networks as independent variables. It should be emphasised that this one example deals with a limited subsector of water policy; its advantage is its capacity to generate dynamic and possibly generalisable insights by referring to experience at the interface between networks and policy implementation in a specific subsector.

To recapitulate: the Water Quality Act of 1987 marked the end of the federally funded project grants approach to supporting construction of wastewater treatment facilities, and the beginning of state revolving loan funds (SRFs). A review of SRF implementation conducted by Heilman and Johnson [*1991*] showed that there was great variation across states in the impact of SRF implementation on relevant subsectoral networks. Specifically, network memberships changed, in some cases dramatically. Some members moved to dominant roles from the latent network, where their inertness but potential for mobilisation placed them prior to passage of the SRF legislation.

As discussed earlier, the consequences in one case were particularly dramatic in terms not only of the transformation of the network but also of the manner in which the network actively undertook policy design and implementation. Network composition shifted to include more private financial consultants and to de-emphasise the role of state regulators; the organisational processes associated with policy design and implementation became much more fluid; the norms that shaped choices in key policy implementation decisions (which kinds of cities were most likely to be supported or even recruited to seek support) shifted perceptibly from an emphasis on environmental need to an emphasis on financial stability. Thus this case, which by no means represents an isolated instance, vividly illustrates a range of specific impacts that networks can have on policy. For example, the SRF reform presented existing policy networks with a new strategy. The goodness of fit between the existing network structure and the new strategy was far from 'perfect' [Döhler, 1992: 240]. It did not allow for 'mutual accommodation'. Rather, a transformation occurred in which a new network emerged and assumed responsibility for local redesign and implementation of the national policy. Thus, the membership and activity of subsectoral issue networks shifts over time, often in response to legislative initiatives. These networks include readily discernible cores of professionals who are consistently active in given policy sectors and maintain the network. There are also present latent networks, each consisting of a congeries of actors, which are potentially mobilisable as the policy arena affords opportunities and incentives.

Such opportunities and incentives can arise in more than one way. Policy change or reform is one possibility. Administration preferences, driven by ideology, pragmatic considerations, or both, may be another. Or, governments under pressure may leave significant policy issues and problems unaddressed through formal policy initiatives. Kenis and Schneider [1992: 36] describe the condition of 'policy overload', and the relevant meaning and function of policy networks, as follows:

> Societal differentiation, sectoralisation, and policy growth render government i]ncreasingly unable to mobilize all necessary policy resources within their own realm, [so that they] become dependent on the cooperation and joint resource mobilization of policy actors outside their hierarchical control. Policy networks should therefore be understood as those webs of relatively stable and ongoing relationships which mobilize dispersed resources so that collective (or parallel) action can be orchestrated toward the solution of a common policy problem.

This definition serves as a convenient vehicle for revisiting the difficult, but potentially very useful, concept of the latent network. In discussing who is

" incompletely illuminated "

active in water policy, survey respondents directed attention to observations that did not fit easily into a definition of 'network' such as the one that Kenis and Schneider offer. The respondents suggested that in order to comprehend the nature of and change in networks, investigators needed to understand that these networks contained members in addition to those displaying 'webs of relatively stable and ongoing relationships'. That is, they called attention to the existence of numerous parties that can become active, but whose relationship to the core is routinely so intermittent and tenuous that they are not among the 'dispersed resources' that the core network routinely 'mobilises'.

The notion of including such a penumbral set of actors in the 'network', and referring to them as a 'latent policy network', may seem to run against definitions that emphasise continuity of relationships, and thus appear troublesome, as suggested in the opening section. The survey respondents were sufficiently persuasive on this point, however, for us to conclude that it is proper to assign the 'latent policy network' a possible place in investigation. Support for doing so comes also from findings on SRF implementation which suggest that members of latent networks emerged to take on an active and even directive role in policy redesign and implementation in individual states.

In sum, one interpretation of what we see about water policy networks that is particularly evident in the US case, and therefore has the potential to be helpful in anchoring at least one dimension of comparative research, runs as follows. Wright [*1993: 530*] challenges the assumption, implicit in some network studies, that networks can routinely be expected to exist at the sectoral level. He urges attention to cases in which no sectoral network can be detected. Here we have one such case. From the network perspective the US case is an outlier in another way as well: its constitutional foundations are designed to support that same decentering of power that the network perspective embraces.

We suggest that this constitutional arrangement helps to explain both the absence of a sectoral network and the presence of latent networks. The fragmented constitutional system is known to support an unusually diverse multitude of interests. In the pluralist conception, these organisations battle one another with policy outcomes as the result. In the network conception, they compete and cooperate with one another and with the official arrangements of the state to provide multiple possibilities and mechanisms for policy design and implementation in a political setting in which government is under pressure and overloaded.

In a context characterised by virtually innumerable actors, participatory or potential, the policy process can accommodate only a finite amount of direct participation.[6] Indeed, it may be that there are practical limits in terms of time, energy, attention span, and financial resources, on the size of networks conceived as stable and continuing sets of relationships. Thus, even leaving aside the issue of political access, networks may inherently be fairly exclusive clubs: there are structural limits on how many participants can get in. It is therefore hardly surprising that over extended periods many actors are found in the latent pool of the sector rather than in the observably-networked core.

When a policy sector is marked by significant change in policy content, or by policy overload or policy hiatus that leaves substantial sectoral needs or interests unaddressed, we may be especially likely to observe mobilisation of latent network members. These observations could of course be discounted as merely reflecting change in network composition: new members are recruited, or self-recruit; the notion of latency seems to be a needless complication that adds little. To the contrary, this study proposes that the latent network represents a reservoir of political power which is distinguishable from the general population of all groups and organisations by its potential for activation in a specific sector or subsector. If detected across many policy subsectors, latent networks might serve a role in investigations of how pressing issues can be addressed quickly and flexibly in a society marked by dispersed government, policy overload, and great organisational variety. The value the latent network adds is the prospect of a mechanism for understanding policy change in extremely complex settings.[7] Of course, the presence of such latent arrays does not imply infinite adaptability, full representation of potentially-affected interests, or unerringly benign policy consequences for those not part of the stable core. Latent policy networks constitute a different constellation than that present in the core; but a 'mobilisation of bias', to use Schattschneider's notion [1960] is possible in the broader structure as well.

The data, then, suggest the following. Under the definition of network adopted in this collection, the US case exhibits neither a US water policy community nor an overall policy network at the sectoral level. At the subsectoral level there is networked activity for policy formation and implementation, carried out through arrays of assorted shapes and sizes. There are varying levels of activity, knowledge, and influence on the part of the actors involved. Within subsectors, small professional cores maintain some degree of network stability. Much larger groups of intermittent participants, whose attention to and knowledge of the sector *qua* sector is limited, make up latent policy networks. The mobilisation of these actors is driven by factors including broad policy changes and the ebb and flow of power in a federal system of government. Once mobilised, latent policy network members can strongly influence the norms and institutional processes that frame policy design and implementation.

Beyond these conclusions, the research reported here also suggests some implications concerning possible limitations facing those who wish to pursue systematic investigations of policy networks. The article closes with a brief statement on the promise and also the limitations of the network theme.

It appears plausible, almost self-certifying, that in late welfare-state settings structures of interdependence operate in which actors make decisions and take actions that affect policy outcomes, such that these structures are not fully contained within the formal institutions of government. These arrangements can exhibit not only cores but also peripheries that are diffuse, even latent. The matter of who occupies these structures, and where the actors are structurally placed within them, is affected by broad (meta-) features of and directions in public policy. Since network structure matters for policy – the nature or identity of the actors who are in or close to the core, for instance, can affect policy outcomes – these arrays should be significant objects of scholarly attention. Networks make a difference as media of action, change, and control. In particular, network structure (for instance, membership and tightness of organisation) can affect policy outcomes (in both formation and implementation).

It is unclear, however, how much value network analysis can add to even moderately general, moderately fine-grained explanations of even moderately subtle features of policy outcomes. How does this conclusion follow? It derives from important conceptual and measurement limitations encountered in the present study and other recent efforts, and also from some of the complications of comparative research more generally.

Factors that may limit the utility of network analysis in this regard include, first, problems of precision, reliability, and validity and measurement; secondly, the possibility that the 'network' concept may prove intractable in terms of clearly distinguishing between its status as an independent variable and its status as a dependent variable; thirdly, possible, even likely limitations on the generalisability of findings across policy sectors; and limitations of generalisability flowing from the strong influence on network processes of historical and constitutional considerations as well as political culture.

The US case thus provides evidence of the importance of policy networks, and it also suggests some of the constraints likely to be encountered in developing network research toward better explanations for policy results.

APPENDIX

INSTITUTIONAL AND POLICY CONTEXT IN THE UNITED STATES

A myriad of water policy issues and institutions comprise the context for any examination of water policy networks in the United States. This Appendix offers a contextual overview to place the description and analysis of the article into perspective. The focus here is on governmental institutions and major policies; additional actors as well as network features are omitted.

In the US federal system, water policy has been an object of attention by the national government, as well as the 50 states and many of the thousands of local units, for much of the nation's history. The division of authority has been complex and the boundaries have shifted over time.

At the national level alone, at least 25 separate water programmes function, and these involve hundreds of formal policies [*Rogers 1993: 16*]. Furthermore, some important water issues – including groundwater protection, wetlands, and non-point source pollution – have yet to be dealt with in a comprehensive way. Authorisations are scattered across various policies, and states continue to be the primary *loci* of policy efforts. Some interests and policy advocates have been pressing in recent years for clear and coordinated national responses. Groundwater now provides the main source of water consumption for half the nation's population and faces serious threats to quality; wetlands have been reduced by more than half; and non-point source pollution has been increasingly recognized as a major problem nationwide. All these issues face serious technical and political complications in any extensive national response.

Both the national administrative agencies and the legislative committees and subcommittees charged with dealing with water policy are among the most important policy actors. The key administrative units include 35 national·agencies located in ten cabinet-level departments; 11 independent federal agencies not housed in cabinet units; four agencies of the Executive Office of the President; five river basin commissions; plus two bilateral international commissions (for a full listing, see Rogers [*1993: 99, 239–41*]). The most important of these are the US Environmental Protection Agency, or EPA (for water quality); and, in water resource development, the Bureau of Reclamation (Department of the Interior), Army Corps of Engineers (Department of Defense), and Tennessee Valley Authority (a regional federal authority).

The US Congress is a pre-eminent force in water policy formation. Most of its work is conducted through an elaborate system of jurisdictionally-based committees and subcommittees. One recent count of those units charged with some aspect of water policy indicates that 102 subcommittees in the House of

Representatives (representing 14 committees) and 82 subcommittees of the Senate (from 13 committees) are currently active in forming water policy and overseeing its implementation (for a complete listing, see Rogers [*1993: 99, 243–49*]).

Many additional units are active at the state and local levels. Their degree of importance in policy formation and implementation depends greatly on the water issues being dealt with.

Water law itself, particularly regarding water rights and supply, is primarily a state responsibility. In the United States the rights to surface water are decided by states, as a part of property law. In the eastern part of the country, states generally take the riparian rights approach, derived from English practice. The principal policy instrument is a set of state permitting schemes controlling withdrawal. Criteria and priorities vary by state and have altered over time. In the arid West, water rights are based principally on the doctrine of 'prior appropriation', from earlier eras when mining and agricultural uses predominated. These schemes have come under renewed challenge as the level of demand has increased.

Groundwater rights are handled under various state frameworks, including common law rights to unlimited withdrawal restricted by rules of reasonable use; allocation in proportion to ownership of overlying land; and (especially in the West) more restrictive priority-based allocations. Implementation takes place primarily via permit arrangements handled by state agencies (see Schmandt, Smerdon, and Clarkson [*1988*]). Disputes are resolved at the state level, and interstate differences are dealt with in the federal court system.

The United States has been a heavy user of water supplies. Water use per capita has declined during the last 30 years, but consumption remains more than twice as high as in any other country. The national government's role in water resources policy has been focused primarily on the development of large projects to increase supply, control flooding, and promote economic development. The era of very high national spending for such projects has ended, and some federal effort has been devoted in recent years to improving the management of existing supplies. Nevertheless, the several Water Resources Development Acts, enacted in even-numbered years since 1986, have authorised hundreds of specific projects. In earlier decades, these enactments provided heavy subsidies, primarily to benefit large agricultural interests. In more recent versions, the degree of subsidy has declined and the variety of beneficiaries has grown. Recent water resource development policy has included projects aimed at addressing concerns of urbanites, environmentalists, and others. The important national agencies for these activities are the Corps of Engineers in the East, and the Bureau of Reclamation in the West. Related recent policy initiatives at the national level in this subsector include the Reclamation Projects Authorization and Adjustment Act, along with administrative rule changes in the Bureau of Reclamation that have opened the door to the trading of water rights.

The national government's role in water quality policy has increased significantly, particularly since 1970. Yet some of the most important actors involved in implementation appear at other levels: states are generally responsible for enforcement of compliance standards (some states have enacted their own enhanced regulatory requirements as well), while local governments are charged with the construction and operation of water and wastewater facilities.

The Clean Water Act amendments of 1987 (modifying earlier policy initiated in the Water Pollution Control Act of 1948, with changes enacted in several later years) constitute the core of the national response to the water quality issue. The Act is undergoing reauthorisation. Policy charged federal regulators with establishing ambient quality standards for water bodies and, under more recent versions, developing a permit scheme for the control of point source discharges: the National Permit Discharge Elimination System. Standards were substantially tightened in 1987, with the inclusion of a number of toxic chemicals. The administering agency is the EPA, working with state regulators, and actions are backed by the possibility of administrative or court orders and financial penalties. The federal government also established under this legislative authorisation a major construction grants programme for building municipal wastewater treatment facilities. During the past 20 years, this programme was first enhanced and then trimmed. It was replaced starting with the 1987 law by an EPA-administered Revolving Loan Fund Programme designed to capitalise state-administered wastewater construction programmes for future years. The national role in this effort is under debate in 1994 as a part of the Clean Water Act reauthorisation process.

The Safe Drinking Water Act of 1986, also scheduled for reauthorisation in 1994, imposes severe regulatory standards on the quality of drinking water supplied. The law lists hundreds of contaminants and requires exceedingly high levels of purity. Regulators at the EPA have not yet been able to issue specific standards for many of these by the dates specified. Management of many local water systems have complained of excessive compliance costs, and the law has been only partially executed. Nevertheless, US drinking water quality is now higher than it has ever been (see Rogers [*1993*]). It is possible, perhaps even likely, that the 1994 reauthorisation process will result in a reduction of drinking water requirements.

NOTES

1. The descriptions presented in this article are based on two sources of data: published reports of earlier empirical investigations of water policy networks and the results of a telephone survey of selected major actors in the field (conducted during November 1992, August 1993, and February and May 1994). The survey was designed to elicit from the respondents a description of US water policy sectoral structure using as points of reference both water quality and water supply, for both policy formation and its implementation. Respondents were prompted to describe the sector in terms of networks, using the dimensions described in the preceding section, and were asked about changes in interactor structure and operation during recent years. Potential respondents were selected through a reputational process designed to ensure informed coverage of important features of the water policy sector.

   The final list included respondents from two professional water policy associations (the American Water Works Association and the Water Environmental Federation); a representative of the US Environmental Protection Agency; the US Congress (a professional staff member of the major Senate committee on water policy); a federal agency administrator with some responsibility for an important subsector, wetlands; officials from each of the US Army Corps of Engineers and the Bureau of Reclamation; and a representative of the Sierra Club. A long-time academic observer of the water policy process was also consulted. Many other actors would need to be included in any thorough survey, including additional environmental organisations, professional and industrial associations, regional and state public and private units, and other federal-governmental agencies. The present survey was used to frame a general depiction of the US water policy sector.

2. However, an executive representing the latter organisation reports that in actuality approximately 40 per cent of the Association's time is spent on water quantity, with the remainder on water quality. Within water quality the specialisation is more pronounced. The AWWA is interested in quality issues only with regard to drinking water and not, for instance, wastewater.

3. We mean by a 'significant' linkage here a regularly-used connection sufficient to influence water policy formation and implementation.

4. Metapolicy is defined as 'policy about policymaking'. See Dror [*1968*]; also see Johnson and Heilman [*1987*] for an examination of the effects of changes in metapolicy on wastewater treatment and privatisation.

5. By meeting certain guidelines and conditions, states could opt to become the primary actor in water quality standards enforcement, thereby reducing the active federal role yet another notch.

6. The policy process here is conceived broadly, to include arrangements, such as networking, that extend beyond traditionally conceived (in functional terms) arrangements for interest articulation and aggregation and for hierarchical coordination (again, for a very useful discussion of why such arrangements have emerged, see Kenis and Schneider, [*1992: 34*–36]).

7. It is likely that a portion of the set of actors occupying the periphery of the latent network are, in turn, linked in more overtly-networked relations around additional subjects of interest, including policies outside the water sector. Needless to say, these further structures of interdependence have not been traced in the current effort. However, where such less visible connections can be found, they may help to explain how the 'paradox of fragmentation and accommodation' [*McCool 1989: 272*] is addressed by certain clusters of policy actors.

REFERENCES

Bachrach, Peter and Morton S. Baratz (1963), 'Decisions and Nondecisions: An Analytical Framework', *American Political Science Review*, Vol. 57, No. 3, pp. 632–42.

Cohen, Michael, James March and Johan Olsen (1972), 'A Garbage Can Model of Organizational Choice', *Administrative Science Quarterly*, Vol. 17, No. 2, pp. 1–25.

Döhler, Marian (1992), 'Policy Networks, Opportunity Structures and Neo-Conservative Reform Strategies in Health Policy', in Bernd Marin and Renate Mayntz (eds), *Policy Networks: Empirical Evidence and Theoretical Considerations*, Boulder, CO: Westview Press, pp. 235–96.

Dror, Yehezkel (1968), *Public Policymaking Reexamined*, Scranton, Pennsylvania: Chandler.

EPA [US Environmental Protection Agency] (1984), 'Study of the Future Federal Role in Municipal Wastewater Treatment', unpublished report, Washington, DC: EPA.

Foster, Charles H.W. and Peter P. Rogers (1988), *Federal Water Policy: Toward an Agenda for Action*, Cambridge, MA: John F. Kennedy School of Government.

Heclo, Hugh (1978), 'Issue Networks and the Executive Establishment', in Anthony King, ed., *The New American Political System*, Washington, DC: American Enterprise Institute.

Heilman, John G. and Gerald W. Johnson (1991), *State Revolving Loan Funds: Analysis of Institutional Arrangements and Distributive Consequences*, Auburn University, Alabama: Final Report Submitted to the US Geological Survey, Department of the Interior.

Johnson, Gerald W. and John G. Heilman (1987), 'Metapolicy Transition and Policy Implementation: New Federalism and Privatization', *Public Administration Review*, Vol. 47, No. 6, pp. 468–78.

Judge, David (1993), *The Parliamentary State*, London: Sage.

Kenis, Patrick and Volker Schneider (1992), 'Policy Networks and Policy Analysis: Scrutinizing a New Analytical Toolbox', in Bernd Marin and Renate Mayntz (eds), *Policy Networks: Empirical Evidence and Theoretical Considerations*, Boulder, CO: Westview Press, pp. 25–59.

Kenski, Henry C. (1990), *Saving the Hidden Treasure: The Evolution of Ground Water Policy*, Claremont, CA: Regina Books.

Knoke, David and James H. Kuklinski (1982), *Network Analysis*, Beverly Hills, California: Sage.

Laumann, Edward O. and David Knoke (1987), *The Organizational State: Social Choice in National Policy Domains*, Madison, Wisconsin: University of Wisconsin Press.

Light, Stephen S. and John R. Wodraska (1990), 'National Water Policy: A Prospect for Institutional Reform', *Public Administration Review*, Vol. 50, No. 5, pp. 594–98.

McCool, Daniel (1989), 'Subgovernments and the Impact of Policy Fragmentation and Accommodation', *Policy Studies Review*, Vol. 8, No. 4, pp. 264–87.

McCool, Daniel (1992), 'Water Welfare and the New Politics of Water', *Halcyon*, Vol. 14, pp. 85–102.

Pappi, Franz Urban, David Knoke and Susanne Bisson (1993), 'Information Exchange in Policy Networks', in Fritz W. Scharpf (ed.), *Games in Hierarchies and Networks*, London: Westview, pp. 287–313.

Polsby, Nelson W. (1980), *Community Power and Political Theory: A Further Look at Problems of Evidence and Inference*, 2d ed., New Haven: Yale University Press.

Rabe, Barry G. (1986), *Fragmentation and Integration in State Environmental Management*, Washington, DC: The Conservation Foundation.

Rhodes, R.A.W. and David Marsh (1992), 'New Directions in the Study of Policy Networks', *European Journal of Political Research*, Vol. 21, Nos. 1–2, pp. 181–205.

Rogers, Peter (1993), *America's Water: Federal Roles and Responsibilities*, Cambridge, MA: MIT Press.

Rosenbaum, Walter A. (1985), *Environmental Politics and Policy*, Washington, DC: CQ Press.

Schattschneider, E.E. (1960), *The Semisovereign People*, New York: Holt Rinehart and Winston.

Schmandt, Jurgen, Ernest T. Smerdon, and Judith Clarkson (eds) (1988), *State Water Policies: A Study of Six States*, New York: Praeger.

Schneider, Volker (1992), 'The Structure of Policy Networks: A Comparison of the "Chemicals Control" and "Telecommunications" Policy Domains in Germany', *European Journal of Political Research*, Vol. 21, Nos. 1–2, pp. 109–130.

Schubert, K. and Jordan, G. (1992), 'Introduction', *European Journal of Political Research*, Vol. 21, Nos. 1–2, pp. 1–5.

Smith, Zachary A. (1992), *The Environmental Policy Paradox*, Englewood Cliffs, New Jersey:

Prentice–Hall.

van Waarden, Frans (1992), 'Dimensions and Types of Policy Networks', *European Journal of Political Research*, Vol. 21, Nos. 1–2, pp. 29–52.

Wright, Maurice (1993), untitled book review, *American Political Science Review*, Vol. 87, No. 2, pp. 529–30.

Water Policy-Making in England and Wales: Policy Communities Under Pressure?[1]

WILLIAM A. MALONEY and
JEREMY RICHARDSON

Over a 20-year period the nature of the water policy process in England and Wales has changed quite radically. Contrasting and contradictory images of the policy process can be constructed, reflecting the episodic nature of the policy process. However, some long-term trends are discernible. Policy network concepts (particularly policy communities) have been helpful in understanding some of these changes, but the model has significant limitations in accounting for sector-level policy change. Moreover, institutional reform and institutional structures have proved to be important in creating both constraints and opportunities for different policy actors. In general, the sector has become more open, more conflictual, and a wider range of interests, concerns, and ideas have been drawn into the policy process. All of these changes have taken place in the context of the increasing Europeanisation of policy-making – itself the biggest challenge to conventional analysis of British policy-making.

Policy Communities Under Challenge in Britain

Most areas of public policy in Britain have been subject to very considerable change in the 1980s and 1990s [*Richardson, 1994*]. The causes of these changes can be categorised as follows. First, growing financial and economic pressures have forced policy-makers to re-examine existing policies and existing rules of the game. Secondly, a new ideological climate developed, starting in 1976 but accelerating after the election of Mrs Thatcher's first Conservative government in 1979. Thirdly, the Europeanisation of both policies and the policy process presented an enormous challenge to British policy-makers. Each of these factors represented a major source of exogenous change to existing policy networks. Different policy areas faced different challenges. For example, the water sector has been caught up in the resurgence of environmental concern to the high levels first witnessed in the 1970s. This strong interest – what Gregory [*1971*] had earlier called the 'halo

William Maloney is Lecturer in the Department of Government, University of Strathclyde, UK; and Jeremy Richardson is Director of the European Public Policy Institute and Professor of European Integration, University of Warwick, UK.

effect' for environmental policy – has been exacerbated by the transfer of the water industry from the public to the private sector, raising the political salience of water enormously.

Existing water policy networks were subject to the same forces as policy networks in other areas. Each sector was subject to an unusual degree of 'turbulence' which changed the meso and micro level politics of the sectors. The (by then) conventional model of British politics as dominated by policy networks (see Richardson and Jordan [*1979*]; Marsh and Rhodes [*1992*]) was being tested to its limits. There is little doubt that post-1979 changes in British politics have exposed the limitations, as well as the continuing utility, of network analysis.

The Changing Configuration of Water Networks

Since the early 1970s water policy in England and Wales has been transformed from an area of extremely low to extremely high political salience. This change has seen the introduction of radical new policy ideas, the involvement of new actors hitherto not involved in either the formation or implementation of water policy, and the creation of new regulatory institutions. Furthermore, water policy is a good example of the Europeanisation of British policy-making, with existing policy networks changing as the focus of power has been shifting to Brussels.

The story is one of considerable change in terms of participation, relationships between policy actors, and policy outcomes. Existing policy networks (be they policy communities or issue networks) have been subject to considerable stress, the magnitude of which forces a reconsideration of the analysis of British water policy solely in terms of policy networks. Thus, earlier characterisations of the water policy process [*Jordan and Richardson, 1977, Jordan* et al., *1977*] need to be recast in order to take account of its episodic nature. There is much more to the analysis of British water policy than simply an analysis of policy network behaviour. Indeed, to some extent, existing policy networks have been the *product* of policy change rather than its *creator*. In effect, the politics of water policy has shifted from the private management of public business to a relatively transparent and often conflictual process.

This major shift in the political context of the sector makes a single characterisation of the politics of water policy difficult. One effect of the increased political salience of water is that participation opportunities have increased and new actors have entered the process, although often as 'sporadic interventionists' [*Dowse and Hughes, 1977*]. For example, surfers played no part in water policy in the 1950s, 1960s and 1970s, yet sporadically intrude into the policy process via high profile media campaigns highlighting the dumping of raw sewage into the seas in which they surf. Less dramatic interventions are secured by long-established groups who were previously confined to their own sector – such as the poor, homeless and disabled – all of whom have begun to impinge on the policy process in some way. Thus it appears that the hitherto well-defined boundaries of the sector have begun to erode. Participation within the sector is now more complex and less predictable and water policy is characterised by numerous cross-sectoral linkages. The number of policy actors who might participate in some aspect of water policy is now potentially in the hundreds rather than the tens.

The remainder of this article describes the nature of the water policy process prior to the major exogenous changes which occurred in the 1980s; the ways in which these shocks to the existing configuration of actors emerged and the ways in which they were processed; and the utility (and limitations) of the policy community concept in these new situations.

Restricted Policy Networks: The Traditional Role of Technocrats in the Policy Process

In the British context, Rhodes [1988] has argued that technocrats are probably among the most successful interest groups and that 'professional influence is exercised via traditional interest group activities (for example, lobbying); it is institutionalised in policy networks; and it sets the parameters to decision-making through national level ideological structure' [Rhodes 1988: 79]. Their insider status has allowed them privileged access to government through their membership of tightly drawn policy communities, which has enabled them to develop and maintain their influential position in many policy sectors. As Dunleavy argues, they constitute a professional community which is 'likely to have major and direct implications for the substantive content of public policies' [Dunleavy, 1981: 8]. By defining issues as technical and apolitical, political salience is reduced – and the cosy milieu of decision-making within closed policy-making arrangements remains stable and unthreatened. Professional power is also enhanced by the relatively strong sectorisation that has characterised most policy-making in Britain [Richardson and Jordan, 1979]. If a sector becomes relatively self-governing it can insulate itself from other potentially relevant policy areas, and this can facilitate the development of a stable exchange relationship between policy-making professionals.

In the case of water, Saunders identified the (pre-privatised) publicly owned water industry as a component part of the 'Regional State' within which all the members shared a common bond – that is, none of the agencies were subject to popular election. The Regional State apparatus developed as a result of the decentralisation and devolution of central government functions to non-departmental public bodies, and via the erosion of the powers and responsibilities of local government [*Saunders, 1983*]. Thus, because the Regional State apparatus is outside electoral control and is completely discrete from the pluralistic processes of political competition: '... decision-making appears curiously non-contentious and uniquely apolitical precisely because most of us have enjoyed precious little opportunity to make our voices heard ... The Regional State tends to be strongly non-contentious and readily lends itself to technical and apolitical approaches to highly politicised questions' [*Saunders, 1983: 23-24*]. Thus, prior to the reform process (our main focus in this article), water policy had been tucked away from public debate and was largely the result of intramural policy-making by water professionals. It seemed to conform, rather closely, to the policy community model outlined in the introduction to this volume.

Even the beginnings of the reform process did not necessarily challenge this professional power. Thus during the 1973/4 reorganisation (see below) the continuation of engineering dominance was ensured by the application of two recruiting principles, 'passing on the torch' and 'ring fence' [*Parker and Penning-Rowsell, 1980: 48*]. Indeed the Water Act 1973 which created the new Regional Water Authorites (RWAs), and began the demise of local authority involvement, was largely shaped by the inputs of these professions [*Jordan* et al., *1977*]. Moreover, the Ogden Report (on management structures) reinforced the calls for a technically and managerially efficient industry through its advocation of corporate management principles. Thus, in the early period of reform, institutional change re-enforced rather than challenged professional power. The managers of the water industry in Britain perceived themselves to be politically neutral, and were 'wedded to an ideology grounded in positivism . . . which stresses "facts" over political "prejudices" and expertise over personal values' [*Saunders, 1983: 34*]. In holding these views, they merely reflected broadly-based public sector values at that time. It was, therefore, accurate to characterise the water policy process as a relatively closed policy-making arrangement, akin to a professionalised network or a policy community.

Policy Networks and Legislative Developments[2]

The stable, private and professionalised world began to change in 1973, which saw the introduction of major structural changes in the water industry. This major piece of legislation, to which we now turn, was the first in a whole series of changes, which are still incomplete. As we shall see, the total impact of these changes was to transform completely the nature of water policy networks in England and Wales.

The Water Act 1973: Intramural Policy Change

The Water Act 1973 created ten Regional Water Authorities out of 198 water supply and over 1,000 sewage disposal units (mainly local government controlled). The 1973 Act had a technical imperative at its roots – the integration of water supply and sewage disposal functions to meet anticipated water supply difficulties. The boundaries of the RWAs were hydrologically drawn and were based upon the concept of Integrated River Basin Management (IRBM) with the river basin (or groups of river basins) chosen as the basic water management unit. The major policy change in setting up the RWAs is more an example of endogenous rather than exogenous change, however. Indeed, Richardson and Jordan argue that it was a good example of policy community politics in that change occurred only when an internal consensus emerged among water professionals about its necessity, and about what shape change should take [*Richardson and Jordan, 1979*].

Yet the 1973 Act – certainly a meta-policy change in terms of the sector as whole – challenges the notion that policy communities prevent policy change, or indeed, that they are always characterised by consensus. Thus local authority interests were major losers in the reform process, partly because they were preoccupied with what they saw as the major challenge to their position – the reorganisation of local government.

In practice, the 1973 Act created a RWA membership dichotomised along two lines of legitimation, each rooted in competing ideologies – technical and electoral. Within this arrangement the domination of professionals, whose legitimacy derived from their technical competencies, sat somewhat incongruously with local authority nominees whose legitimacy derived from popular election. Local authorities decried the RWAs' lack of democratic accountability. The RWAs were not directly elected yet they enjoyed the power to raise taxes. The RWAs maintained that they were democratically accountable because a majority of their members had to be local authority nominees and the RWA's were responsible to Parliament via the appropriate minister. Also they were open to public scrutiny and pressure from numerous sources.

Local authority nominees on RWAs were the result of a concession to the local authority associations during the passage of the 1973 Act. Their membership was – *de facto* – placebo in nature. It gave an air of having met local authority claims. However, in reality local authority members were swamped with the technical details during RWA meetings. Their role was never envisaged as that of bringing any semblance of democratic accountability to the RWAs. Indeed the Ogden Committee Report recommended that all members of RWAs should view water problems from a corporate management perspective, and relegate their special interests to a secondary position.

That the relationship remained cordial was probably a result of a process of depoliticisation. Saunders argues that the reduction (and ultimate elimination) of local authority involvement in policy-making meant that there was little scope for conflict [*Saunders 1984: 12*].

Thus although the 1973 Act was a major reform in that it both drastically reduced the number of authorities and introduced an integrated system based on hydrological boundaries, it did not yet challenge existing professional power. The real losers were the local authorities. They had been moved from running the water industry to playing an ineffectual role in the new institutional structure. In terms of network analysis, a member of the core policy community had been pushed to the periphery (and was eventually excluded altogether under the Water Act 1983; see below). As an original key member of the 'network' they neither agreed to their change in status and position, nor were they able to stop it. Neither was this a simple case of an impositional policy style by government, as the original reform proposals were more or less generated from within the industry. Essentially, the water professionals seized an opportunity for change and were able to mobilise the necessary governmental backing to push the reforms through against a rather ineffective (and heavily distracted) local authority resistance.

The Water Act 1983

The complete demise of the local authorities occurred under the Water Act 1983 which finally abolished the institutionalised link between the RWAs and local authorities. It removed the statutory requirement that local authority nominees comprise the majority of RWA membership. The size of the RWAs was reduced to between nine and fifteen and the relevant ministers were given powers to appoint all RWA members. RWAs were permitted to terminate sewerage agency arrangements with district councils if they were dissatisfied with the quality of the councils' service, and the two representational bodies – the National Water Council (NWC) and the Water and Space Amenity Commission – were abolished. Although the RWAs were to make special arrangements for consumer representation, the Act dealt decisively with the issue of democratic accountability by removing any pretence of a democratic basis. Insofar as changes in policy networks were taking place, they were designed to restrict participation still further. The policy process was becoming more closed rather than more open. The policy community was still very much in place, but one of its members had been shown the door.

The Water Act 1983 also impacted on the shape of policy networks in other ways. For example, the abolition of the National Water Council lead RWAs to liaise directly with the Department of the Environment (DoE). Consultation and negotiation occurred directly between DoE officials, chairmen of the RWAs and ministers. In practice much of the interaction concerned ceilings for RWA borrowing and the setting of RWA water charges. Once agreement was reached over the total financial package, the RWAs had the power to distribute the resources as they wished. The relationship can be described as one where the RWAs determined their own objectives within the strict financial framework laid down by the government. Saunders summarised the relationship as follows:

> ... the RWAs make policy while the government controls the purse strings, and while this certainly does not indicate autonomy, nor does it suggest subordination. Important policy decisions are taken at the regional level by the chairmen and his senior officers, and it is for this reason that private sector groups with an interest in water find it more than worthwhile to try to cultivate relations with them [*Saunders, 1984: 9*].

The implication here is of some kind of layered system of policy communities with wider participation only at the regional level. The relative autonomy view has been subsequently confirmed to us by the chairman of one of the (subsequently) privatised RWAs, Yorkshire Water plc, Sir Gordon Jones. He said that:

> ... although my experience of the public sector is limited to about five or six years in Yorkshire Water, the degree of Government interference in the water industry was quite low, and we were left on a fairly loose rein subject only to severe financial constraints on how much we could borrow. There were, of course, second order targets, such as reductions in operating costs, numbers employed, disposal of assets and the like, but they were fairly minimal: in addition, there were nudges about charges, but no explicit directives [*correspondence, 28 May 1991*].

Here we see the beginnings of a second major exogenous change to affect water networks which eventually caused seismic changes in the sector as a whole. As elsewhere in the public sector at this time, financing began to come to the fore as an issue of concern. Public sector finances were increasingly pressurised post-1976 under the Labour government, a trend which accelerated rapidly after the election of the Conservatives in 1979. The increasing governmental pre-occupation with financing may have contributed to a decline in the government's own expertise in the sector, alongside a general trend to reduce the size of the central bureaucracy. Thus, we see two possibly conflicting trends emerging. First, the increasing pressure from government regarding the financing of the industry – that is, a rather more *dirigiste* style. Secondly, a decline in government's interest in and capacity to interfere in the details of the sector, so long as the financing was kept under control.

At the same time, the organisational culture of the RWAs was changing – at least at the senior management levels. As Sir Gordon Jones put it to us:

> . . . most, if not all, of the Water Authorities started to think of them-selves as businesses, albeit publicly owned and subject to financial and other constraints . . . all ten introduced business practices to the maxi-mum extent compatible with that . . . there is no doubt that the prevail-ing culture and ethos within the water authorities changed markedly after 1983 or so, with more of an emphasis towards the definition of corporate goals and objectives, the introduction of Business Plans, management training and on quite a large scale, and a greater degree (albeit still not very much) of customer orientation [*correspondence, 28 May 1991*].

These broad cultural changes were as exogenous as they were endogenous. Members of the water policy sector were as affected by these new cultural forces as were actors in other sectors – such as universities and the health service. The water sector had to respond in its own way, but it was a common enough task in the 1980s [*Richardson, 1994*]. In the case of water and in others such as British Telecom) some interests were able to exploit and bene-fit from these value changes. However, exploiting the new values often needed a new type of professional – not necessarily the engineer.

These broad changes still left the uncomfortable question of accountability. The important political symbol of accountability did not end with the disenfranchisement of directly elected local representatives. Consumer Consultative Councils (CCCs) were established in each RWA and were com-prised of between 10-40 members representing a wide variety of interests (local authorities, industry, agriculture, voluntary associations and so on). In addition to the CCCs, Regional Recreation Conservation Committees (RRCCs) were created and were composed of numerous recreational and environmental groups. In theory, therefore, quite a wide range of groups were recognised as stakeholders in the policy sector. However, the rather symbolic nature of these bodies is demonstrated by the absence of any interest shown in them by major producer groups – the Confederation of British Industry (CBI) and the National Farmers Union (NFU), for example, who also claimed (and were granted) a stake in water policy. These groups continued to lobby as core insiders [*Maloney et al., 1994*] through the traditional routes – informal and regular contact with the regional headquarters of the water authorities – rather than through the official consultative structures. As the Southern Water chairman informed Saunders:

> ... we have regular meetings with groups like the NFU, the CLA and the CBI ... so all that's been going on irrespective of these consultative

councils ... I can't speak to every bloody shopkeeper. We have been in constant discussion with the major groups. I think the consultative councils will widen the discussion ... I will continue to talk with these groups so that I shall have two lots to talk to instead of one lot [*Saunders, 1984: 15*].

In reality two types of access to the implementation process were being used. As Parker and Penning-Rowsell [*1980: 248*] argue, while access to the RWAs was not restricted solely to 'mutually self-interested' groups – that is to agricultural, industrial and professional bodies, these '...traditionally strong and politically astute interests ... make better use of these opportunities and generally present arguments with which the Government (and the RWAs) are likely to agree'.

The operation of a privileged or weighted access system was also a consequence of existing behavioural norms. It was not possible to consult every conceivable interest. In any case, intensity of interest is always an important factor in influencing participation, especially as the focus of policy change moves towards the implementation phase. Here the old notion of core groups is useful. In most policy areas there is usually a core of actors whose interests are vitally affected by a particular policy or by the actual ways in which a chosen policy instrument is to be implemented. These actors are likely to devote more time and resources to participation, are more likely to see continuous participation as cost-effective, have more knowledge as a result, and arguably have more to win or lose.

While the post-1974 and 1983 reforms were being implemented by these core actors, contextual and exogenous changes regarding managerial styles and financial constraints were beginning to have a more profound effect on the distribution of power within existing networks – the balance between the professions was beginning to change. Almost without the old water professionals realising it, a new agenda was being set, and new values were being introduced. These long term changes culminated in the arrival and processing of the privatisation issue. It was this event which proved to be an enormous shock to the existing policy networks. It also raised important questions relating to notions of stability of policy communities and the conditions under which change takes place. Moreover, the 1970s and 1980s had seen the arrival of a completely new institutional structure (Integrated River Basin Management and the RWAs) which made further radical change possible.

Privatisation as Exogenous Shock

Privatisation of publicly owned industries had gradually moved up the Conservatives' agenda, even though it was not a significant policy commitment when they were elected in 1979. As the momentum of privatisation grew, more and more policy areas were subject to major shocks as this metapolicy began to be applied more systematically. To the surprise of many in the industry and outside it, water proved no exception.

Agenda Setting and the Role of Policy Communities

Although water privatisation itself had its specific origins within at least part of the water policy community, its eventual formulation presented an enormous shock and challenge to the existing policy process. The emergence of privatisation as a policy issue is one of the most remarkable examples of the privatisation process in Britain. Initially, there was no governmental intention to privatise the industry. Yet today, England and Wales have a totally privatised sewage disposal and water supply system.³ Over a two year period 1984 to 1986 the Conservative government executed a complete U turn on the issue, as the following three quotations illustrate clearly:

> *We have absolutely no intention of privatising the water industry.* The government have no plans to urge that upon the water authorities. There has been some press speculation about it in the past, but there is no intention to do so'[*Mr Neil MacFarlane, Parliamentary Under-Secretary of State for the Department of the Environment, HC Debates, 20 December 1984, col. 457* – emphasis added].

> ... my right hon. Friends and I will be examining the possibility of a measure of privatisation in the Industry.' [*Mr Ian Gow, Junior Environment Minister HC Debates, 7 February 1985, col. 1142*].

> *In the last six years we have made the water authorities fit and ready to join the private sector ... Privatisation is the next logical step.* It will bring benefits to the customers, to the industry itself and to the nation as a whole.' [*Mr Kenneth Baker, Secretary of State for the Environment HC Debates, 5 February 1986, col. 287* – emphasis added).

As suggested earlier, the pre-privatisation history of the industry had seen major institutional restructuring, particularly the major rationalisation of the publicly owned industry into ten Regional Water Authorities. The industry had also begun to develop a more managerial culture in common with other public sector organisations at the time. Thus, in one sense, the eventual decision to privatise may not have been quite as radical as it initially appears, in that both structurally and attitudinally, the industry had changed in a direction which at least facilitated, if not provoked, privatisation. As is often the case in the reform process, a spark is needed to provoke change and to mobilise change champions within the sector. In the case of water, it was a specific event derived from the broad contextual changes in the industry's financing.

In February 1985 the Treasury Orders on Rate of Return for the water industry provoked and annoyed the management of some of the RWAs. Indeed, in January 1985 several of the RWA chairmen had reminded their customers that the government was to blame for the increases in charges. In particular, the Thames Water chairman, Roy Watts, stated that his Board objected to the repayment to government of an extra £40m in loans and to the consequent increase in charges of 10 per cent to cover it – Thames had budgeted for a six per cent increase. Watts claimed that Thames could provide a better service if it was in the private sector, and that Thames had become a revenue-raiser for the Treasury. Mr Watts played a key role in the initial stages of the privatising process and his intervention heralded the beginning of 'a long period of confusion and false starts' [*Kinnersley, 1988: 136*]. It would be wrong, however, to see Watts' intervention as a random event. Since being appointed he set in train a process of organisational change, bringing to Thames a completely new perspective, culminating in an organisational culture which was more akin to the concept of an American utility company than to a British public service organisation. Therefore, this initiative from one part of the industry did not come out of the blue. It reflected the values of the industry's new managers, even though it did not reflect any involvement of the water policy community as a whole.

Following Mr Watts' comments, the late Ian Gow, the junior Environment Minister announced, during the Treasury Orders debate on 7 February 1985, (it is believed without the knowledge of his department) that the government was *at least prepared* to consider radical change. However, as late as 31 January 1985, the Prime Minister (PM) had been unenthusiastic about the prospects of water privatisation. Indeed, in December 1984 the government had issued a categorical denial that it had any intention of privatising the water industry. In response to a written parliamentary question, the PM replied that, 'The government would welcome new ideas on privatisation. However, the Water Authorities are natural monopolies for many of their functions and we need to be particularly careful when considering replacing a public monopoly by a private one. *Because of the environmental and public health responsibilities, any proposal to privatise them would also raise issues of regulation*' [*HC Debates, 31 January 1985 col. 292* – emphasis added]. Yet one week later Mr Gow said that 'Some of my right hon. and hon. Friends have suggested that the Water Authorities might be transferred to the private sector and I understand that the prospect would not be unwelcome to the Chairman of Thames ... The transfer of Water Authorities, which form a natural monopoly, presents special problems, not least because of their regulatory functions. Nevertheless, my right hon. Friends and I will be examining the possibility of a measure of privatisation in the industry' [*HC Debates, 7 February 1985, col. 1142*].

Privatisation of the water industry therefore arrived on the agenda suddenly, although we believe that Mr Gow had previously discussed the possibility of privatisation with the Chancellor of the Exchequer and some Conservative backbenchers. A threatened Conservative revolt over the Rate of Return Order was also influential in catalysing the government's interest in privatisation. There had been no departmental consideration of models for a privatised industry or of the complex regulatory issues which the Prime Minister had recognised. Water privatisation was near the bottom of the Treasury's list of possible privatisations and there was no need for active departmental consideration. The hitherto well-ordered policy community in water had not considered the issue, the government had not really considered it, and even the main proponents appeared to have no clear ideas of how it might be achieved, or of what political obstacles might be encountered with rival interests, or of the possible legal implications because of Britain's membership of the EC.

At the policy initiation stage, therefore, the evidence strongly suggests an absence of policy community influence or of widespread consultation processes. However, once the government had declared its willingness to examine water privatisation, it started a consultation process which followed the standard operating procedures for processing political issues. On 1 April 1985 the Department of the Environment circulated a discussion paper to water authority chairmen and others, partly to buy time in view of the lack of preparation, and partly to gauge the industry's opinion before consulting more widely. At the outset the Department had a rather partial conception of who really mattered. This led to a narrow definition of the policy community.

The Water Minister, John Patten, revealed that the government received 43 responses to the discussion paper of which 'seven supported the principle of privatisation and eleven opposed it. The remaining 25 commented on practical issues, without expressing a view on the merits of privatisation itself' [*HC Debates, 16 January 1986, col. 680w*]. Leaders of the industry, represented by the Water Authorities Association (WAA) (now the Water Services Association [WSA]) were divided, but not sufficiently so for the Watts' initiative to be stalled by opposition from his own colleagues. Despite the managerial enthusiasm for greater freedom, there was a reluctance to enter into controversial political territory. The stance was that the decision to privatise was a political one, whereas the practicalities of such a decision were of central concern to the industry. Insofar as the WAA had an official (public) view, in 1985, it believed that the authorities should be privatised as they stood, with their environmental, service, and regulatory obligations embodied in the general terms of the licences issued to each authority. The Association rejected a suggestion that private authorities could not exercise regulatory functions. Internally, however, the Association recognised that privatising in toto could lead to internal conflicts between commercial and regulatory objectives and that a new regulator might be needed.

The government's 1986 White Paper, *Privatisation of the Water Authorities in England and Wales,* in fact stated that the RWAs were to be privatised *in toto.*

> The principle of integrated river-basin management ... introduced by the Water Act 1973 will be retained. The water authorities will be privatised on the basis of their existing boundaries ... and should continue to carry out their responsibilities for the management of rivers, control of pollution, fisheries, environmental conservation, recreation and navigation [*DoE, 1986: 2-3*].

Land drainage and flood protection were to remain under public control reflecting the long-standing influence of a very well organised subsectoral policy community in land drainage.

In fact the whole process soon ran into trouble – both political and legal. Again, this suggests an important qualification to the policy community model. The internal logic of maintaining consensus and, above all, keeping decisions within the confines of an existing trusted group quite clearly failed. In the event, the whole issue first entered the public domain causing the policy community to lose control and was then internalised by the relevant Minister who took what was a personal, but key decision.

The Interlude: Policy Failure and Extended Consultation

The government faced a deluge of opposition to its proposals from bodies of varying degrees of influence, including the Council for the Protection of Rural England (CPRE), the Institute for European Environmental Policy (IEEP), the Country Landowners Association (CLA), the Institute of Water & Environmental Management (IWEM) the CBI, and the trade unions. Even the Ministry of Agriculture, Fisheries and Food (MAFF) was unhappy about certain aspects as its policy space was being threatened. One obvious interest was the local authorities. In comparative European terms the expectation would be for local authorities to be significant policy actors. Not so in Britain. They had gradually been excluded from the sector and failed to seize this opportunity to re-enter the policy area.

There were three decisive factors which forced the government to shelve its 1986 proposals. First, widespread opposition (in particular, the CBI) was important. Whilst the CBI argued that the RWAs were not the most natural candidates for privatisation, it nevertheless welcomed privatisation, but rejected the proposed model. It argued that it was wrong in principle that one privatised company should exercise statutory control over the affairs of another private company. (The landowning interests made the same point.) Secondly, the late Nicholas Ridley's arrival as Secretary of State in May 1986 was a major influence on events. Thirdly, the legal controversy raised by environmental organisations such as the CPRE and the IEEP over the question of whether the private water companies would constitute *competent authorities* under EC law was a key issue. For example, Nigel Haigh, Director of the IEEP had written to *The Times* on 13 May 1986, questioning whether the privatised water companies would constitute such competent authorities pointing out that, unless this was resolved, the government could at any time be challenged in the European Court [*The Times, 13 May 1986*].

This issue seems not to have been adequately addressed by the government even though elements within the WAA had already anticipated that it could prove difficult to resolve. In the end, most participants finally recognised that water policy was subject to the same exogenous forces as other policy areas – namely Europeanisation – with a shift in the locus of power from Whitehall to Brussels. However, both the government and the majority of interests normally consulted in this sector were slow to recognise the full implications of this shift, in terms of lobbying. Outsider groups were, in contrast, quick to exploit this potential [*Mazey and Richardson, 1993*], and had a better grasp of the significance of EC membership than did some of the core groups. Eventually, the European Commission issued a 'carefully worded warning' that the proposed transfer of pollution control functions to the private sector might be inconsistent with EC legislative requirements:

> The Commission does not know of any private body operating in a Member State as a competent authority under Council Directive 76/464 EEC (which deals with discharges of dangerous substances) ... the Commission takes the view that the 'competent authority' in the sense of the said Directive can only be an authority, empowered by each Member State, which acts, in performing its functions, in the general interest' [*OJ No. L 129, 18 May 1986: 23*].

The EC issue illustrates the *ad hoc* development of the government's plans. The plans were drafted without reference to this issue, and without effective dialogue with the Commission. Again, this is an example of an initially unrecognised exogenous influence over the network of actors involved in the sector. The Commission was a key player yet others appeared not to notice that it was on the field! Only by late May 1987 did the Department of the Environment finally concede that the proposed private water companies were unlikely to qualify as competent authorities. The water industry itself eventually recognised the government's need to accommodate certain influential non-water groups such as industrial and landowning interests and began looking for satisfactory solutions with them. Although it was an insider group, it recognised that the issue might be processed within a much wider network. It therefore began to search for a consensus within this more extended network of policy actors.

As a result of strong opposition and the specific difficulty of the competent authority issue, the privatisation of the water authorities was, therefore, postponed. This failure of the original proposal for the privatisation of the water industry reflected an inappropriate choice of consultation processes by the government. It had misjuged the anticipated reactions, believing that it could process the initial (and crucial) policy developments via a very tightly drawn policy community – consisting of the relevant government organisations and the water authorities. There was also a failure to recognise the increasing significance of trans-national politics – the EC had become an important policy actor and could not be so easily discounted.

Lonely Decisions: Internalised Policy-Making and the Creation of the National Rivers Authority

After an initial process limited to core members of the water policy community, the policy development phase had seen very different patterns of interaction. The period of limited consultation was followed by a more open phase in which actors outside the usual policy community played an important role. This period of wider involvement was followed by a short period when policy-making became internalised [*Jordan and Richardson, 1982*] – that is, the government virtually ceased consultations with the affected interests, even those normally part of the inner circle of groups. Thus, for a time, a third model of policy-making appears a more appropriate description of events. This presented the opportunity to resort to an 'impositional policy style' [*Richardson* et al., *1982: 13*], in which the policy community and the policy network as a whole were excluded.

The government's shift was, however, not simply due to the considerable external pressures being exerted on it. The change reflected much more closely the new minister's views. His single-mindedness was not the only factor which led him to impose a radical solution. He recognised that the RWA chairmen had by then reached a consensus over the desirability of privatisation. There had been a gradual shift of opinion within the WAA, with some doubters and opponents having become enthusiasts and others having left the industry. The regulatory question could be resolved by governmental imposition, providing that the industry was guaranteed the right to substantial involvement in the negotiations over the functions of the new regulatory body, and over many issues such as land assets, pensions and land drainage, all of which were crucial to the financial future of the priva-tised companies. Departure from the policy community model was in part conditional on its re-introduction at a lower level of decision in order to maintain the political support of this key interest.

The final decision of the minister, Nicholas Ridley, was that it was no longer possible to consider handing over the environmental regulatory functions to the proposed private water companies. Thus, when they were privatised, the Regional Water Authorities would have to lose their existing regulatory functions. The minister conceded that the government had failed to convince the opponents to the original proposal and indeed, he expressed the personal view that their objections should not be resisted. He, therefore, announced that only the water supply and sewage disposal functions were to be privatised and that a new regulating body – the National Rivers Authority (NRA) – was to be established. The new public body would take over the functions of environmental regulation. Essentially, this key decision was imposed on the industry but the industry concluded that the benefits (to it) of privatisation still outweighed the costs.

The industry finally decided to accept the imposition of the NRA, and to play its full role in the decision-making processes relating to the many remaining issues to be resolved. By November 1987 the government had received 349 responses to its proposals to establish the NRA. Of that total, 179 supported the creation of the NRA, 39 opposed it, and 131 expressed no view but offered comments on aspects of its operation [DOE, 1987].

The government had successfully brought the WAA back into the detailed processing of the privatisation issue. In that sense some kind of policy com-munity was re-established, via the switch from 'high' to 'low' politics [Hoffmann, 1966]. This was crucial because of the pivotal position of the Water Authorities vis-à-vis their role in both their flotation and subsequently in implementing privatisation, and the need to maintain their public support for the main thrust of a controversial policy. The high political salience of privatisation was being eroded into a series of more manageable sub-issues which were bargainable. This had a number of advantages for both the government and the industry. Issues could be processed in private consulta-tions between government and water industry officials. The proposals could be de-politicised and transformed into a series of technical problems to be resolved by fellow professionals. Having adopted an impositional policy style in deciding to set up the NRA, the government then shifted back towards a more consensual and negotiative policy style in order to secure delivery of the policy as a whole. In other words, the original network characteristics were re-introduced, and issues began to be processed again, via the policy community model. The approach of the privatisation date increased the pressure on the government to settle all remaining issues. A re-establishment of the rules of the game had occurred, and both government and industry moved forward on the basis of mutual self-interest.

One important qualification to the picture of the re-introduction of normal politics needs to be made, however. The settlement at the sectoral level facilitated the rebuilding of a recognisable policy community but it also introduced a new institutional structure to the industry – the new regulatory system. As we shall see below, the politics of water is played out under a different set of institutional arrangements and rules, as well as in the context of continued high issue salience. These two factors have fundamentally changed the politics of the sector in the post-privatisation period.

Political Salience and the Influence of Policy Networks on Policy

The reality of the politics of water post-privatisation is quite different from the pre-privatisation situation. There is now much greater conflict within the sector than was ever the case under public ownership; the range of organisations involved is undoubtedly greater; the power to decide the main lines of policy is increasingly in Brussels rather than in Whitehall or Westminster; and the policy network as a whole is more open and vulnerable to external influences than at any time in its previous history. Moreover, the state has not gone away, either. In broad terms, the shift has been from a sector in which a fairly coherent network linking identifiable policy communities could be distinguished to a sector where its boundaries are indistinct, the agenda setting process is unpredictable, and decisions emerge from a rather loose extended issue network of actors constrained by the complex national regulatory structures and subject to considerable extra-territorial influences.

Why has this rather unstable and unpredictable situation arisen? Several answers seem plausible. Privatisation itself has had unintended and profound consequences for all existing actors. Privatisation was controversial and brought the industry more fully into the political spotlight – raising water consumers' expectations. When sewage disposal and water supply were a local government service paid out of general or local taxes (property rates) then a particular set of public perceptions and attitudes followed: legitimacy was high and expectations were low. Providing the service via profit-maximising private companies produces a rather different set of perceptions and expectations which manifests itself in at least four ways. First, general consumer bodies such as the National Consumers' Council have began to articulate consumer interest in water policy. Secondly, the industry's own consumer bodies see themselves in a different and more proactive light. Thirdly, individual consumers appear to be more demanding in their relations with the companies. Lastly, as a consequence of the above, all actors appear to be more conscious of the consumer interest and of its potential to cause trouble. The last point is of special significance to our interest in the changing nature of policy networks. In a very real sense consumers now 'participate' in a way which never used to be the case. They occupy what Dudley terms an empty seat during policy discussions [*Dudley, 1994*] and their potential political reactions have to be anticipated.

A second new factor is that environmental interests have continued to play a significant role in influencing the policy agenda at both the national and European levels. To some degree they are directly involved as participants in the consultative process and, increasingly, in the legal process. For example, Friends of the Earth (FOE) has begun reporting breaches of the Drinking Water Directives to the European Commission and has challenged the UK interpretation of values for such parameters as nitrates [*Fawell and Miller, 1993*]. The main resource of such groups is, of course, publicity and their position as some sort of surrogate public opinion. However, resorting to legal processes is a relatively new strategy for British interest groups and is similar to that adopted in the US.

The constant pressure from the environmentalists is very much a feature of the sector in the 1990s. These groups are also becoming more technically oriented and are seeking to challenge water professionals on equal terms. For example, Greenpeace's activity prompted the DOE to commission studies of organic pollutants in water which showed that, in the Mersey estuary and Liverpool bay, many chemicals exceeded values recommended by the World Health Organisation (WHO) [*ENDS, September 1991: 21*]. Groups such as FOE, Greenpeace, the CPRE, the Royal Society for the Protection of Birds (RSPB) and the Royal Society for Nature Conservation (RSNC) manage to play a significant role in the agenda-setting process and are now regularly included in the consultation process, and can, at least, be termed 'peripheral insider groups' [*Maloney et al., 1994*].

Environmentalists also participate indirectly by presenting a constant threat to those water policy-makers who may be said to still constitute the core policy community (see below). Environmentalists are 'present' in most deliberations and can invoke the law of anticipated reactions, to a considerable degree. Simply by being out there they exercise influence on those who participate intensely (and full-time) in the water policy (and regulatory) process(es). Thus, an important qualification to the utility of network analysis is that focusing on actual, regular and observable participation can mislead the observer into neglecting some broad contextual factors. Today, water policy is made in the context of high political salience, including influences from the Labour Party, anxious to exploit any post-privatisation implementation problems. Making policy in a goldfish bowl is a more accurate analogy than the old description of water policy as the private management of public business. The irony is that a privatised industry which was literally intended to be the private management of what used to be public business, is now much more public than under public ownership.

A third reason for a more open and less predictable style of policy-making and implementation is the existence of the new regulatory structure. In detail the new structure is much more complex and more open than under public ownership, involving at least six regulators. In practice two of the regulators – the NRA and the Office of Water Services (OFWAT) – have emerged as the key regulatory players, with the Drinking Water Inspectorate (DWI) involved in auditing drinking water quality. Since privatisation, both the NRA and OFWAT have developed their own organisational cultures and regulatory styles.

The NRA is primarily concerned with environmental questions and the need to secure environmental and quality improvements. OFWAT is concerned to see that costs and charges are commensurate with the benefits likely to accrue to water consumers, that the industry remains viable and, increasingly, with the social welfare and distributional consequences of policies. The fact that England and Wales have two different institutions dealing with these two sets of objectives has had the beneficial (but uncomfortable for the government and for the industry) effects of exposing these real issues to wider public scrutiny. Of particular interest in terms of network analysis, these two agencies appear to be mobilising (and perhaps creating) their own *constituencies* of groups and organisations.

A fourth factor leading to significant changes in the politics of water is the diminished role of the sponsoring department – the Department of the Environment. It would be very misleading to suggest that the Department is no longer an important actor, but quite clearly it has lost a significant amount of its former leverage – both to the two independent regulators as well as to Europe. To a degree, therefore, government has lost some of its ability to steer and control the sector and may have become a more equal player than used to be the case.

The cumulative effect of these changes has been to create new opportunities for a more extended form of participation in the water policy process. For example, in terms of Whitehall politics, the Department of Social Security is beginning to exhibit some limited participation because of the welfare implications of rising water charges needed to pay for environmental improvements. Also, the Treasury may be re-entering the sector because of its general concern with the costs of regulation – particularly of European regulation. In November 1993 the Chancellor of the Exchequer, Kenneth Clarke, called for a delay in the implementation of the Municipal Wastewater Directive on the grounds that the costs of compliance within the current time limits had risen substantially and were 'unacceptable' (*Financial Times, 23 November 1993*).

In terms of extra-Whitehall politics, those groups representing the poor, the disadvantaged, and the disabled, have begun to claim some stakeholder status in the sector just as the environmentalists have done. Similarly, city investors now have a very real stake in the industry and certainly secure the attention of the industry's managers. Increasingly, some aspects of the water sector now resemble Heclo's issue network model, with potentially large numbers of participants in the water policy process. For example, the Department of the Environment and the Welsh Office issued a deregulation consultation paper in November 1993 and sent it to over 80 organisations for comment, in addition to other relevant government departments (see Appendix II for details). Even this list did not include many organisations who have specialised interest in water policy – such as the Industrial Water Society, the Filtration Society, numerous research establishments, and dozens, if not hundreds of sectoral trade associations. The CPRE was (accidentally) excluded from the original list. (The eventual response rate was approximately 50 per cent, although some 50 additional organisations wrote in, once they gained knowledge of the consultation document.)

Thus, the maximum possible number of organisational participants must run into several hundreds and would include quite esoteric associations such as the Swimming Pool and Allied Trades Association, the Box Culvert Association (part of the British Precast Concrete Association), the Construction Industry Environment Forum, and the Royal Society of Chemistry. In practice, noone in the water sector has a definitive consultation list – not even the DOE. Each division of the DOE (and of the NRA and OFWAT) has rather separate consultation lists reflecting that division's sub-sectoral special interests. It is at this level that notions of policy community seem more applicable.

However, the temptation for observers to exclude the esoteric and part-time participants and to concentrate on full-time core participants is risky, especially in terms of agenda setting. This may be especially true for scientific research organisations whose findings can be translated into public issues at some stage particularly via the megaphone effect of environmental groups (see Richardson elsewhere in this volume). For example, as one practitioner has commented in relation to oestrogen substances in water, '... the recent television programmes on oestrogen substances have made public questions being raised by research workers. Whether this will become a real water quality issue or not will depend on the outcome of further research' [Fawell 1994: 2]. Because of the high political salience of water, and, the new openness of the sector, what may have remained esoteric in the 1960s is less likely to be so in the 1990s. As a member of OFWAT has commented:

People are very concerned by health issues and public opinion is hardening against environmental pollution, both atmospheric and water. There are arguments to the effect that on some issues public concern is exaggerated, but public opinion is understandably risk averse, and the burden of proof must always be on those who claim that a particular level of pollution is safe [*Howarth, 1994*].

The central difficulty, for any researcher, is to distinguish between, on the one hand, rather loose participation in consultation which is so general as to be sham and, on the other, effective influence over the details of policy-making. At what stage does the action move from open consultation to a smoke filled room with only the few that matter present? As Jordan noted in his study of the reform of the engineering profession, large numbers of con-sultees can mask the fact that the crucial decision can eventually be made by a handful of key players [*Jordan, 1993*]. Here, the level of analysis is of para-mount importance. What level of decisions are we discussing? Much of the stuff of politics is the politics of detail – indeed, it is the preoccupation of most interest groups, particularly of the professions. Thus, at the level of technical detail, it seems possible to continue to characterise water policy in England and Wales in terms of policy communities as described in the intro-duction to this volume. At this level, much of the actor behaviour relates to detailed implementation. Thus, a typical example is the one day symposium on 'Odour Control and Prevention in the Water Industry' organised by the Institute of Water and Environmental Management. All the speakers were water professionals from the industry and its associated consultancy sector. None of the issues was likely to attract media, public or parliamentary atten-tion, and the nature of the symposium was typically esoteric. These gatherings probably group together the relevant policy community for these technical subsectoral issues. Even so, they are also held against a backdrop of potential public concern and have the potential to mobilise a broader network of actors.

The notion that quite small issues have a big issue potential is an important one. Policy-makers in water can never be sure which problems can be expanded into public issues or of what groups and organisations will be drawn into the policy process as a result. In one case, for example, the Water Cress Association became particularly active in response to certain proposals yet on any reputational study of water policy-making over the past twenty years it would not merit a mention. For many groups, the devil is in the detail. Even minor changes in the regulatory environment or in the details of implementation can provoke significant – if sporadic – levels of participation from a potentially vast array of actors. Again, this suggests some caution in claiming that there is something out there called the water policy network.

Implementing Privatisation: Regulatory Instability

Space does not permit a detailed review of the implementation process. However, certain key issues have arisen. The most central is the cost and pace of investment required to bring the system up to European and national standards. Related to this are the mechanisms for distributing the costs of that process and the incidence of those costs. If we return to the concept of a water policy community or core group of actors who have to deal with these problems on a day-to-day basis, the following would be included on anyone's list. First, the 'sponsoring' department – the Department of the Environment; secondly the Office of Water Services – OFWAT; thirdly the National Rivers Authority – NRA; and lastly, the Water Services Association – WSA.

In order to capture the essence of the new politics of water, it is useful to review the central position of those four key actors. First, the lead department, the DOE. In a real sense, the DOE was potentially the biggest loser under the new arrangements – because the public sector of which it had been formally in charge is now a private industry in the hands of independent (and so far uncaptured) regulatory agencies. Moreover, many key policies are decided in Brussels via the Commission and/or the Council of Ministers. Indeed, one could say that a central intention of privatisation was to distance the Department deliberately from policy-making. In a sense, water was potentially an example of the retreat of the state from a well established policy community. In practice this retreat has been limited for three reasons. The state is very much part of the EU policy process. Britain is currently one of the most active of the national governments within the EU in trying both to amend existing EU legislation on water and to slow down the reform process. It is also necessary for the state to move back into the policy area (in addition to the natural tendencies of bureaucracies to want to expand their policy space) because of the public interest in the sector and because OFWAT has specifically requested the government's involvement. Thus, the senior civil servant in change of water policy at the DOE has remarked that '... the economic regulator of the water industry has been anxious to have the help of ministers in clarifying an important aspect of the framework within which he and the water industry has to operate' [*Summerton, 1993*].

In its 1993 paper *Water Changes: The Quality Framework* the government stated its position. The basic thrust was a continued commitment to improved standards, and therefore increased investment, but a caution in pushing the pace of reform too far or too fast, with plenty of references to the need to take costs into account, where this was legally possible. Crucially, however, the Europeanisation issue was identified as the key variable. For costs to be contained 'to levels which people and ministers would consider tolerable', action to change or re-phase European legislation was necessary. Adopting a cautious approach to the prospects of achieving this, Mr Summerton warned that the task should not be underestimated '... particularly in view of the constitutional changes which result from the introduction of the Maastricht changes to the treaty on November 1st' [*Summerton, 1993*]. In other words this was a clear message that Her Majesty's Government might have great difficulties as a member of that other policy community – the Council of Ministers.

OFWAT has gradually emerged – ahead of the government in some ways – as the champion of the restrain costs argument. Thus, in a series of papers and statements, OFWAT has been raising the stakes in the debate over environmental and quality improvements versus costs to consumers. In a now much quoted passage, the Director of OFWAT, Ian Byatt, has argued that there is a general concern about price increases for water consumers, especially for customers on lower incomes. Thus:

> There is a world of difference between a necessary, once for all, adjustment in the price of something and an unending escalation in prices. The first will inevitably be accompanied by some protests, but, when complete, will often be accepted. The second would be intolerable. The escalator has, at some stage, to be stopped. Unless this is tackled through the current regulatory arrangements, public dissatisfaction will grow, putting pressures on government for change ... The escalator started with the combination of privatisation and the decision rapidly to meet new objectives for the quality of drinking water and waste water. It is now in danger of being driven ever upwards by new obligations added to existing obligations with little regard for costs or either willingness or ability to pay [*Byatt, 1993*].

This increasingly robust line on the cost effects of the escalator has brought OFWAT into open conflict with the NRA. The environmental case has been put equally robustly by the NRA's Chairman, Lord Crickhowell, who said that he makes '... no apologies for the vigorous way that I have sometimes openly disagreed with Mr Byatt. He, for his part, has provoked controversy and has been right to do so' [*Crickhowell, 1993a*]. A particularly difficult situation arose between the two regulators concerning OFWAT's estimate of the likely cost of some of the proposed improvements. Thus, Lord Crickhowell had complained about the exaggerated estimates of the likely costs made by OFWAT [*Crickhowell, 1993b*] and about the effects of these estimates on the consultation exercise which followed their publication. This dispute, which was regularly reported in the press, is a fascinating insight into the strengths and limitations of the policy community/network approach. Thus, the conflict between two of the key participants was bitter and public – no consensus, no agreement on values, no agreement on quantitative measures even – yet the key players ended up working closely together in order to reach an agreed cost analysis. Thus throughout the summer of 1993 '... the NRA, the Drinking Water Inspectorate worked closely with OFWAT, the DOE and the WSA, in clarifying requirements and obligations, and in seeking to get a much more accurate picture of the real costs' [*Crickhowell, 1993a*].

Amid conflict, there was a recognition that there were still mutual advantages in cooperating via private discussions. But this was not the private management of public business. Indeed, the NRA commenced its own public opinion survey, 'in the light of all the comments that had been made, and the criticism that we were not taking sufficient account of customer interests ...' [*Crickhowell, 1993b*]. The results showed high levels of concern about the quality of the water environment, high level of support for EC standards and quite high (over half) support for paying more for improvement in river and coastal waters [*Crickhowell, 1993b*].[4] The NRA – backed by a belief that the high salience of the issues demanded the continuation of improvements and by a vociferous environmental lobby – had a relatively clear position. Thus, Lord Crickhowell was able to confirm that '. . . the NRA will seek to ensure that excessive regulatory caution is avoided while insisting that necessary and appropriate standards are maintained' [*Crickhowell, 1993b*].

The industry, represented by the WSA, was, of course, in the middle of this controversy. Under one scenario, the pressure for higher standards should be no worry to the industry. Indeed it is to the advantage of an industry which cannot really expand its market significantly. Basically, higher standards raise the value of the product. This is true, however, only if the industry secures a comfortable cost-pass-through agreement from OFWAT in order for industry to meet its statutory obligations – the so-called RPI + K factor. (RPI is the rate of inflation and K is the amount by which charges can be raised in any one year. It is set for each individual company and reflects the level of charges needed to finance the provision of services, including financing its capital expenditure programme.) The potential for a cosy regulator/industry relationship is obvious. In practice it has not materialised. Indeed, open conflict between OFWAT and the WSA is sometimes apparent. Thus, the classic regulatory issue – to secure efficiency gains from a monopoly supplier – has proved so controversial that members of what we might expect to be a model policy community have been swapping arguments in the national press. The politics of the sector has escaped into the public domain, indicating that the core actors have been unable to re-establish an effective policy community for the bigger issues.

Conclusion

How then, can we best characterise the present policy system in the water sector in England and Wales? Inevitably, multiple images are needed. As we have seen, the story has been one of the destabilisation of an existing and stable policy community, based upon the role and power of professions. Once this policy community had been opened up, the system has passed through various stages, as outlined in our case study. At times, policy communities have been important and at times the process has been more characteristic of open issue networks on the Heclo model. At other times neither model has been appropriate – for example during the period of internalised policy-making by Nicholas Ridley.

Moreover, conflict rather than consensus has often been a feature of the policy process – and continues to be so. This is in part due to institutional factors, particularly the regulatory structure, but also because new actors have become involved in the sector on a more or less permanent basis. Thus, a wider set of interests has to be accommodated. And, of course, the Europeanisation of the sector has been enormously important, with a major shift in the locus of power from London to Brussels. As described elsewhere in this volume, policy-making at this new level draws in a very large number of actors and has seen the formation of a variety of advocacy coalitions in which British interests are but one factor.

Yet the notion of policy network retains considerable capacity to enlighten our understanding of the water policy process in England and Wales. For example, we have suggested that technical, subsectoral, issues can still be processed via recognisable policy communities. There is also a core of central actors – the so-called quadripartite meetings of the Department of the Environment, the two main regulators (the National Rivers Authority and the Office of Water Services), and the Water Services Association representing the industry. There is significant disagreement between these core actors – and open conflict on occasions – but they each recognise the need to live together. In that sense they exhibit many policy community properties. Yet they continue to operate in a context of a much more open and public system and recognise the need to accommodate and bargain with a wider range of actors. It seems likely, therefore, that the models appropriate for describing water policy in the 1950s, 1960s and 1970s are likely to remain rather obsolete.

ACRONYMS

CBI	Confederation of British Industry
CCC	Consumer Consultative Council
CPRE	Council for the Protection of Rural England
DOE	Department of the Environment
DWI	Drinking Water Inspectorate
FOE	Friends of the Earth
IEEP	Institute for European Environmental Policy
IRBM	Integrated River Basin Management
IWEM	Institute of Water and Environmental Management
MAFF	Ministry of Agriculture, Fisheries and Food
NFU	National Farmers' Union
NRA	National Rivers Authority
NWC	National Water Council
OFWAT	Office of Water Services
RRCC	Regional Recreational Conservation Committee
RSNC	Royal Society for Nature Conservation
RSPB	Royal Society for the Protection of Birds
RWA	Regional Water Authority
WAA	Water Authorities Association
WHO	World Health Organisation
WSA	Water Services Association

NOTES

1. This research was funded by the Anglo-German Foundation for the Study of Industrial Society and was co-directed by Jeremy Richardson, Wolfgang Rüdig, Martin Jänicke and Lutz Mez. We would also like to acknowledge the willing assistance of many people in the British water industry. Finally, we owe a debt to our colleague Wolfgang Rüdig for his contribution to our earlier work on British water policy
2. For a full chronology, see Appendix I.
3. It is worth noting that private water companies in the United States supply water to approximately 17 per cent of the population. Private companies serve some 31 million consumers, while public bodies serve around 180 million [*Savas, 1987*].
4. Anglian Water PLC have surveyed their customers and found that the majority were prepared to pay more for improvements in water quality. The Chairman, Bernard Henderson, told the Annual General Meeting in July 1993 that, 'Some 70% of the company's customers are prepared to pay slightly more for improved water services ... and this should be heeded by OFWAT' [*ENDS Report 222, July 1993: 10*].

REFERENCES

Byatt, Ian (1993), 'Economic Regulation: The Way Ahead', Address to *The Economist* Conference on Water Policy, London, 9 November.

Crickhowell, Lord (1993a), 'Regulation: Water and Pollution – UK Water Quality Objectives', *Financial Times* Conference, The European Water Industry, London, 15/16 March.

Crickhowell, Lord (1993b), 'Water Service Quality and Water Bills', Address to *The Economist* Conference on Water Policy, London, 9 November.

Department of the Environment (DoE) (1986), *Privatisation of the Water Authorities in England*

and Wales, Cmnd 9734 , London: HMSO.

Department of the Environment (DOE) (1987), *The National Rivers Authority: The Government's Policy for a Public Regulatory Body in a Privatised Water Industry*, London: HMSO.

Dowse, R. and J. Hughes (1977), 'Sporadic Interventionists', *Political Studies*, Vol. 25, pp. 84-92

Dudley, Geoffrey (1994), 'The Next Steps Agencies, Political Salience and the Arm's Length Principle: Barbara Castle at the Ministry of Transport 1965-68', *Public Administration*, Vol. 72, pp. 217-238.

Dunleavy, P. (1981), 'Professions and Policy Change: Notes Towards a Model of Ideological Corporatism', *Public Administration Bulletin*, No. 33, pp. 3–16.

Fawell, J. K. (1994), 'Water Quality Issues', paper presented to Institution of Water and Environmental Management Seminar, *Satisfying Drinking Water Standards*, Cambridge, 15 March 1994.

Fawell, J. K. and D. G. Miller, (1993), *UK Drinking Water – A European Perspective*, paper presented to IWEM Conference 'Water Regulation 3 Years On', Harrogate, 2 /3 March 1993.

Gregory, Roy (1971), *The Price of Amenity*, London: Macmillan.

Hoffmann, S. (1966), 'Obsolete or Absolute? The Fate of the Nation State and the Case of Western Europe', *Daedalus*, Vol. 95, No. 3, pp. 862-915.

Howarth (1994), 'Implications for Customers', paper presented to Institution of Water and Environmental Management Seminar, *Satisfying Drinking Water Standards*, Cambridge, 15 March 1994.

Jordan, Grant (1993), *Engineers and Professional Self-Regulation. From the Finniston Committee to the Engineering Council*, Oxford: Clarendon Press.

Jordan, Grant, Richardson, Jeremy and Richard Kimber (1977), 'Outside Committees and Policy-Making: The Central Advisory Water Committee', *Public Administration Bulletin*, Vol. 24, pp. 41-58.

Jordan, Grant and Jeremy Richardson (1977), 'The Origins of the Water Act 1973', *Public Administration*, Vol. 55, pp. 317-34.

Jordan, Grant and Jeremy Richardson (1982), 'The British Policy Style or the Logic of Negotiation?' in J. Richardson, (ed.), *Policy Styles in Western Europe* (London: George Allen and Unwin), pp. 80-110.

Kinnersley, David (1988), *Troubled Water. Rivers, Politics and Pollution*, London: Hilary Shipman.

Maloney, W. A., Jordan G. and A. M. McLaughlin, (1994), 'Interest Groups and Public Policy: The Insider/Outsider Model Revisited', *Journal of Public Policy*, Vol. 14, No. 1, pp.17–38.

Marsh, David and R. A. W. Rhodes, (1992) (eds.), *Policy Networks in British Government*, Oxford: Oxford University Press.

Mazey, Sonia and Jeremy Richardson, (1993) (eds.), *Lobbying in the European Community*, Oxford: Oxford University Press.

Parker, D. and E. Penning-Rowsell, (1980), *Water Planning in Britain*, London: George Allen and Unwin.

Rhodes, R. A. W. (1988), *Beyond Westminster and Whitehall*, London: Unwin Hyman.

Richardson, Jeremy J. (1993), 'Public Utilities Management', in Eliassen, K. A. and Kooiman, J. (eds.), *Managing Public Organizations: Lessons from Contemporary European Experience*, London: Sage.

Richardson, Jeremy (1994), 'Doing Less by Doing More: British Government 1979-93', *West European Politics*, Vol. 18, No. 1, pp.116–39.

Richardson, Jeremy, Gunnel Gustafsson, and Grant Jordan, (1982), 'The Concept of Policy Style' in Richardson, Jeremy (ed.), *Policy Styles in Western Europe*, London: George Allen and Unwin, pp. 1-16.

Richardson, Jeremy and A. Grant Jordan, (1979), *Governing Under Pressure: The Policy Process in a Post-Parliamentary Democracy*, Oxford: Martin Robertson.

Saunders, P. (1983), *The 'Regional State': A Review of the Literature And Agenda for Research*, Working Paper 35, Urban and Regional Studies: University of Sussex).

Saunders, P. (1984), *We Can't Afford Democracy Too Much: Findings from a Study of Regional*

State Institutions in South-East England, Working Paper 43 Urban and Regional Studies, Sussex: University of Sussex.

Savas, S. (1987), *Privatisation: The Key to Better Government*, New Jersey, Chatham House.

Summerton, Neil (1993), 'Water: Paying For Quality', Address to *The Economist* Conference on Water Policy, London, 9 November.

Taylor M. and B. Lee-Harwood, (1993), *An Environmentalists' Perspective*, paper presented to IWEM Conference 'Water Regulation 3 Years On', Harrogate, 2 and 3 March.

APPENDIX I

A CHRONOLOGY OF THE MAIN DEVELOPMENTS IN THE WATER SECTOR

1945	Water Act 1945 establishes a national water policy.
1963	Water Act, 1963 created 29 River Authorities and the Water Resources Board.
1972	Consultation begins on proposals for the integration and regionalisation of water services.
1973	Water Act setting up ten Regional Water Authorities (RWAs) is passed.
1983	Water Act 1983 ends local government link with RWAs and pushes the industry firmly towards commercialisation.
1985	The government announces that it is 'examining the possibility of a measure of privatisation in the industry'.
1986	The White Paper, *Privatisation of the Water Authorities in England and Wales* (Cmnd 9734) is published and proposes transfer of the RWAs to private sector as they stand.
1986	Government postpones privatisation.
1987	National Rivers Authority (NRA): government publishes its policy for a public environmental regulatory body in a privatised water industry.
1989	Water Bill receives royal assent
1989	The two new regulators – the NRA and the Office of Water Services (OFWAT) established.
1989	*Impact Day* – government publishes the prospectus which offers 2182.9 million Ordinary Shares in the ten Regional Water Holding Companies at 240p per share.
1989	Share Offer closes. Share offers to the general public 5.7 times oversubscribed.
1990	The Drinking Water Inspectorate established.

APPENDIX II

WATER DEREGULATION: LIST OF CONSULTEES IN ENGLAND AND WALES

All water companies
Assembly of Welsh Counties
Association of County Councils
Association of District Councils
Association of Independent Business
Association of Metropolitan Authorities
British Agrochemicals Association
British Association of Chemical Specialists
British Ceramic Manufacturers Federation
British Chemical Engineering Contractors
  Association
British Clothing Industry Association
British Coal
British Colour Makers Association
British Dam Society
British Ecological Society
British Gas plc
British Leather Confederation
British Nuclear Fuels Inc
British Paper and Board Industry Federation
British Petroleum
British Waterways Board
British Wood Preservers Association
Building Research Establishment
Chemical Industries Association
China Clay Association
Ciba Geigy plc
Confederation of British Industry
Confederation of British Wool and Textile
  Manufacturers
Council of the Isles of Scilly
Council of Welsh Districts
Country Landowners Association
Countryside Council for Wales
Electronic Components Industry Federation
English Nature
Environmental Control Consultancy Service
Farmers Union of Wales
Fertilizer Manufacturers Association
Fibre Building Board Organisation
Fire Extinguishing Trades Association
Friends of the Earth

Greenpeace
Health and Safety Executive
Her Majesty's Inspectorate of Pollution
ICI Laboratory
Institute for European Environmental Policy
Institution of Civil Engineers
Institution of Water and Environmental
  Management
Lighting Industry Federation
London Boroughs Association
Metal Finishing Association
Motor Manufacturers Association
National Association of the Launderette
  Industry
National Farmers' Union
National Federation of Self-Employed and
  Small Businesses
National Rivers Authority
North Sea Working Group
Packaging and Industrial Films Association
Paintmakers Association of Great Britain
Photographic Waste Management
Road Haulage Association
Royal Commission on Environmental
  Pollution
Royal Society for Nature Conservation
Royal Society for the Protection of Birds
States of Guernsey Water Board
Telecommunication Engineering and
  Manufacturing Association
Textile Finishers Association
The British Photographic Association
The Jersey New Waterworks Company Ltd
UK Nirex Ltd
UK Petroleum Industry Association Ltd
Union of Independent Companies
United Kingdom Agricultural Supply Trade
  Association Ltd
Water Companies Association
Water Research Centre plc
Water Services Association
World Wide Fund for Nature

EU Water Policy: Uncertain Agendas, Shifting Networks and Complex Coalitions

JEREMY RICHARDSON

European Union (EU) water legislation is now very extensive in scope and has major cost implications for the member states, for the water industry, and for consumers. Although participation in the policy formulation process was fairly narrowly based in the early development of this programme of legislation, more recently participation has become more extended. The EU water policy process is an example of a rather loose and more open issue network or constellation of actors, rather than a closed and restricted policy community. It is, however, possible to identify a core of central actors within this loose configuration. Even so, the agenda setting process remains unpredictable and issues are processed via the interaction of a series of advocacy coalitions which link epistemic communities of scientists (especially toxicologists) into a wider and more visible political world. Because of the high salience of water policy throughout the Union, issue expansion, rather than issue contraction, is likely to remain the norm. The end result may be rather 'garbage can' in its characteristics – namely 'organised anarchies characterised by problematic preferences, unclear technology and fluid participation'.

The EU Policy Process

Before considering the nature of the relationships between policy actors in the water sector within the EU, we need to sketch briefly the unique nature of the EU policy process. Almost any firm characterisations of the process are unreliable, simply because it is so highly sectorised and segmented, different levels of issue are treated in different ways, competing policy models are advocated, and there is a degree of both institutional and 'processual' instability which all make the process singularly difficult to capture.

Jeremy Richardson is Director of the European Public Policy Institute and Professor of European Integration, University of Warwick, U.K. This paper is part of a project on the selection of policy instruments by the Commission and is funded by the Nuffield Foundation. I would like to thank the many Commission Officials, MEPs, national civil servants and interest group personnel who agreed to be interviewed for this study. The lengthy interviews, conducted over the period September 1993—June 1994, were supplemented by the analysis of documents (both published and unpublished) produced by various public and private organisations connected with the European water industry. In one or two cases, access to files was granted.

Despite this almost 'garbage can' [*Cohen* et al., *1972*] nature of the policy process, it is clear that the EU has a considerable capacity to make 'authoritative allocations' for society – that is, the EU has acquired for itself at least the policy-making attributes of a modern state. Indeed, much of the criticism of the European Commission during the Maastricht debates was centred upon the alleged excessive policy-making role of the EC in general and of the Commission in particular. The anti-Maastricht argument was that the EC had become a nanny state, over-regulating the economic and social life of the member states. This particular argument has been especially strongly put by some EU member states in the case of EU water policy. As a result, EU water regulation has recently acquired a new political salience in debates about the fundamental nature of the EU and has become some kind of litmus test in the debate between federalists and anti-federalists as they battle over the future of the Union. Thus, in considering the range of actors involved in EU water policy, one needs to remember that there are some parallels between current debates within the EU and the long debate in the US concerning federal versus states' rights. We also need to remember that the policy process in modern democracies is multi-faceted and multi-phased, suggesting that a multi-model approach to analysis is essential if one is to capture the reality of policy-making over time. At different times and at different stages of the policy process, different models of analysis may be necessary. As in the British example of water privatisation [*Richardson* et al., *1992*], the policy process might be episodic, with network analysis being appropriate at some stages and highly inappropriate at others. In the case of water policy within the EU, some actors – particularly national governments – have only recently started to recognise the full costs and implications of EU regulation and have, therefore, become much more active within the policy process. Also, in some sectors of EU water policy, as for example with groundwater, it is virtually impossible to identify any coherent network of actors as such, simply because the range of actors is so diverse and unstructured.

In general, the EU policy process is best described as a multi-national, neo-federal system, extremely open to lobbying by a wide variety of organisations [*Mazey and Richardson, 1993*] with an unpredictable agenda setting process [*Peters, 1994*] creating an unstable and multi-dimensional policy-making environment. Even the relationships between key institutions such as the Commission, the European Parliament (EP), The Council of Ministers (CM) and the European Court of Justice (ECJ) are not yet settled. We know that the EP (although generally weak) will further increase its influence and that the extended use of qualified majority voting (QMV) post-Maastricht will further erode the power of individual member states. Nevertheless, there is little doubt that the Commission will remain at the centre of the policy process. This is likely for a number of reasons. First, the EU has no government as such, backed by a governing party. Though perfectly obvious, this fact is of enormous importance in terms of analysing the policy process. Unlike nation states, the EU is not led by a government elected on a policy platform, however vague. In the absence of such policy leadership, any bureaucracy would move to fill the vacuum. Moreover, in the case of the EU, the Commission is given the formal power of policy initiation under the Treaty of Rome – that is, it has a constitutional right and duty to initiate policy. Of equal importance is the pivotal position of the Commission as a broker of interests and *bourse* for the exchange of policy ideas [*Mazey and Richardson, 1994a*]. Thus, if policy networks exist at the EU level, they will almost certainly be centred around the Commission as the initiator of policy. In this respect the EU is no different from individual states in western democracies, when, habitually, interest groups focus their attention on bureaucracies [*Richardson, 1993*]. This is especially the case where policy debate often concerns technical and detailed issues, as is the case in water policy.

Regulation is, of course, another important feature of the EU policy process. If the Common Agricultural Policy is excluded, the EU is unusual in being a government with few tangible financial resources to distribute. It is not a government of big money, with all of the influence that brings. Hence, as Majone argues, the Commission often resorts to regulation as a resource [*Majone, 1991*]. From the Commission's perspective, regulation has two favourable features. First, it is extremely cheap in the sense that the only resources needed in order to produce regulations are knowledge, expertise, and an ability to construct and mobilise a winning coalition. Though regulations are often costly in practice, the costs are born elsewhere – either by the national governments of the member states, by regional and local authorities, or by private bodies and ultimately consumers. In a sense, the Commission has power without the financial responsibility to carry through its recommendations. Secondly, the loading of potential costs and benefits is differential. The benefits of new regulations – for example on drinking water quality – are front-loaded in the policy process. Only much later are the costs and disbenefits of regulation more apparent, as the process of implementing EU policy is developed. Thus, at the policy formulation stage it is possible that a rather different set of actors will be mobilised, compared with the set of actors who are likely to be involved in the implementation process at a much later stage – many years later. Quite often the implementers are in any case otherwise engaged – busily trying to make the previous set of regulations work. They often lack the political resources (or awareness) to take their eye off the ball that is already in play in order to see where the next ball may come from! Water policy appears to be a particularly good (or bad) example of this phenomenon, as much of the (now extensive) EU water legislation was not strongly opposed by those interests now singularly vociferous in their criticisms. Indeed, member states who now object to some of the legislation, did not use their power to block it when it was being passed.

The EU is now notorious for both a lack of policy coordination and for a poor implementation record. These features are, of course, common at the national level too, but they seem particularly acute within the EU. The highly sectorised nature of the Commission has inhibited attempts (currently being intensified) to produce the kind of routine inter-departmental co-ordination that would be common in Whitehall, for example. The Court of Auditors was highly critical of the lack of coordination between Directorate General (DG) XI, responsible for environmental policy, and DG XVI, responsible for regional policy [*Court of Auditors, 1992*]. The Court's report produced many examples of contradictory policies being pursued by the two Directorates General. These criticisms have provoked a more determined attempt to secure better coordination within the Commission, and better integration of environmental policy with the rest of the Commission's policy-making [*Mazey and Richardson, 1994b*]. The gradual shift from an un-coordinated and individualistic approach to policy-making, to a more coordinated approach within the Commission has implications for our analysis of water policy-making. The more there is an attempt to coordinate environmental policy (including water policy) with other sectors such as regional development and agriculture, the more the process will shift from a narrowly based set of actors to a more extended network (*mélange* might be a more accurate term) of actors. This may be more akin to Heclo's concept of an issue network [*Heclo, 1978*] than to the narrowly defined policy com-munities originally identified in Britain [*Richardson and Jordan, 1979*] and in the US by Walker.[1] As the nature of the policy process changes, then so do the models of analysis needed to describe it. In the water case, it seems possible to argue that, over time, the number and range of actors has increased, moving the system from a relatively private and limited range of participation to a more open, conflictual and public system of decision-making.

However, as we shall argue, there is still an inherent 'logic' within the Commission which leads it to identify and nourish certain key actors, again reflecting national experience where notions of inner and outer circle con-sultation are familiar. Whatever trends and counter-trends may be evident, bureaucracies usually get to know, over time, which organisations really matter and which do not. Defining who matters is, of course, subjective and has at least two aspects. At the formulation stage, organisations who matter may be those which define what the problem is and suggest how it might be processed, or those who can block the passage of legislation by mobilising political support – either in the EP or in the CM. As suggested above, a rather different set of actors may matter at the sub-national implementation phase.

Here, the EU's poor record in evaluation and enforcement is relevant as it may have actually facilitated much of the rapid policy development in the environmental field. The relative lack of really strong and effective resistance to the considerable amount of EC/EU environmental legislation during the developmental phase may have much to do with the perception of many potential actors at the time that much of the legislation could be ignored in practice. If implementation and enforcement are lax, why get exercised about the legislation in the first place? Under such circumstances, it is relatively easy to sign up to new regulations, in the knowledge that there are so many opportunities for policy erosion at the implementation stage that it is not worth the risk of being seen as a bad European by opposing the process of European integration. This tendency is exacerbated by lack of knowledge on the part of those carrying out the implementation and by those affected by it – particularly knowledge about the costs of actually implementing legislation. Again, this observation seems especially relevant to EU environmental legislation and to water legislation in particular. Only now, as Commission, ECJ, and public pressure develop for more effective implementation, is a wider network of actors – particularly national governments and industrial interests, as well as the water industry and its national regulators – realising the true cost implications. Consequently, we are seeing a greater degree of interest mobilisation, further expanding the constellation or configuration of actors in the water sector as a whole. In earlier phases of policy development, the link between policy inputs and policy outputs was, perhaps, somewhat tenuous. More recently, under post-Single European Act (SEA) pressures for a level playing field, the links between inputs and outputs are becoming more apparent. As the laggards in the EU implementation process come under increasing pressure to implement EU laws, we can see a greater degree of actor mobilisation in many policy areas.

This brings us to a final observation on the EU policy process – namely that we need to take account of the institutional context of the process. Policy actors – and networks of actors where they exist – operate within institutional constraints. Moreover, institutions are important actors in their own right. They do not simply reflect their own constituency. For example, however important the Commission might be, national governments, through the CM, play a central and crucial role in the policy process. In the current post-Maastricht phase of the EU's development, there appears to be a resurgence of the will of national governments to defend their national interests. This is matched by a new (possibly temporary) caution on the part of the Commission in the development of new policies, in order to avoid too many 'nanny state' accusations. Like all sensible bureaucracies, the Commission knows when to consolidate and when to advance. It also knows, as Downs suggested more generally [Downs, 1967], that in times of threat it is useful to mobilise the constituency that it in part created. As part of what Downs termed the jockeying for policy space, the EP also knows that mobilising a constituency of some kind is useful. Hence, we can see the EU policy process as a rather messy amalgam of interrelationships between non-governmental actors and formal institutions.

Quite clearly there is a potentially large constituency of European level interest groups interested in a policy area such as water. (One senior official suggested that a figure of between 200 and 300 was a reasonable estimate.) These groups are mobilised in differing degrees and have different types of interrelationships. Some, such as EUREAU (Union of National Associations of Water Suppliers) and ECPA (European Crop Protection Association) are continuous participants. Others will participate only intermittently. For example, one Commission official was initially surprised to receive a telephone call from the European association representing dentists, only to discover that it had a particular concern with fluoride regulations. The picture is further complicated by the fact that national governments are linked to national networks of groups and thus particpate in a two level game as suggested by Putnam [*1988*]. Before considering the dynamics of this rather fluid set of interrelationships, however, it is useful to review briefly the actual contents of EU water policy.

EU Water Legislation

EU environmental legislation is now a classic example of how the Commission has successfully extended and expanded its area of competence. The original Treaty of Rome did not include references to environmental policy. The Commission, as a key policy actor, has been an effective policy entrepreneur in the use of the Treaty in order to develop its environmental competence. For example, it has used Article 100 of the Treaty, covering the harmonisation of laws in member states directly affecting the establishment or functioning of the common market. Also, article 235 has been used concerning measures which 'prove necessary to attain ... one of the objectives of the Community' in the absence of specific delegation of power by the Treaty. Until 1987, all Community environmental legislation was based on one or the other (or both) of these articles [*EEC, 1992*]. It was the passage of the SEA in 1987 that formalised the power of the EU in the environmental field. Article 100a lays down criteria for environmental protection legislation affecting the internal market and allows legislation to be adopted by QMV in the Council. Articles 130r, 130s and 130t lay down the goals, means and procedure for the adoption of legislation regarding the environment by unanimous decision [*EEC, 1992*].

By 1987 some 200 items of environmental legislation had been agreed under Articles 100 and 235 [*Haigh, 1994: 2.1*]. The passage of the Maastricht Treaty further strengthened the power of the EU in the environmental field. In article 2 of the Treaty, one of the EU's basic tasks is defined as promoting 'sustainable and non-inflationary growth respecting the environment'. Environmental policy has to be based on the precautionary principle. The SEA's provision that environmental policy should be integrated into other EU policies was also reinforced [*Haigh, 1994: 2.3*]. In addition to legislation, the EC has so far produced five Environmental Action Programmes, indicating the general direction of EC/EU environmental policy. The Fifth Environment Programme is especially interesting in terms of the focus of this article. Thus, it places great emphasis on the active involvement of all parties concerned with the environment on a voluntary and preventative basis and on the detailed consultation of interested parties in the preparation of major decisions.

The EC itself has identified some 27 items of EC water legislation which had been passed by 1990. The list, not surprisingly, consisted of some measures which are relatively minor and narrow in scope – such as Directive 82/242/EEC, Testing of Detergent, to legislation which is of major importance in the water industry and beyond, such as Directive 80/778/EEC, Water for Human Consumption. Since then, further legislation, both major and minor, has been developed. For example, the Council adopted Directive 91/676/EEC on nitrates from agricultural sources and Directive 91/271/EEC on urban waste water. Both are very major pieces of legislation and have very considerable cost implications. In total it is fair to say that EC/EU water legislation is now as comprehensive – and more so in many cases – than are many national systems of water regulation.

As Haigh argues, water policy was the first subsector of EC environmental policy to be developed and is now also the most comprehensive sector [*Haigh, 1994: 4.2.1*]. Space does not permit a detailed analysis of the nature of this legislative portfolio. Suffice to say that, ultimately, it has plenty of regulatory force and has major financial implications for those authorities responsible for its actual implementation. For example, much of Britain's multi-billion pound investment programme in the water industry is directly related to the need to comply with various aspects of EU water policy (see *Maloney and Richardson* elsewhere in this volume.) If we take the Drinking Water Directive 80/778/EEC as an example, it lays down maximum admissible concentrations (MAC) levels and guide levels (GL) for 62 parameters and minimum required concentrations (MRC) for four parameters in seven categories: organoleptid parameters; physio-chemical parameters; substances undesirable in excessive amounts; toxic substances; microbiological parameters; and MRC for softened water. Similarly, the Council Directive on Bathing Water lays down 19 physical, chemical, and microbiological parameters for the quality of bathing water, 13 of which are mandatory imperative values and the rest of which are non-binding guides. A significant proportion of the legislation governing water is also justiciable, through the ECJ. For example, several member states have been brought before the ECJ for non-compliance with EC water laws. Moreover, legal force and the threat of the ECJ are not the only sanctions behind EU water policy. The mere fact that there is EU legislation, setting out limits on such matters as pesticide and nitrate levels, is of political salience in most of the member states – particularly those such as Britain, Germany, Denmark, and the Netherlands with well developed and well organised environmental and consumer groups. The charge that a national, regional, or local authority is not complying with EU standards for drinking water, for example, is politically damaging for any administration, bearing in mind the psychological and emotional commitment we all have to being able to drink so-called pure water. Consequently whistle blowing by ordinary citizens and their representative organisations is a significant and important aspect of the EU water policy process and gives the policy area a rather special feature when compared with, say, EU policies for R&D. For example, the Commission received some 12,000 letters from Germany alone concerning the 1993/4 revisions of the Drinking Water Directive. Whatever policy networks and policy communities might now be in existence or might develop, they all have to operate in the context of rather wide and unregulated participation by individuals. In that sense, policy making discussions are always conducted with an additional but empty seat at the table – representing the threat of individual citizens who regard water quality as of high salience. This is of crucial importance in understanding the water policy process, because of the possibility of issue expansion [*Sedenius, 1992*] at any time.

The Range of Actors Involved in EU Water Policy: Institutional and Non-Governmental

As suggested earlier, the range of organised groups who can claim some stakeholder status [*Richardson, 1995a*] in EU water policy is probably between two and three hundred. We must add to this a rather larger number of groups potentially active at the national level in the twelve member states but who do not participate directly in water policy formulation at the EU level. Even so, they can have an indirect influence via their national and regional administrations and, indeed, via national regulatory agencies of various types. In many respects, national regulatory agencies can themselves be at the core of a network of constituent organisations within the nation state. It is, therefore, reasonable to argue that if network is an appropriate term to use we should generally see EU water networks as open rather than closed. Indeed, a more accurate image might be extended issue networks with potentially large numbers of participants, who may not have regular inter- action and who share few apparent resource dependencies. Yet, on occasions, and at certain stages of the policy process, an inner core of actors may be identifiable, albeit operating within this broader and looser context described above. In an attempt to make sense of this rather messy image of the EU water policy process, it is useful to categorise the various actors, as follows.

Institutional Actors

Three institutions are involved in the formation of EU water policy – the Commission, the European Parliament, and the Council of Ministers. In addition, it might be argued that the European Court of Justice also plays a policy-making role in that it is able to make important adjudications having major policy implications.

The Commission   As suggested earlier, the Commission is in a pivotal position and has been largely responsible for the development of water policy to date. It has in the past been able to operate in a rather favourable policy- making environment, as witnessed by the fact that it developed an extensive programme of legislation, notwithstanding the absence of clearly defined duties under the Treaty of Rome. The SEA marked the formal legitimisation of what had already taken place. The Commission, in the shape of DG XI, has been assisted by having a politicised, mobilised, and effective con- stituency of environmental groups. These groups have, in turn, been backed by a no less effective and political constituency of scientists and other experts – producing a rather good example of the type of advocacy coalition described by Sabatier [*1988*]. In terms of any network analyses, the Commission as an institution looms large. Thus, DG XI – responsible for Environment, Nuclear Safety and Civil Protection – is at the crossroads of all of the water policy traffic at the Euro-level. (More recently, however, DG III (Industry) is increasingly playing a role in challenging DG XI's preroga- tives.)

The European Parliament   The European Parliament has, despite its un- doubted general weakness as a legislature, played a significant role in EU environment policy generally and in water policy specifically. As always in politics, individuals can play an important role. Thus, the President of the Parliament's Environment Committee, Ken Collins, Member of the European Parliament (MEP), has been a vigorous and effective policy entrepreneur and has secured for the EP an important place in the policy initiation and process- ing stages of water policy. The Environment Committee is said to be unusual in the context of EP committees because it has produced a considerable flow of own initiative reports [*Jacobs and Corbett, 1990: 106*]. As Judge notes, '...the Environment Committee has had several notable successes in prompting the Commission into legislative action . . . several of these successes *pre-date* the SEA' [*Judge, 1992: 190*]. It should be noted, however, that it would be wrong to assume that the EP is generally *forcing* the Commission to take on board proposals. Quite often both DG X1 and the Environment Committee of the EP can be on the same side, in some kind of institutional coalition, each backed by a similar network of environmental groups. Thus, as Judge discovered when interviewing one DG XI official '. . . For a long time DG XI wasn't taken too seriously within the Commission. In this context DG XI would lobby the EP to act on its behalf . . . in fact the Council still sometimes thinks that there is an incestuous relationship between the EP and DG XI, with the Environment committee used to turn the screw' [quoted by *Judge, 1992: 199*]. Both DG XI and the EP Committee tap and speak to the same constituency of groups. As one of Judge's interviewees commented, 'MEPs need a network, we all need information and, as a rapporteur, groups will come to you' [*Judge, 1992: 200*].

It would be foolish to suggest that the EP Environment Committee and DG XI always see eye to eye. However, their primary objectives – stronger environmental regulation – are very similar. Also, the Environment Committee can assist DG XI in trying to ensure that other DGs in the Commission do not undermine environmental policy. A recent example in the water field is a good illustration of this function. In December 1993 Ken Collins noticed that the meeting of agriculture ministers, in the Agricultural Council, was considering a Belgian proposal to relax the pesticide parameters for the introduction of plant protection products into the market place. Collins was quick to mobilise his Committee. He then persuaded the EP as a whole to adopt a resolution calling upon the Commission and Council to uphold the current standards for the quality of drinking water, by withdrawing the proposal concerning the placing of EEC-accepted plant protection products on the market [*EP resolution B3-1736/93 Collins*]. The proposal was duly withdrawn.

More generally, the EP's Environment Committee is a useful source of 'pressure' for DG XI when faced with demands from countries like the UK and for the so-called 'repatriation' of some aspects of water policy, under the principle of subsidiarity. A good example of this 'pressure' on the Commission is Ken Collins' after dinner speech to the major conference on Drinking Water held in Brussels in September 1993 (see below). As he pointed out, the conference was dealing with technical matters. However, he wanted to remind his audience that scientific matters are contained within a political context. Specifically he warned that '... there can be no change in the Directive without proper consultation of the democratic institutions of the

EC, and in particular without full participation of the EP and my committee'
[*Ken Collins' speech, September 1993*]. Earlier, in 1988 the Committee had
tabled its own report on the implementation of European Community water
Directives, which was somewhat critical of DG XI for its consultation procedures. The Committee felt that the procedures were too biased towards
specialists representing national governments. Consequently, it recommended
that the Commission should be '... required to study its consultation procedures with a view to increasing participation of the scientific community,
environmental bodies and industrial specialists, among others' [*Document
A2-0298/87*]. Again, this seemed to be a warning that water policy could not
be de-politicised and confined to the specialised policy communities. Broader
and more open participation was being demanded. All decision-makers are,
therefore, fully aware that the EP's Environment Committee is capable of
making a fuss on water quality and other related issues and that this can place
the Commission, the Council of Ministers, and national government in a bad
light.

The Council of Ministers   Some analysts of the European Union would be
surprised by the focus of this collection – policy networks often consisting of
interest groups – because they see the EU as primarily an *intergovernmental*
institution. For example, Andrew Moravcsik challenges the popular notion
that the SEA was the result of an elite alliance between EC officials and pro-
European business interest groups. In his view, 'the negotiating history is
more consistent with the alternative explanation that EC reform rested on
interstate bargains between Britain, France and Germany' [*Moravcsik, 1991:
42*]. His preference is for an 'intergovernmental institutionalism' approach,
with states as the principal actors in the international system and interstate
bargains reflecting national interest and relative power [*Moravcsik, 1991:
48*]. In a crucial passage he argues that:

> the importance of interstate bargains is consistent with the broader
> experience of the EC since the mid 1960s. European integration did not
> proceed steadily and incrementally; it proceeded in fits and starts.
> Moreover, since the Luxembourg compromise, decision-making has
> moved toward intergovernment ('state-to-state') decision-making
> centred in the council and summit meetings, rather than toward
> increasing authority for international bodies such as the Commission
> and Parliament [*Moravcsik, 1991: 67*].

Whether this was actually the case for the SEA, as Moravcsik suggests, may
itself be open to doubt. In the case of water policy formation, until fairly
recently, this model would be a very inaccurate characterisation of history.
Clearly, national governments have always and continue to take up national

positions on water policy proposals. Proposals can be and are hard-fought in the Council of Ministers where, ultimately, decisions are made. For example, Haigh notes that the negotiations on the Drinking Water Directive 80/778 were lengthy with, for instance, the Netherlands wanting stringent standards for sodium chloride and conductivity, so as to control the activities of countries of the upper Rhine. In contrast, Britain campaigned for a more lenient standard for lead [*Haigh, 1994 4.43*]. But this is rather different from seeing the CM as the *central* institutional actor in water policy even though it is the final authority. It would be odd, indeed, if nation states took no view on water policy, bearing in mind the cost implications, but this is often more a reaction to proposals originated elsewhere than setting the policy agenda as such. Even with the Drinking Water Directive, Haigh reports that there was relatively little difficulty over the nitrate parameters (now seen as very problematic) with only the UK expressing reservations [*Haigh, 1994, 4.44*]. Even so, the UK of course signed up to the Directive. While it is always the case that the CM is very important in water policy – in the end policies have to be agreed by the CM – it would be wrong to see the *development* of water policy to date as CM driven. More recently, however, national governments, especially Britain and France, have begun to play a more significant role in agenda setting. For example the current review of EU water legislation, of which the September Conference on Drinking Water (see below) was part, appears to have two main origins. First, implementation experience and the advance of scientific and technological knowledge necessitate periodic reviews. More importantly, perhaps, water policy has been caught up in the whole subsidiarity debate. This has applied significant pressure to the Commission which, in December 1993, announced that it would be proposing new Directives in place of some of the existing Directives. The thrust of the new Directives will be to 'reorient rules and regulations towards compliance with essential quality and health parameters, leaving Member States free to add secondary parameters if they wish' [*COM (93) 545*]. Both the Nitrate Directive (91/676/EEC) and the Urban Waste Water Directive (91/271/EEC), cited earlier, already reflect this new approach, introducing greater flexibility for the member states. Thus, the Deputy Director of DG XI, Tom Garvey, has claimed 'the more recent Directives are quite different in approach from earlier texts. They attack the source of pollution and describe a general aim which is to be achieved and rely less on specific quality objectives for various parameters and situations. This new approach clearly reflects a considerable change in attitude in how the Community's policy is realised' [*Garvey, 1993*]. However, Member States face the uphill task of reversing some previous decisions. This is not going to be easy, because both the Commission and the EP will defend territory already won and can mobilise a range of national and European interests in their support. Various groups of actors are mobilising in order to defend the *status quo* – rather like a magnetic field holding policy in place.

When participating in the CM, national governments of course face their own sets of organised interests with which they have to deal. Some of these are discussed elsewhere in this volume. Suffice to say that it would be wrong to assume that it is a simple task for national governments to control and direct these interest group systems. All of these systems are developing their own European focus, are increasingly independent of their national governments [*Mazey and Richardson, 1993*], and are just as likely to exert pressure on their national governments to maintain and strengthen EU water policy as they are to want to see it eroded or 'repatriated' under subsidiarity. Thus, the behaviour of national governments may be understood only with reference to the need to manage national as well as international politics. In Tsebelis' terms, we can understand the behaviour of actors only if we are aware that they are involved in what he calls a series of 'nested games' [*Tsebelis, 1990*]. Thus, whilst the British government may feel able to press for the relaxation or deletion of some water pollution parameters, other nation states, such as Denmark and Germany, may be under counter-domestic pressures. Also, they may have funding and cross-subsidy systems for water supply and sewage disposal which make the cost question less visible and less relevant in the short term. And they may have a constituency (as in Germany) more willing and able to pay the price of clean water. Thus, we return to the need to examine the range of non-governmental actors in the water policy process.

Non-Governmental Actors

We suggested earlier that the range of possible actors was rather large – in the hundreds rather than in the tens. It is also quite varied and, hence, it is quite difficult to scale the influence of participants. Fortunately, however, DG XI is probably the most advanced Directorate within the Commission in terms of identifying and mobilising the relevant constituency of groups and individuals. Having initially developed a long-standing and close (some would say symbiotic) relationship with environmental groups, it has identified a much broader range of actors with whom it has some relationship, consistent with the statements in the Fifth Action Programme. Having consciously expanded the range of groups consulted (a process encouraged by the transfer to DG XI of some officials who had worked in DGs closer to manufacturing industry) it has also faced a need to *structure* these relationships, in order to make the process of consultation more effective and manageable.

In terms of environmental policy generally, in December 1993 DG XI set up a General Consultative Forum on the Environment in order to bring together representatives from the sectors of production, the business world, regional and local authorities, professional associations and environmental protection and consumer organisations. Some interests represented in the forum have specific water interests, for example the Deputy Director General of Lyonnaise des Eaux, the President of the European Environment Bureau, and the President of COPA (Committee of Agricultural Organisations in the European Community). The Forum is quite clearly a broad church and we have yet to see how it will work in practice. However, because key EU water legislation is currently under review, including the Drinking Water Directive and the Bathing Water Directive, a major consultation exercise is being undertaken by DG XI. The Directorate has faced the task of identifying the full range of stakeholders in water policy. A central feature of this exercise was the convening of a major conference on drinking water, in Brussels in September 1993. The function of the conference was to hear the views of all interested parties. The difficulty, of course, is in defining 'interested party'. Potentially the number of interested parties could run into thousands across the EU as a whole. For example, every industry and service is in some way affected by water policy, some more directly than others. In practice, those interests where water is central to their activities – either because they use large quantities of water or because their activities are a major polluter of the water supply – have become more actively mobilised, although DG XI retains the power to decide.

The perception of policy-makers and others interviewed for this project is that DG XI's September conference brought together more or less everyone who mattered in water policy or who could claim some legitimate stakeholder status in the sector. Indeed, one of DG XI's objectives was to maximise participation, rather than to be restrictive. (However, in the event, it had to reject some requests to attend.) A number of factors lead DG XI down the path of identifying the maximum relevant constituency of actors. First, it was seen as part of the general thrust towards greater transparency and openness of EU decision-making, albeit rather well controlled. Secondly, there appears to have been a genuine desire to get it right – that is, to ensure that the full range of arguments relating to the review of drinking water policy should be aired. Bearing in mind that the Commission is a very small bureaucracy for the tasks it has to perform, the conference can be seen as part of the general phenomenon whereby the Commission seeks information, expertise and advice. Thirdly, it may also have been part of the phenomenon noted by Henderson in the context of the British policy process – namely an attempt at risk sharing by officials [Henderson, 1977]. At a time when the Commission is generally under attack for being over-enthusiastic in its pursuance of the process of European integration, trying to mobilise some consensus around any revised drinking water Directive seems a sensible political strategy. If all of the relevant voices have been heard and if proposals can indeed attract a broad coalition of support, then dealing with the CM, for example, ought to be somewhat less troublesome. What stronger argument can a bureaucrat put than to claim that everyone has been consulted and that the proposed measure has the support of those directly affected? A fourth factor (which is impossible to verify) was put to the author by one interviewee who had participated in the conference. It may have been a skillful exercise in massaging the interests who were represented there, conducted via skilled stage management by the Commission in order to be able to produce the Commission's desired result. Under this version, the consultation was sham rather than real. In Henderson's terms, the appropriate seats had to be warmed by the appropriate organisations! In fact this does raise a difficult (perhaps fundamental) methodological problem in analysing actor involvement in the policy process – namely it is extremely difficult to correlate participation with influence, especially as the conference produced lists of issues to be resolved, rather than agreed solutions (see below).

Whatever the reality of the processes which took place at the conference (in truth, probably none of the participants – including Commission officials – can really know the effects of the conference as it was a complex process of mutual learning) the gathering swept in large numbers of stakeholders. Thus, over 250 people participated. Clearly the national governments were seen by the Commission as the leading stakeholders and all were invited to send representatives. Thus, the list of participants included a large number of representatives from the member states. However, the Commission asked the member states to be restrained in their participation in the conference discussions, in order to avoid them dominating the proceedings. This was consistent with the Commission's main purpose of taking soundings amongst the non-governmental actors within the sector. The non-governmental actors present at this key conference can be grouped, approximately, as follows.

Water Suppliers   Here the main Euro-association – EUREAU – played a central role in the selection/nomination of the many representatives from the industry itself who participated in the conference. Effectively, EUREAU was given the power to decide who would attend on behalf of the water industry itself. Typical examples of industry representatives sailing under the EUREAU flag were individuals from the Associação Portuguesa dos Distributores de Agua; Lyonnaise des Eaux-Dumez; Services des Eaux; Water Services Association; GEW Köln; and Severn Trent Water.

Polluting Industries   Typical examples included representatives from COPA; CEFIC (European Chemical Industry Council); Confederation of Industries Agro-Alimentaries; UNICE (Union of Industrial and Employers' Confederations of Europe); European Salt Producers' Association; and ECPA.

Environmental Groups and Organisations   The main environmental groups concerned with water were represented at the conference by FoE; Greenpeace; World Wide Fund for Nature (WWF); European Environmental Bureau (EEB); plus some less well known groups such as Pesticide Action Network (PAN FRG/Europe), based in Germany.

Consumer Organisations   Just as the water industry has a mainstream or lead organisation (EUREAU) which the Commission sees as representative, so the Commission sees BEUC (Bureau Européen des Union de Consommateurs) as the lead organisation representing consumers. Several BEUC representatives were present. (An additional channel of consumer input to water policy not represented at the conference [the effectiveness of which is impossible to gauge] is the EU's Consumer Consultative Council [CCC]. This has discussed a range of environmental issues, alongside more traditional consumer concerns, including the question of nitrates in water. Also, the European Community of Consumer Co-operatives [EUROCOOP] came out strongly against the proposed relaxation of pesticides regulations cited above.)

Scientific Experts   Much of the 'stuff' of EU level water policy is now micro not macro policy-making. The main policy framework is now in place – for example legislation on drinking water, bathing beaches, and dumping at sea. Big issues remain, of course, such as possible repatriation under the guise of subsidiarity and the whole question of securing the future of Europe's groundwater supplies. However, the politics of water is often the politics of detailed regulations. Indeed Ken Collins' speech, cited above, was meant to warn against the simple transferring of water into detailed technological issues. The debate tends to be about scientific, medical and technological issues concerning what substances should or should not be regulated, what parameters for them should be set, and how they should be monitored and measured. Even so, for many policy-makers these are matter of great uncertainty and, as Haas notes, under conditions of uncertainty, policy-makers are likely to turn to epistemic communities of various kinds [*Haas, 1992: 12*]. Not surprisingly, therefore, the conference included a long list of scientific and other experts.

Other Participants – Institutional and Non-EU   As the conference was designed to bring together all of the key players in EU policy it was inevitable that the *institutional* actors should be there too. For example the Commission was well represented. Many officials were from DG XI but also from other DGs operating cognate policy areas such as DG XII (Science, Research and Development), DG III (Industry), DG XV (Financial Institutions, Company Law and Internal Market), DG XXIII (Enterprise Policy, Distributive Trades, Tourism and Co-operatives), DG VII (Development), and DG VI (Agriculture).

Many of these officials could be said to represent, indirectly, their own specialised networks of non-governmental organisations on the agency/ principal notion. In some sense, therefore, participation by a wide range of DGs was some kind of surrogate participation for a very diverse 'network of networks'.

The EP was strongly represented at the conference, led by Ken Collins and several members of his Environment Committee. Several members of the Economic and Social Committee (ESC) of the European Union were also present, essentially representing the social partners, and reflecting the functions of the (relatively weak) ESC.

It is also important to note that extra-EU actors have some stakeholder status in the process. Of particular note (see below) is the representation of the World Health Organisation (WHO) – an important but little-recognised player. Other non-EU bodies represented were several of the EFTA countries, the American Chamber of Commerce in Brussels (probably the best organised lobbyists in the EU); a member of the US government's Mission to the European Communities; and a representative of the US Environmental Protection Agency. The participation of non-EU actors was a reminder that it is not only the autonomy of nation states that is in question when one analyses the EU policy-process. There are important questions to be asked concerning not just the globalisation of economic markets, but the globalisation of policy-making in such areas as pollution and crime prevention, particularly through transnational regulation. Hence any network analysis designed to capture the reality of extra-national policy-making would probably need to go well beyond the EU and would certainly need to include a detailed analysis of the role of WHO.

The Water Policy Process: Who Matters, Who Decides? The Inner Core

The September 1993 conference can be considered to be a gathering of the good and the great in European water policy. Interviews with participants suggest that the Commission had done an excellent job in identifying the stakeholders in the policy area – not an easy task bearing in mind that there are actually very few organisations, particularly at the Euro level, who are *exclusively* concerned with water policy. As always, such gatherings risk being ineffective simply because of problems of size and because of the sheer diversity of representation. Under no stretch of the imagination could this gathering be described as a policy community in the sense described in the introduction to this volume. The question also arises, was it even a policy network as such, if one takes network to mean (as it undoubtedly does in proper English usage) some kind of interconnections between the participants? The answer is 'yes' but only in the very loose sense of issue network as used by Heclo [*Heclo, 1978*]. There is certainly not a regular and stable set of interactions between this large group of actors – more an awareness of each other's existence, often incomplete understandings of each other's policy positions, and quite large divergences of views both about problem definition and problem solving. If there is a glue binding this constellation (or 'configuration' to use Lehmbruch's term [*Lehmbruch, 1991*]) of actors together it is related to the notion of stakeholder status suggested earlier. There is a common recognition that the various parties have a legitimate interest in the policy area, underpinned by an increasing awareness that, as Pareto maximisers, there are mutual gains for everyone in participating in a common venture [*Richardson, 1995a*]. This reflects a learning process over the past decade or so, during which the main interests who find themselves in conflict have each begun to recognise that compromise is both necessary and possible. Many of the disputed issues – particularly parameters for pollutants – are infinitely bargainable. This is not to suggest that there is anything like a consensual approach to policy-making, but there is the emergence of an acceptance that actors may behave differently in different policy-making arenas, that is, they are involved in nested games, and that this does not preclude a degree of cooperative effort in private.

In terms of the practicalities of policy-making, this large collection of diverse organisations is manageable first because the Commission is a skilled broker of interests (as suggested above) and, secondly, because it is possible to identify a core of key actors, along the familiar model of inner and outer circle consultation. The Commission's brokerage skills (in the terms of this volume, 'network management skills') were clearly evident in the management of the September conference. Thus, the Commission was able to use the conference in two ways. First, the conference forced the disparate members of the issue network/constellation to be more aware of each other's positions. Secondly, it helped the Commission define what the political and technical issues were. The key question, of course, is how these issues will be resolved. It is here that the notion of core groups or actors is useful. It is they who will need to be drawn into the process more closely before proposals can be made to the CM.

In trying to identify the core actors and groups, it needs to be noted that any core which can be identified is not static. If one looks back, the drafting of the existing Drinking Water Directive 80/778 was prepared in the 1970s. During that process there was virtually no formal consultation with water suppliers! It was a decision-making process which for a period may have been superficially close to Moravscik's intergovernmental model. It was,

however, not a case of politics of exclusion – that is, it would be wrong to see
the early process as a deliberately closed system. Basically, participation was
restricted because so few actors actually recognised their interest in the policy
area. This is not untypical of the process of European integration. Many
policy areas appear to exhibit this lack of appreciation of the potential effects
of early Euro-legislation, essentially because interests were still absorbed
with national politics and policies. For example, the main European association representing the suppliers (and undoubtedly at the core of any policy network) – EUREAU – was not formed until 1974. It emerged out of a gradual
realisation that the Commission would become increasingly responsible for
water policies which were hitherto the responsibility of national governments. Even then, the Commission played an indirect role in the emergence
of EUREAU. The Commission approached the General Manager of the
Brussels Water Supply Company for information on European practices
involving cold water meters. He contacted his own personal network in
Europe and it was eventually decided that it would be useful for the supply
industry to form a Euro-level association. Even then it took some time for the
significance of Europeanisation to be fully appreciated. Thus, in the early
years of the development of European water policy, the preconditions for the
emergence of policy networks were absent – namely a proper recognition of
the policy relevance of the EC. As the impact – particularly costs – of Euro
regulation has become much more apparent, so has the awareness by groups
and other organisations of their own interest in the matter. We have little
evidence on how this early legislation came about, as many of the actors now
mobilised were not particularly active. The most likely explanation seems to
be an advocacy coalition of scientific and technical experts, environmental
groups and an entrepreneurial Commission. Today, at the centre of the core
of non-governmental actors is, of course, the water industry itself.

The Water Industry

The supply industry has certainly learned the significance of EU water policy
and the importance of being involved in the early stages of the policy process
in the hope of influencing the problem definition phase. However, it does face
problems. EUREAU itself represents an industry that is both public and
private. England and Wales (see elsewhere in this volume) are unusual in
having a totally privatised system, whereas elsewhere in Europe a more
mixed pattern is usual with individual communes often being important.
Indeed, some observers see EUREAU as being divided into two camps – a
mostly privatised, business-driven industry and a great number of small community works still in the public sector. More importantly, the water industry
is still divided into the so-called clean and dirty water interests. In terms of
the latter, a relatively new body – The European Waste Water Group – was

set up in 1992. It originated in Britain and is currently housed in the Water Services Association offices. Although it has developed quite rapidly and is well recognised, it still does not cover the whole of the EU in terms of its membership. This division between clean and dirty water undoubtedly reduces the efficiency of the industry's lobbying efforts. In due course, some kind of merger seems inevitable so that the whole industry can speak with one voice. An additional supplier interest, of considerable importance to the Commission, is the local authority water suppliers. Thus, the structure of the sector – in this case water supply and wastewater and sewage disposal – is a key determinant of 'network' structure too. That is representational structures reflect industry structure to a considerable degree. This structure is in turn influenced by a combination of technical, political and administrative criteria.

Agro-Chemical Industries and Agriculture

Currently three associations appear to be of central importance in representing the chemical and agro-chemical industries. ECPA is especially important because of the high political salience of the pesticides issue. Although formed only in 1992, it represents 17 national associations including the 13 leading research-based crop protection product manufacturers operating in Europe. ECPA's role is a difficult one because its main opponents in the core community of actors, the environmentalists, are able to present themselves as being on the side of the angels, as it were. It is an especially difficult job to convince a sceptical public (and European Parliament) that pesticides are not necessarily harmful and, indeed, can be beneficial. ECPA's strategy has two main elements. First, it has recognised the need to operate in the policy-making arenas largely dominated by the environmentalists and their associated scientific networks – the public and parliamentary arena – as well as dealing with the Commission. For example it has conducted (and published) a survey of public attitudes to crop protection [*ECPA, 1992a*]. Some 6,000 respondents were surveyed (in Denmark, France, Germany, Italy and the Netherlands). Soil pollution and pesticides were seen as important by approximately one third of respondents. Worryingly for the industry, only 30 per cent had heard or read anything about registration schemes for regulating the use of crop protection products. Only around 18 per cent felt that crop protection products were necessary and desirable, with a significantly higher number (40 per cent for males and 34 per cent for females) conceding that they were necessary but undesirable. Over 50 per cent felt that farmers might be tempted to overdose crops to get results. ECPA's survey of the EP was perhaps more alarming for the Association's members. It found that over 62 per cent of MEP's had not even heard of ECPA. Some 80 per cent of MEPs felt that farmers used unnecessary quantities of pesticides, and crop protection products were seen as having a poor record by 49 per cent of MEPs [*ECPA, 1992b*]. (Thus, there appears to be little evidence of some of the characteristics which, in the introduction to this collection, were seen as defining features of, say, policy communities, for example shared values and common perceptions, familiarity amongst participants and so on.) ECPA's strategy in the public and parliamentary arena has been both to increase awareness of the Association (almost certainly achieved since 1992) and to increase understanding of the importance of the industry and of the rational arguments for the use of pesticides. Its second strategy has been to argue for much greater emphasis to be placed on the use of scientific and technical information in the policy-making and regulatory process. A constant theme of ECPA's publications and submissions to the Commission and MEPs is the need to base policy on reliable scientific evidence. For example, in its position paper of May 1993, on the revision of the Drinking Water Directive, it argued that MAL levels should be based upon '. . . thorough review of all available scientific data, in particular the toxicological data . . .' [*ECPA, 1993*]. The fundamental difficulty, of course, is that the Association has to fight the argument that *any* measurable quantities of pesticides in water should be banned. Moreover, it believes that there is a danger that policy will not be based on proper scientific knowledge.

Similar problems face the fertiliser industry represented by EFMA (European Fertiliser Manufacturers' Association) because of the high political salience of the nitrates issue. The industry's difficulties in responding to this issue are compounded by the fact that it is in very serious recession. In 1992, EFMA members alone made a loss of $1.1 billion on a turnover of $8.4 billion [*EFMA, 1993*], and it continues to face overcapacity of approximately 20 per cent. The preoccupation with economic decline limits EFMA's lobbying strategy on water issues, even though these issues are potentially crucial to the long-run business environment of EFMA's members. The timescale of the potential threat is long, but the threat is nevertheless real. The internal problem is for EFMA as an organisation to ensure that its members pay sufficient attention to the issue and agree to devote the necessary resources to lobbying. Nevertheless, there is evidence that EFMA is increasing its capacity to participate in the water policy process and is beginning to accept that the industry must develop solutions to the nitrate problem, alongside publicising the benefits of fertilisers to the European economy. (Interestingly, the industry appears to have been aware of the nitrate problem as early as the 1930s and 1940s, as it had data on the build-up of nitrates in water. It is ironic, therefore, that non-industry scientists and pressure groups like Greenpeace and FoE picked up the issue and publicised it much later, wrong-footing the industry.)

Despite its difficulties, EFMA is an important player but, as with ECPA, operates in a rather difficult policy-making environment. It too emphasises the need for better decision-making rules as well as the need for better decisions. Thus, it jointly published a document with the Commission in December 1991, entitled *The Fertiliser Industry of the European Community: The Issues of Today and Tomorrow [EC/EFMA, 1991]*. The document argued that it was inappropriate to think in terms of Community-wide regulations governing the specific details of product use because fertiliser use needed to take account of the specific crop, soil type and local climate. Hence it argued for framework directives, outlining broad objectives for the use of fertilisers, but leaving member states with the responsibility of adapting the most appropriate and effective solutions. The whole tenor of EFMA's strategy is to emphasise scientific data and scientific problem-solving – for example by arguing that there are many scientific data to indicate that applications of fertilisers at the optimum levels does not lead to a high loss of nutrients into the water supply. (One consequence of a more devolved and decentralised decision-making process would be to force the environmental movement to spread its resources across a whole range of different decision points throughout the member states.)

Behind the agro-chemical industries are of course the European farmers – represented by COPA. They are perhaps the most effective industry in terms of EU lobbying generally, securing enormous financial support via CAP. Moreover they have their own DG (DG VI) which has in the past been adept at defending its clients. There is, however, evidence of the gradual erosion of this enormous power and it may be that COPA's fall-back position might be to press for compensatory payments for farmers – as with the set-aside policy designed to reduce production. Even so, the farmers are a powerful and well organised lobby – as witnessed by the fact that, so far, the agricultural industry has succeeded in transferring its costs (from pollution) to others, in the classic 'externalities' fashion.

Finally, the chemical industry as a whole has an obvious stake in the case of key players. Represented by CEFIC, the industry faces a range of threats in the water field – for example, in 1994 it is concerned with several major 'water' issues. These are the three Maritime Conventions dealing with Best Available Technology; proposals from various industry sectors proposing bans of certain products: the proposed framework Directive on Ecological Quality of Water; the Drinking Water Directive; and the updating of the Black List Directive (Discharge of Dangerous Substances, 76/464); as well as the intended prioritisation of the Black List and the North-Sea-List ID. CEFIC liaises closely with both ECPA and EFMA (indeed EFMA is in the same building in Brussels). It too is conscious of the difficult task of balancing the need to project a much better environmental image for the industry (under its Responsible Care campaign) with the need to argue for a more rationalistic/scientific decision-making process based upon hard and reliable scientific and toxicological evidence and research.

The Environmental and Consumer Interests

The environmentalists are, of course, quite different organisations – both in terms of organisational structure, in terms of their tactics, and in terms of the policy-making arenas in which they operate. Interestingly, although every interviewee referred to the environmentalists as powerful and important actors, the actual Euro-level resourcing of the specific water campaigning efforts of these groups is small. (They do, however, have access to a world-wide network of expertise.) For example, Greenpeace's European office in Brussels has no specialist in water policy and sub-contracts its Euro-water campaigning to its German association. Similarly, other important environmental groups – such as WWF and the EEB see water as just one part of a broader campaign strategy. Their strength is not large organisational resources, but an ability to play a key role in setting the agenda in the environmental sector as a whole, including water. Indeed, as policy actors, they often explain their role as being in the agenda-setting business [*Mazey and Richardson, 1992*]. In playing this role very effectively (many of the other key players admit that they themselves are usually reacting to the agenda set by the environmentalists) the environmental groups access a range of scientific and technical data. They can out-match the big chemical companies in some respects, simply because the groups access a different range of scientific expertise than even a large chemical company can command. (How many chemical companies have their own scientific experts on whales or on the effect of nitrates on small babies, for example?) The links between the environmental organisations and the scientific community are complex, but it seems reasonable to see the environmentalists as producing a megaphone effect for scientific findings. They have a well developed skill in popularising and marketing scientific knowledge and are classic 'movement entrepreneurs' [*Schmitt, 1989*] seeking out new market opportunities for organisation growth and membership renewal [*Richardson, 1995b*]. Other actors – the water industry, polluters, national governments – continue to be vulnerable to this marketing strategy.

   The other category of non-producer groups involved in water is, of course, consumers. As always, they are less effective as organisational actors – though BEUC was both represented at the September Drinking Water conference and is sometimes listed by other key water actors as important. As an organisation, however, it has a very wide range of interests to cover and insufficient resources to match. Hence water is not central to BEUC's concerns in the way that water is to EUREAU or even to ECPA. However, the empty chair concept is important in terms of representing consumers' interests. All participants in the European water policy process know that consumers are politically important and there is a constant concern for the perception of consumers and for how they might react to policy change.

Scientists and Technologists

We conclude with a brief discussion of a rather different set of actors who may not always see themselves as policy actors at all – scientific researchers in various fields such as toxicology and ecotoxicology. Here we enter the world of knowledge, ideas, and problem definition. It is here that power ultimately lies.

If we stand back from the complexity or *mélange* of different actors in EU water policy, it is clear that the agenda-setting process is of crucial importance. We fail to capture what Schattschneider termed the supreme instrument of power – the power to set the political agenda [*Schattschneider, 1960*] – if we merely concentrate on the discussions and actor involvement in the processing of such issues as, say, nitrates or lead in water. The key question, in terms of political power, is why is there a debate about the precise levels of these pollutants in the first place? Adler and Haas posed the question in more elegant terms when they argued that the study of the political process is 'a question of who learns what, when, to whose benefit and why?' [*Adler and Haas, 1992: 370*]. Water policy is, *par excellence*, an example of the power of science and technology to drive policy by setting the agenda of politics. Put simply, it is the scientific community which ultimately has the power to set the EU's water agenda in that it is only via science that we know (or think we know) that certain pollutants are harmful, and it is only via technology that we know (albeit often in total ignorance of the actual costs and benefits) that these pollutants can be removed from (or prevented from entering) the water supply. It would be naive to believe that science is objective or that it is a fairly simple matter to translate science into public policy. One cannot fail to be struck by the importance of scientific evidence and counter evidence, and scientific dispute, as one analyses documentary sources relating to water policy. For example, EUREAU's proposals for the modification of the Drinking Water Directive 80/778 ran to some 187 pages and dealt with such detailed technical issues as the advantages of ortho-phosphate over polyphosphates for reducing lead solubility and the limits set on anionic surfactants [*EUREAU, 1991*]. Though adopting a counter-position, the EEB also concerned itself with specific values for parameters – for example arguing for a lowering of the MACs for arsenic and cadmium [*EEB, 1993*]. In reality the process by which these scientific and technical disputes are resolved is at best opaque and at worst highly politicised. It is to this political process that we now turn, briefly, in our conclusion.

Concluding Speculations: The Importance of Institutions, Specialised Communities, and the Formation of Advocacy Coalitions

In concluding this overview of the EU water policy process, it is important to return to the notion of complexity – not because social scientists make their living by claiming that the social world is complex (they do!) but because of the EU water policy process is still in the developmental phase. As in all policy sectors, there are increasingly intense and dense cross-sectoral linkages operating in a complex institutional setting. Equally there are many sub-sectoral features. Thus, in one sense it has been rather misleading to talk about EU water policy or the EU water policy process. There are many policies and many processes and they may have rather different network characteristics. Commission officials responsible for 'managing' the whole policy sector have a distinct perception of a series of specialised networks, configurations, or constellations. Some sub-sectors are more structured, organised and predictable than others. Drinking water is probably the most structured and stable (relatively) compared with groundwater (the most crucial sub-sector in the long run, perhaps). The actors in the groundwater subsector are so numerous, varied and diffuse, that talk of network is as yet fanciful. In the end, the Commission will have to tackle this mess and will have to mobilise and organise the subsector, however difficult, time consuming and controversial that might prove to be.

Other sub-sectors, such as drinking water, seem set for a rather more familiar pattern of decision-making, albeit not entirely predictable. At the heart of this process is likely to be the Commission's role as broker, as suggested earlier. Thus DG XI has a range of groups whom it recognises on a regular basis and on whom it draws for advice. It also has an official Network of National Correspondents and a formal committee of scientific experts – the so-called Scientific Advisory Committee to examine the toxicity and eco-toxicity of chemical components. Some of these experts are drawn from national administrations and regulatory agencies and others are drawn from academic and other research centres. (Their names and country affiliations are published, but not their organisational affiliations.) Whatever their organisational and national backgrounds, however, they are on the Committee because of their standing as experts in the sense described by Haas. It seems likely that these experts – linked as they are to a whole network of other experts in the scientific community – correspond to Haas's understanding of what an epistemic community looks like, namely:

... a network of professionals with recognised expertise and competence in a particular domain and an authoritative claim to policy-relevant knowledge within that domain or issue area' [*Haas, 1992: 3*].

In one sense (if our speculation is correct) we could interpret this phenomenon in terms of a policy community, as defined in the introduction to this volume. The group is tightly drawn, continuous, shares *some* fundamental values and understandings grounded in scientific knowledge and approach, and is fairly exclusive. In more colloquial terms, the Committee on Toxicity and ,Ecotoxicity (CSTE) risks being portrayed as the private management of public business. The Committee is, of course, by no means the *exclusive* source of advice to DG XI. It can and does hire experts on an *ad hoc* basis and can commission full studies on an open or restricted tender basis. Insufficient evidence is available to analyse this process and its effects, however, although it is interesting that the politics of expertise appears to be the politics of a particular kind of expertise. For example, there is no equivalent committee of economists to CSTE, yet the whole question of the use and management of water resources and the control of pollution quite clearly raises economic issues. Thus, one possibility is that although it is unlikely that any one part of the Commission is subject to the American phenomenon of regulatory capture [*Mazey and Richardson, 1993*] there is at least a possibility that particular professions may have achieved an especially influential position within the water sector at the EU level.

Yet water remains a very volatile political issue. As noted earlier, the issue is of such continuing political salience that issue expansion, rather than issue contraction, is likely to remain the norm. If this is correct then we can best characterise the EU water policy process as a linkage of specialised epistemic communities into the public domain via a series of changing advocacy coalition on the Sabatier model. Thus, as Sabatier suggests, within a policy subsystem '... actors can be aggregated into a number of advocacy coalitions composed of people from various organisations who share a set of normative and causal beliefs and who often act in concert' [*Sabatier, 1988: 3*]. In practice, advocacy coalitions can include elected and agency officials, interest group leaders and researchers. Some of these coalitions will be relatively stable over time, as for example within the agricultural and agrochemical coalitions, but there will always be the possibility of new, often temporary, coalitions emerging. These coalitions will be constructed according to the nature of the issue and the nature of the different interests surrounding the issue. Quite clearly, different organisations have different interests and have different reactions to the cost/benefit calculation of water regulation. Water supply, typically, is a cost-plus industry and, within reason, can benefit from regulation as it turns a low value product into a higher value product. In contrast, some interests – pesticide or fertiliser manufacturers – face tremendous risks if regulation gets too tough. Interests will seek coalitions on an *ad hoc* basis, reflecting how the particular issue affects their fundamental interests. In this process, today's opponents can be tomorrow's allies. For example, the possible relaxation of the regulation governing the introduction of pesticides into the marketplace cited earlier, produced a coalition of EUREAU, Greenpeace and the EP, with the pesticide industry in opposition. Yet proposals to introduce new regulations on the use of atrazine to a level which was a surrogate for zero, saw EUREAU and the crop protection industry on the same side, against the environmentalists. In this case EUREAU had as much interest in opposing a regulation which would have been impossible for its members (putting them at serious risk in terms of fines and so on), as it was in the interests of the pesticide industry in avoiding the banning one of its key products.

We may, therefore, expect what are often quite detailed technical and scientific issues to be regularly exported from the relatively closed world of technical and scientific debate, into the more public world where advocacy coalitions form and campaign for support. Even the detailed toxicological questions, which often seem the very stuff of policy debate, cannot be confined to the world of technical advisory committees such as CSTE. For example, much of the current debate about drinking water is about whether or not to accept or modify WHO guidelines. In broad terms, opponents are lined up for or against WHO guidelines. Polluters often see WHO as the line in the sand because some WHO guidelines specify more flexible parameters than existing or proposed EU guidelines. In contrast, the environmental and consumer bodies want tougher standards than WHO, claiming that the EU should be at the forefront of the regulatory process, not simply following WHO. Whatever the outcome, it has to be recognised that WHO plays a major if not central role in this whole process – that is, to a considerable degree the action is outside the EU. That, of course, is another story. Suffice to say that once issues are in this public arena, participation can be extensive, suggesting that EU water policy-making will be difficult to capture using single policy models. If one had to select one, rather than several models, to describe the nature of the process, the Cohen *et al.* garbage can model suggests itself. This model has three main properties. The first is problematic preferences – organisations operate on the basis of a variety of inconsistent and ill-defined preferences. The second is unclear technology – organisations operate on the basis of trial and error, learning from accidents of past experience. The third feature is fluid participation – the audiences and decision-makers for any particular choice vary capriciously [*Cohen* et al., *1972: 1*]. All three features seem to be central to our understanding of how EU water policy is made.

Finally, we must, of course, return to the institutional actors. These coalitions, networks and communities all operate in an institutional context. Thus, they all have to recognise the relative and changing powers of the key institutional actors – the Commission, the EP and the CM. Everyone, in turn, needs to keep an eye on the European Court of Justice. In the end, EU laws do bite!

NOTES

1. Jordan *et al.* suggest that Jack Walker first used the term policy community in an occasional paper on *The Diffusion of Knowledge* in 1974 (see Jordan, Grant, Maloney, William A. and McLaughlin, Andrew (1992), *Assumptions About the Role of Groups in the Policy Process: The British Policy Community Approach*, British Interest Group Project Paper, No. 4, Aberdeen.

REFERENCES

Adler, Emanuel and Peter Haas, (1992), 'Conclusion. Epistemic Communities, World Order and the Creations of a Reflective Research Programme', *International Organisation*, Vol. 46 (1), pp.367–390.
Cohen, Michael, March, James and Johan P. Olsen, (1972), 'A Garbage Can Model of Organization Choice', *Administrative Science Quarterly*, Vol. 17, pp.1–25.
Court of Auditors (1992), *Special Report No. 3/92 Concerning the Environment, together with the Commission's Replies*, Official Journal, 92/C245/01, Vol. 35.
Downs, Anthony (1967), *Inside Bureaucracy*, Boston: Little Brown.
EC/EFMA (1991), *The Fertilizer Industry of the European Community: The Issues of Today, The Outlook for Tommorrow*, EC/EFMA: Brussels.
ECPA (1992a), *The Public View*, ECPA: Brussels.
ECPA (1992b), *What Members of the European Parliament Think*, ECPA: Brussels.
ECPA (1993), *ECPA Position Paper on the Revision of the Drinking Water Directive (80/778/EEC)*, ECPA: Brussels.
EEB (1993), *Comments on the Possible Revision of the EC Drinking Water Directive*, EEB: Brussels.
EEC (1992), *European Community Environment Legislation*, Vol. 7, Water, EEC: Brussels.
EFMAU (1993), *Annual Review* 1992/3, EFMA: Brussels.
EUREA (1991), *Drinking Water Directive 80/778/EC. Proposals for Modification. Views of EUREAU*, EUREAU: Brussels.
Garvey, Tom (1993), 'Regulation: Water and Pollution – Water Policy in the European Community', *The Financial Times*, London, 15/16 March.
Haas, Peter (1992), 'Introduction: Epistemic Communities and International Policy Co-ordination', *International Organisations*, Vol. 49, pp.1–35.
Haigh, Nigel (1994), *Manual of Environment Policy: The EC and Britain*, London: Longman.
Heclo, Hugh (1978), 'Issue Networks and the Executive Establishment', in King, Anthony (ed.), *The New American Political System*, Washington DC: American Enterprise Institute.
Henderson, P. D. (1977), 'Two British Errors: Their Probable Size and Some Possible Lessons', *Oxford Economic Papers*, Vol. 29, No. 2, pp.159–205.
Jacobs, F. and R. Corbett, (1990), *The European Parliament*, London: Graham and Trotman.
Judge, David (1992), 'Predestined to Save the Earth: The Environment Committee of the European Parliament', *Environmental Politics*, Vol. 1, No. 4, pp.186–212.
Lehmbruch, Gerhard (1991), 'The Organisation of Society, Administrative Strategies and Policy Networks', in Czada, R. and Windhoff-Heriter (eds.), *Political Choice: Institutions, Rules and the Limits of Rationality*, Frankfurt, Campus Verlag.
Majone, Giandomenico (1991), *Market Integration and Regulation: Europe After 1992*, Euro-

pean University Institute, Working Papers, SPS 91/10, Florence.

Mazey, Sonia and Jeremy Richardson, (1992), 'Environmental Groups and the EC: Challenges and Opportunities', *Environmental Politics*, Vol. 1, No. 4, pp. 109–128.

Mazey, Sonia and Jeremy Richardson, (eds.), (1993), *Lobbying in the European Community*, Oxford: Oxford University Press.

Mazey, Sonia and Jeremy Richardson, (1994a), 'The Commission and the Lobby' in G. Edwards, and D. Spence, (eds.), *The Commission of the European Communities*, London: Longman.

Mazey, Sonia and Jeremy Richardson, (1994b), 'Policy Co-ordination in Brussels: Environmental and Regional Policy', *Regional Politics and Policy*, Vol. 4, No. 1, pp. 22–44.

Moravcsik, Andrew (1991), 'Negotiating the Single European Act', reprinted in R. Keohand, and S. Hoffmann, *The New European Community: Decision Making and Institutional Change*, Boulder, CO: Westview Press.

Peters, Guy (1994), 'Models of Agenda Building: Is the European Community Different?', *Journal of European Public Policy*, Vol. 1, No. 1, pp.9–26.

Putnam, Robert (1988), 'Diplomacy and Domestic Politics: The Logic of Two Level Games', *International Organisation*, Vol. 42(3), pp.427–460.

Richardson, Jeremy (1993), 'Introduction: Pressure Groups and Government' in Richardson Jeremy (ed.), *Pressure Groups*, Oxford: Oxford University Press pp. 1–15.

Richardson, Jeremy (1995a), 'Actor Based Models of National and EU Policy-Making: Policy Communities, Issue Networks and Epistemic Communities' in Kassin, H. and A. Menon, (eds.), *State Autonomy in the European Community*, London: Routledge.

Richardson, Jeremy (1995b), 'The Market for Political Activism: Interest Groups as a Challenge to Political Parties', *West European Politics*, Vol. 17, No. 3.

Richardson, Jeremy and Grant Jordan (1979), *Governing Under Pressure: The Policy Process in a Post-Parliamentary Democracy*, Oxford: Martin Robertson.

Richardson, Jeremy, Maloney, William and Wolfgang Rüdig (1992), 'The Dynamics of Policy Change: Lobbying and Water Privatisation', *Public Administration*, Vol. 70, No. 2, pp. 157–175

Sabatier, Paul (1988), 'An Advocacy Coalition Framework of Policy Change and the Role of Policy Orientated Learning Therein', *Policy Sciences*, Vol. 21, pp.128–168.

Schattschneider, E. E. (1960), *The Semi-Sovereign People. A Realist's View of Democracy in America*, New York: Holt.

Schmitt, R. (1989), 'Organizational Interlocks Between New Social Movements and Traditional Elites: The Case of the West German Peace Movement', *European Journal of Political Research*, Vol. 17, pp. 583–98.

Sedenius, James K. (1992), 'Challenging Conventional Explanations of International Co-operation: Negotiation Analysis and the Case of Epistemic Communities', *International Organization*, Vol. 46 (1), pp.323–365.

Tsebelis (1990), *Nested Games: Rational Choice in Comparative Politics*, Berkeley: University of California Press.

Water Management Networks in Hungary: Network Development in a Period of Transition

KENNETH HANF and MARCEL ROIJEN

In the countries of Central Europe the dynamics of network change are more marked than in most countries of Western Europe. The discontinuities between traditional patterns of water management and the new political and economic conditions that are presently emerging are quite dramatic. An examination of the way in which post-communist developments are modifying the traditional system of Hungarian water management illustrates nicely the processes of institutional development and network change which are likely to be important in other countries of Central and Eastern Europe as well. Although things are in a state of flux – and even though we have relatively little empirical information on actual operations – a brief description of the current arrangements for water management in Hungary provides a useful baseline from which to describe the institutional and societal context as well as the task environment out of which new patterns of water policy networks will develop. Such an analysis can suggest ways in which network relations and formal institutions interact and mutually shape one another in the daily practices through which 'real' policy is developed and applied. The Hungarian case makes clear how broader system changes modify the context of sectoral networks and how these become embedded in larger political and social structures. It is this set of more extensive changes that has created the need for new network relations and has, simultaneously, changed the rules and the conditions under which these will emerge. At the same time, a focus on the need actively to design and create such networks suggests the value in looking more closely at the nuts and bolts questions of how such cooperation can be brought about.

Managing the Dynamics of Institutional Change: The General Relevance of the Hungarian Experience

Water management in Hungary has a long and venerable tradition. Both the institutional arrangements and the networks of relationships between the

Kenneth Hanf is Senior Lecturer in Public Administration at the Erasmus University in Rotterdam and Adjunct Professor of International Environmental Policy at The Netherlands Business School at Nijenrode. Marcel Roijen is a Research Assistant in Public Administration at the Erasmus University.

actors involved that have grown up around them have evolved gradually over the last two centuries. Even the changes initiated by the Communist takeover after the Second World War did not completely disrupt the tight professional community that was the core of the state water management network. However, the impact that the current process of system transformation is having on these relationships indicates that even long-standing structures of management can only take so much before they, too, must yield and adapt to the forces of change. Under pressures from within and outside the country, the immediate sectoral institutions as well as the broader political and socio-economic context within which water policy is formulated and carried out are being radically transformed.

Like other countries in Central and Eastern Europe, Hungary is experiencing extensive political and institutional discontinuity as a result of its transition from a system of central state direction of the economy to a parliamentary democracy and free-market economy. The period 1987–1990 marked the beginning of a period of adjustment which is still in progress. A start has been made at abolishing institutions and ways of doing things associated with the old regime to make way for those more appropriate to the emerging order. Under both domestic and international pressures, an effort is being made to design a completely new set of functional institutions while trying, at the same time, to perform the basic functions of daily government. The presently emerging patterns of water management in Hungary are being shaped by the effort to redefine the tasks and organisation of water management to fit the new demands made by a new socio-economic formation whose shape is not yet clearly visible.

The Hungarian system of water management is, therefore, undergoing re-institutionalisation – shedding, in part, the institutional shell of the previous regime while searching for a form more appropriate for the new political economy. The water regime will need a new legal basis; the balance between the demands of water management and environmental protection will have to be worked out; the relations between different actors involved in performing the various water management tasks will have to be redefined on the basis of a new allocation of functions and powers for the policy strategy selected. These choices regarding institutional (re)design cannot be made by a process of 'rationally' weighing of potentially most appropriate forms and arrangements. They will be made against the background of and as part of the general process of radical economic and politico-administrative and social transformation presently underway in Hungary. The pattern of relations between the different levels of actors in water management will be shaped by more fundamental constitutional decisions with respect to the relations between central government and local self-government. Similarly, the range of regulatory strategies and instruments available to water managers will be determined by the demands and possibilities of the emerging market economy. It is interesting to note that whereas the efficient performance of water management functions may require new patterns of collaboration and cooperation – between quality and quantity managers, between levels of government, between government and the economic sector – forces of radical change are at work that tend to pull apart and isolate different actors. Having long been forced to live together under central direction, both local government and economic actors are suspicious of any measures that look as though they would threaten newly-won independence and reintroduce old regulatory mechanism in new forms. Understandably, as new institutional arrangements develop, the traditional pattern of relationships and ways of 'doing things', the patterns of relationships within and across existing jurisdictions and organisational boundaries are disrupted. New patterns of interaction emerge slowly, either following the path laid out by the new institutional arrangements or developing informally to bridge the uncertain division of labour and unclear allocation of responsibilities and authorities that characterise the initial period of transition.

In Hungary, as in the other countries of Central and Eastern Europe, there has been a significant amount of (perhaps) unavoidable institutional lag in adapting existing politico-administrative structures to new social and political forces. The initial efforts to transform the political and social landscape together with the rules of the game must be undertaken within the institutional constraints of the old regime. Responses of these actors to new challenges and disruptions of the old system – even with the best intentions in the world – will be based on familiar habits of mind and the legal-administrative instruments immediately available. During the interregnum 'hold overs' from the previous regime will have to be used to prepare and carry out the changes envisioned. Along with the continuing 'fundamental tasks' of water management there will be new objectives and modes of operation flowing forth from the new division of labour between state and society, and between central state organs and the organs of local self-government.

In any case, the shape of the new networks of relationships through which water management policy will be formulated and carried out in the countries of Central and Eastern Europe is not yet clear. A number of factors will, however, influence the way in which these patterns develop. Internally, there will be the decisions taken regarding the transformation of the economy, the redefinition of the constitutional division of labour between central and local governments, policy choices of the sitting government and the support from the politically mobilised public for economic development and the conditions under which acceptable standards of material well-being and social security can be achieved. All this will have consequences for the substantive direction of water policy, the institutional context within which it develops and the relative power of the different actors in determination of these objectives. At the same time there are significant pressures from different parts of the international community (multinational lending institutions, international organisations, most notably the EU, and bilateral agreements) all pressing Hungary to undertake various institutional reforms and to commit itself to particular substantive courses of action.

As we have seen in the other country studies, water policy networks are undergoing gradual but constant change. In the countries of Central Europe the dynamics of network change are more marked and the discontinuities between inherited or traditional patterns and the adjustments to the new situation are more dramatic. This intertwined process of institutional change and network development is clearly visible in the case of water management in Hungary. An examination of the way in which these developments are modifying the traditional system of Hungarian water management offers an intriguing example of a network in transition or reconstruction. As such the Hungarian story illustrates nicely the processes of institutional development and network change which are likely to be important in other countries of Central and Eastern Europe in the area of water policy and management. Although things are in a state of flux – and even though we have relatively little empirical information on actual operations – a brief description of the current arrangements for water management in Hungary can serve as a useful baseline from which to describe the institutional landscape and the task environment out of which the new patterns of water policy networks will develop.[1] In this sense, empirical research on the changes in Hungary, as well as its neighbouring countries, should provide interesting case studies documenting the processes of network development in one important policy area. Such studies provide a chance to follow the way in which network relations and formal institutions interact and mutually shape one another in the daily practices through which 'real' policy is developed and applied.

In keeping with the major questions (and analytical tasks) identified in the introductory essay, we will first examine the general characteristics of the water policy network in Hungary, as these can be distilled from the formal institutional arrangements that now exist. This will serve as a baseline from which to speculate over the kinds of developments that are likely to be in the offing in the near future as a consequence of changes in the fundamental institutions of Hungary state and society. Subsequently, we will look at how this pattern of relationships has developed over time and pinpoint some of the factors that have shaped these dynamics. We will then try, in conclusion, to provide an answer (however tentative) to the role that these can have in shaping the substance of Hungarian water policy.

Continuity and Change in Hungarian Water Management: Historical Development

Water policy and management have long been important responsibilities of central government in Hungary. Historically, the tasks of water managers have been dictated by the particular hydrological features of the country. The basic challenge that the natural environment sets for Hungarian water management has been vividly captured in the popular quip that asserts that there are really only two kinds of water in Hungary: too little or too much, and usually at the wrong time of year or in the wrong place [*Hinrichsen and Enyedi, 1990: 67*]. Of the total water resources, only 50 per cent is due to direct precipitation. Much of the Hungarian plain has low rainfall with the summers being particularly dry. Consequently, large areas of Hungary are prone to water shortages. At the same time, many of the most productive and populous parts of the country are threatened by flooding. This has meant that significant resources have had to be allocated for flood control and drainage measures. Furthermore, the water resources within the country are also very unevenly distributed: the demand for water does not coincide with its physical presence. A further peculiarity of Hungary's political geography also influences the tasks of water management: most of its water resources arise outside its national borders. More specifically, 90 per cent of its surface water is provided by just three rivers – the Danube, Tisza and Drava – all of which arise in other countries. This classical 'downstream character' of the country means that some of the key participants in decisions regarding the protection of both the quantity and the quality of water resources in Hungary will be external to the national network of actors and institutions [*Somlyody and Hock, 1991: 44*].

Coping with this situation has kept Hungarian water managers occupied since the nineteenth century building countless kilometres of flood protection dams, canals and channels and irrigation systems to control flooding and provide necessary drainage and run-off, to make available sufficiently deep water ways for transportation and to deliver water for industrial and agricultural use.

The basic tasks of water management along with the first legal and organisational measures for their realization were already in place by the second half of the eighteenth century [*Zotter, 1993: 2–3*]. In keeping with the character of the state at that time (absolute and later constitutional monarchy), a centralised system of technical management was set up to deal with problems of flood protection and river flow regulation. These early developments in water management also laid the groundwork for a second element of the traditional water management system in Hungary: the water management associations. These were voluntary organisations set up by those directly affected by a water management problem at the local level. Although basically self-governing, they operated under the supervision of state water officials, who could also 'force' reluctant partners to participate in the joint effort. These associations have played a basic role in protecting against water damage as well as in dealing with other local water management tasks such as irrigation and drainage. The third element of water management consisted of the provision of water services within the local communities. As in other countries, the organisation of water supply and sewerage was a responsibility of local government. Special public utilities associations were also used to plan and construct facilities that were then brought into the local water service system. Here, too, central state water managers played an important supervisory role to ensure that local services were consistent with the legal and technical conditions stipulated by national policy.

We can conclude, therefore, that the traditional system of water management in Hungary consisted of two distinct but interrelated elements. On the one hand, there were well-organised local networks of key water 'interests' (providers and users). Although these actors enjoyed a good deal of operational autonomy, they were also subject to steering and ultimately control by the water professionals from the central state agencies in charge of national water management tasks.

Post-War Consolidation of State Water Management

Building on the basic legal-administrative framework provided by the water act of 1885, the Hungarian system of water management was characterised by substantial continuity from the late nineteenth century until the immediate post-war period. After 1948, this system underwent a number of dramatic changes [Karászi, 1991]. Prior to 1945, water management functions were divided among state authorities and more local bodies. On the one hand, there were associations organised by the affected agricultural or industrial interests in areas such as flood control, drainage or irrigation; there were also associations for water supply and sewerage collection and treatment companies. On the other hand were the state agencies responsible for things such as navigation, waterway and channel maintenance, hydrographic services, professional training, water-use licensing and general water management. In 1949 all the functions related to water management were made the responsibility of the state. However, these functions continued to be allocated among three, later four, central agencies (ministries or national boards). These dispersed responsibilities were brought together in 1953 in the newly-created National Water Authority. Functions of local importance, such as drainage of agricultural land, irrigation, water supply and sewerage were then once again assigned in 1957 to local associations, while state water management was concentrated on functions of prominent public interest, for example flood control. For this purpose, 12 district water authorities were established to cover on a predominantly catchment-area basis the entire territory of the country. Besides these 12 district authorities, specialised hydraulic construction and engineering companies of national scope were also set up. The local companies of the water supply and sewerage services were organised into larger, regional units while the earlier fragmented system of flood control associations was replaced by a national organisation.

Changes in the political and economic structure of the country after 1945 also transformed the physical context of water management and the range of tasks it performed: developments with regard to the relations of ownership and the scale of agriculture production resulted in different patterns of drainage and irrigation. The increased demands for more water for economic production led to the building of dams to store and provide water for irrigation. These also were used to create the depth necessary for navigation and to generate power for industry and urban centres of population. The water impounded in the resulting reservoirs and other storage basins was also used to meet the water demands of industry. Continuing concern for large-scale flood control led to major levee reinforcement and maintenance projects [Karászi, 1991: 29–30].

Although the basic hydrological characteristics remained the same, the political and socio-economic changes introduced by the socialist regime had important consequences for the organisation and functioning of the water management network. While the system of democratic centralism effectively destroyed the local self-management and service provision, at the same time the system of central state planning and administrative represented – in one sense – the culmination of the strand of integrated state management of water resources. Strategic planning and policy was in the hands of the ministries and national authority, operational tasks were carried out by regional water management authorities. County councils and local councils were primarily administrative bodies with few independent tasks and responsibilities of their own. Water management had effectively been taken out of their hands. During this period the role of water management associations as vehicles for local joint action among water users also declined.

In short, responding to the changing and growing demands for water in the socialist economy worked to reinforce the traditional values and institutions committed to the provision of crucial water services. Water management continued to be dominated by a tightly integrated network of technically trained managers, which was now, however, forced to share control over water policy with a central political elite. In this sense, it can be argued that these water professionals and the political bosses constituted a 'policy community', within which there was a division of labour between the political determination of policy and its technical execution. An important precondition for the continued central role of the water professionals in the network was the high degree of complementarity between the traditional objectives of this sector and the general expectations and requirements of the country and its political leadership. They protected themselves against undue arbitrary intervention by politics (and other sectoral interests) by putting their technical and administrative expertise at the 'disposal' of the central political leadership to carry out water management projects and to provide water services for the benefit of the society as a whole. By defining its role as that of a 'public service' enterprise, protecting citizens against water damage and managing water resources as a precondition for societal development, state water managers were able to withdraw into a closed professional policy community of technically competent and politically neutral water management engineers [*Karászi, 1991: 30*]. The continued dominance of the state water management establishment was, therefore, based on the mutual advantage derived by the political leadership and the water management system from providing important infrastructure and water service to support economic development.

The Environmental Quality Challenge

The dominant position of these professionals at the core of this policy community appeared to be challenged by the growing concern for environmental protection in general and, more specifically, the qualitative aspects of water management. It cannot be said that the traditional water management community ignored or denied the quality issue in order to avoid a threat to the existing establishment. Indeed, since there was little demand for environmental protection generated from outside the party-state leadership, the water management community itself provided a good deal of the institutional support for this issue. Although the water law of 1964 contained important provisions with respect to the avoidance of water pollution, the decade of the 1970s brought a growing realisation, supported by water managers, that there was an important 'quality dimension' to the management of water as a natural resource and that water could no longer be considered a 'free gift' even in a centrally planned economy. The first phase of post-1945 development had stressed making water available and handling the management problems associated with economic and social development. By the mid-1970s it had become clear that 'water could no longer be regarded as a free gift of nature and had to be treated as a limited resource even in the controlled economic system' [*Karászi, 1991: 30*]. Consequently, in addition to the more traditional concern with the quantity aspects of managing water resources, problems of guaranteeing an adequate water quality also acquired greater importance. The rising costs of water treatment together with the limited amounts of clean fresh water available focused attention on the problem of the rational use of water. With a policy of balanced allocation of water to 'realistic water demands' and more investments in waste water treatment and disposal to improve quality of water, water managers sought to promote the incorporation of this new set of values into the existing policy community [Karászi, 1991: 31].

Consequently, a serious effort to integrate the issue and value of water quality into its own structure was quite consistent with the general orientation of the service. As a result, up until the formation of the joint ministry for water management and environmental protection in 1988, water quality management was taken care of by the water policy community. Indeed, it was the professional core of this community that had a monopoly on water quality experts. When the Ministry of Environmental Protection and Water Management was established, it was the water management community that supplied the expertise and trained manpower in area of water quality. Although forced to become part of the administrative structure through which the environmental protection issue network acquired a formal institutional focus, the water managers were able to maintain their position as senior partners and thus, once again, to protect the core integrity of the policy community. Indeed, at the regional level, it was the environmental protection offices that adapted their boundaries to the jurisdictions of the district water offices, organised around catchment areas. In this regard as well, the concern for water quality issues was in important respects integrated into the system of general water resource management.

The National Water Authority and the National Environmental Protection and Nature Conservation Authority were united to form the Ministry of Environmental Protection and Water Management in December 1987. Although this amalgamation was at the time heralded as an appropriate institutional recognition of the interrelations between water management and environmental protection, the new integrated ministry had a short life. Environmental protection tended to be the weaker partner in the face of prevailing special water authority interests. Within the ministry, protection of water quality remained under the jurisdiction of water authorities who were responsible for fulfilling their water resource management plans and were expected to produce income. During this period, the conflicting interests between water protection and water sales continued to be mostly resolved in favour of the latter. These conflicts apparently came to a head in the disagreements between environmentalists and water managers over the necessity for, and the environmental impacts of, the Gabčikovo–Nágymaros dam being constructed by the Hungarian and (the then) Czechoslovakian governments. The dam was seen as being supported and promoted by energy and water management interests but environmentalists were concerned with the likely downstream environmental impact of the project. It was felt that a conflict of interest was inevitable if a single institution was responsible for both water management and the aquatic environment.

This 'defeat' of the traditional water policy community cannot be interpreted only as a failure, on its part, to manage this particular issue well. It can be seen more as a case in which the immediate water management-environmental protection conflict, the immediate issue that 'sparked' the changes in existing institutions, was caught up in a broader set of challenges to the existing political system, in which the environmentalist movement played an important role. Under pressure of the public and political movements two new ministries were established in 1990, one taking over the environmental protection tasks of the old integrated authority, the other absorbing the water management functions. Controversy over the dam triggered serious criticism of the water management establishment. Water management also suffered for its close identification with the development objectives and administrative practices of what was on its way to becoming the *ancien régime*. The environmentalist movement (dubbed the 'blues' instead of greens just because of the importance of the dam issue) was both a carrier of the values of environmental protection and a vehicle of political protest in Hungary. Its strength was sufficient to force a split of the new ministry in order to 'protect environmental' considerations from dominance of the development and infrastructure mentality and coalition represented by water management.

Water Policy Networks in Hungary

The Formulation of Water Policy

At present, water in Hungary can be owned by the state, local authorities or private landowners. In general, owners are responsible for the upkeep of river beds and shorelines. Since 1989 the state has owned the large rivers while local authorities own the smaller rivers and lakes; reservoirs remain the property of the state. Owners of land through which the rivers flow have certain rights of use of the water but they cannot abstract the water without a license from the water authorities. All groundwater belongs to the state, which licences all abstractions from the deeper levels; local authorities regulate water drawn from levels up to 30 metres. Fees are charged for these licenses with the revenues going into a Water Fund from which grants can be made for the financing of water projects.

The so-called Water Act of 1964 established the legal framework for the further specification of the objectives of Hungarian water policy and the way in which the different water management functions are to be performed. It is this law that also has defined the basic institutional arrangement for the management of water resources. In the years since its enactment, the Water Law has been spelled out (and, effectively, amended in part) by means of a large number of governmental decrees, ministerial orders and regulations. These pieces of secondary legislation spell out in detail how the law is to be applied in practice. Not surprisingly, this specification of the material content of the framework law has resulted in a complicated hodge-podge of (often) opportunistic responses to the exigencies of water management practice.

Consistent with the political and economic system of the time, the 1964 law regulates water management as a unified state task within a general system of central economic planning and administration. Since at that time all waters were owned by the state, it followed that all water management activities were also considered to be tasks of state agencies under the control of central decision makers. This included those concerning minor waterways that had been performed earlier by the local councils. At the present moment a new water law is needed because the social field has changed with the result that new and varied actors have appeared on the scene whereas in the past the management process was dominated by state water authorities, at both the national and regional levels. The new water law (along with a new environmental protection law) is ready for parliamentary deliberation. The new legislation that has been drafted is intended to reflect recent changes in property relations and the need to redefine the responsibilities of the central state and local governments as well as other legal persons involved in water management. The main institutional consequences have to do with accommodating new legal facts of privatisation of water services; local ownership of some waters; and, in general, the new status of local self-government. As far as can be seen, the overall institutional framework for the state management tasks will remain the same.

The appearance of new players with effective access to the decision-makers can also be seen in the way in which water policy is formulated. Under the socialist regime, things were in some ways much simpler. The process was more tightly centralised and sectoral policy making was subordinated to the over-arching development objectives set out by the party leadership. The articulation of often conflicting interests and priorities and the search for negotiated solutions were concentrated at the top of the hierarchy. These 'political' processes involved primarily central decision-making elites in the party, planning commission and ministries. Social interests (water users) were 'represented' in these negotiations by the ministry responsible for those economic or social sectors. What 'intermediary organisations' there were, also served to channel what little independent input there was from the 'societal field' through official party-controlled mass organisations. Even if we allow for slippage in efficiency of the planning system and accept the fact that central planning often incorporated (even depended on) suggestions and information from the 'bottom', policy formulation still occurred in a highly centralised, party-dominated system. Within the sector itself, professional water managers exercised strong influence, filtering the perceived needs of other social interests and translating general policy objectives into projects and tasks for the water management portfolio.

As we have suggested, the social field of water policy has presently become much more complex and volatile. There is a fledgling system of more open political articulation that links societal interests to decision makers within political parties and government. More effective institutions are in place both to generate and mobilise public opinion and support regarding water policy issues, among other things. There is still an active and relatively influential environmentalist movement. It has not, however, been able to refocus public and political attention and support for environmental quality issues. Within Hungary, as in other Central European countries, citizens continue to be more concerned with achieving the economic development that they hope will bring the desired level of material well-being and social security. It is in this sense that the political context within which water policy decisions are made – and ultimately enforced – has become less hospitable for water management objectives than before. Nevertheless, at the same time, the water policy and environmental protection agendas are, in important respects, being strongly shaped (even set) by actors outside both the water sector and the country itself. Important non-Hungarian actors such as partners in various bilateral agreements; multilateral financial institutions such as the World Bank and European Bank for Reconstruction and Development; and, most importantly, the European Union are exerting pressures on constitutional structure, policy substance, administrative capacities and specific projects in the water field.

The new water law has been drafted by national and international water experts, with an opportunity for some input from regional water managers. Many of the social interests which normally could be expected to participate in such a drafting exercise do not yet exist in their new institutional guise or are not yet well-organised. At the same time, there continues to be a certain inclination to professionalise and depoliticise the preparation of such laws by emphasising the professional and technical input of the experts and leaving the political discussion (formally) to actors in the parliamentary and cabinet arenas. To the extent that this has been the case, societal or water user interests continue to be virtually represented by the experienced water management officials who have already taken them into account.

The Management of Water Quality in Hungary

Water management tasks in Hungary have been allocated to two ministries. The general division of labour is between quantity and quality tasks, although with regard to the latter functions there is a good deal of overlap and joint responsibility.

The job of establishing national policy and regulations with regard to water quality management is in the hands of the Ministry of Environmental Protection and Regional Development.[2] This ministry has broad responsibility for coordinating and harmonising all activities related to environmental protection and regional development. In this capacity it sets environmental and ecological standards to govern any activity that interferes with or affects the natural conditions of waters. As part of its overall task of monitoring the quality of the environment in Hungary, the ministry is also charged with setting up a system for the evaluation of the quality of the country's waters. In short, by means of the various regulatory instruments at its disposal, it is this national environmental authority that defines the conditions under which activities can be undertaken that could have detrimental impacts on the quality of surface or ground waters.

Although primarily involved in the quantitative management of water resources, the Ministry of Transport, Communication and Water Management and its regional offices are directly responsible for such quality matters connected with waste water management and accidental water pollution accidents such as oil spills. At the same time, to the extent that there are also qualitative dimensions to water quantity management, the environmental protection ministry is responsible. For example, there are situations in which excessive water use might cause environmental damage; then water quantity is also the responsibility of environmental protection ministry. This ministry also sets limits on the use of groundwater and monitors compliance with these allocative decisions. On the other hand, the relationship between the two ministries, and their field offices, is not completely clear. The Ministry of Environmental Protection and Regional Development may be concerned with the impacts of water management decisions on the quality of the water involved, for example the consequences of the regulation of the flow of a river on the condition of a particular aquatic environment, and yet have no direct way of ensuring that its concerns will be effectively taken into consideration by the district water officials. Apparently, where it is a question of the quality of the water resource directly – that is, drinking water or effluent discharges, things are much clearer; there are clear, even if overlapping, procedures. In matters regarding the quality of the water environment in more general terms, the relationships between the two networks is less clear.

In the field, the implementation of this general policy on water quality is, in the first instance, the job of the 12 regional environmental protection inspectorates. District Water Offices are, obviously, also expected to take the relevant quality regulations and objectives into consideration when making decisions in the course of implementing their water management tasks. As we will see, formal administrative procedures ensure that both sets of officials will have to cooperate in the taking of decisions on licences and sanctions in concrete cases. Each of the regional inspectorates has an environmental laboratory attached to it to operate the regional network for monitoring water quality, monitoring and analysing effluents or controlling for specific pollutants. For special tests beyond the capacities of these regional laboratories there are two larger and more specialised regional laboratories. In some cases factories will be used to monitor their own discharges.

Regional inspectorates are also supposed to draw up a 'coherent environmental protection concept' for the region, indicating how water quality concerns are to be realised within this context. Similarly, each District Water Office prepares a regional concept for the management of water resources in the area. At the national level, policy makers work with a classification scheme for classifying different bodies of water according to the water needs of the country as a whole and the quantity and quality required for the different uses for which these waters have been designated. The regional water management plans are based on these national determinations.

The Water Act of 1964 defines the regulatory regime through which the quantity and quality of Hungarian water resources are to be managed. Although provision is made for the use of certain economic instruments, this regime is, by and large, one based on a traditional system of direct regulation. Water quality in Hungary is 'managed' by a system of water use and discharge permits, working with a set of national effluent standards, for discharges into both surface water and sewage systems, and a system of enforcement relying on fines for non-compliance. This regulatory system is intended to ensure that no activity contaminates the waters and that waste water is treated adequately before being discharged into bodies of water or sewers. Over the years, a system of rather strict emission standards has been developed, building upon German norms of the early and mid-1970s. According to a recent study (USAID, 1992), its drinking water standards (issued in 1978 and revised in 1990) are also high and compare favourably with WHO guidelines and standards in other European countries. On the other hand, Hungary's waste water discharge standards are generally not as high as EU standards. It is, however, expected that they will be progressively tightened to meet EU standards in the future.

A system of water use and discharge licenses is the cornerstone of water quality management in Hungary. All activities that involve the use of water or could lead to pollution of the water resources must have a permit specifying the conditions under which they will be allowed. Facilities for the abstraction of water must be licensed by the regional water authorities, who in turn must consult the environmental protection authorities about the potential impact of the abstraction on water quality. Permits for small domestic wells are granted by the local mayor. Licences are also required for discharges into surface waters or into the public sewerage system. National effluent standards are differentiated according to the characteristics of each of six water quality regions. These standards can be adjusted further by the permitting authority to the individual case under consideration. Depending upon water quality interests in the concrete situation, the regional environmental inspectorate can define so-called 'individual limit values' regarding pollutants stipulated in discharges to open waters. These limits may be either more favourable or more restrictive than the general standards set as guidelines by the national regulations. In this way the determination of the 'hazardous contamination' can be based on the conditions of a concrete case and the impact on a specific body of water. These limits can be adjusted as the circumstances of the case at issue change. Such 'individualised' standards can also be revised or withdrawn if this proves to be necessary. The district water office is involved in the making of these decisions in its capacity as a so-called 'professional authority.'

The licensing procedure, and the provisions for enforcing the conditions of such permits, are important determinants of the 'real' water quality management network at the regional level. They provide a good example of the relation between formal institutions and the network of relationships involved in determining the way in which the formal allocation of tasks and authority operates in practice. A closer look at the way in which these procedures define the roles of the different agencies helps make clear in what ways the different actors need to work together if the regulatory tasks involved are to be performed effectively. Even a perfunctory look at the formal procedures for permitting and enforcement decisions makes clear that quite complex networks of actors are involved in the implementation stage of water management. Consequently, it is difficult to speak of a policy community in this phase of the policy process.

Administrative law[3] in Hungary makes a distinction between the agency possessing the first line 'administrative authority', that is, that which actually issues the license, and those agencies involved in the process as a 'specialised or professional authority', that is, those making contributions based on their special expertise to the determination of the conditions under which the permit will be granted. The laws defining the substantive and administrative tasks of sectoral ministries also indicate the scope of this specialised authority in the administrative decisions and activities of governmental organisations.

Even without the participation of these 'professional authorities', the licensing authority is expected to apply all relevant laws and their derivative regulations in coming to its decision. The involvement of the other designated professional authorities provides an opportunity for these 'other' authorities to apply 'their' rules and regulations to the concrete case at hand through their own field offices. Each of the designated professional authorities takes its own 'decision' with regard to the permit application and these decisions are then 'aggregated' into a general overall judgment by the competent licensing authority. This licensing authority cannot deviate from or alter the decisions of the specialised agencies involved. Obviously, a procedure such as this contains a tremendous potential for conflict and delay. Of course, if agreement can be reached among those concerned regarding a particular licence, then the general judgment will reflect this consensus. On the other hand, in cases of disagreement, there is no common superior to which an appeal can be directed.

The most important cooperating actors on water quality decisions will be the regional offices of water management and environmental protection. However, these formal procedures mean that other national agencies can be involved, depending upon the concrete case at hand. For example, the state public health service will act as a professional authority in decisions on water management with regard to such issues as the quality of potable water; public sanitary requirements with regard to surface water; and the evaluation of the 'hazardousness' of waste waters with regard to public health and the testing of waste waters to be disinfected. Its determination will be included in the relevant licences. Officials from this service will also be busy with monitoring the conditions of the waters in question with regard to the health conditions. The enforcement of permit conditions will, in the first instance, be in the hands of the directly responsible licensing authority. But it is clear that there is room for confusion here since other 'professional' authorities are also constantly monitoring conditions on the basis of their own grants of legislative authority and responsibility. Consequently, the efficient fulfilment of these regulatory tasks will ultimately depend on the relationships of cooperation among the different authorities active in a given region.

There is also a division of labour and responsibility between the environmental protection and water management officials with regard to enforcement activities. In Hungary there are actually two different enforcement processes according to whether the action has to do with a permit for discharges into open (natural) waters or a permit for discharges into the public sewer system. In the case of direct discharges, its is the regional environmental inspectorate which enforces compliance with the conditions specified in the discharge licence. However, in keeping with Hungarian administrative law, the district water office must be involved as a 'specialised authority' whose judgment must be incorporated into the authoritative enforcement decision. Enforcement actions regarding discharges into public sewers for pollutants are concerned with non-compliance with the conditions laid down in their waste water discharge permit. Responsibility for initiating these actions and, when deemed necessary, levying fines, is the responsibility of the notary (roughly comparable to a city manager) of the municipality having juris- diction over the sewerage system affected. The public sewage enterprise is supposed to monitor these discharges in order to detect any violations of the licence conditions. In such cases, both the regional inspectorate and the district water office act as professional authorities in 'advising' the local government.

   In general, enforcement of industrial and municipal discharge limits is considered to be rather spotty, with numerous exemptions and a failure to collect fines. In the past these problems were partly due to insufficient resources available for enforcement. Primarily, however, they have been simply a consequence of the political context within which enforcement officials worked. Some regulations created express exemptions for some industries. The whole legal system was unresponsive, with judicial review of administrative decisions unheard of, although the new constitution has at least formally changed this situation. To the extent that there were non- governmental bodies that could have signalled instances of non-compliance, these were in fact parts of the overall system of party-state control. Consequently they lacked the legal and political basis from which to exert effective influence. Although the green movement played a significant role in Hungarian political life in the 1980's, after the high point marked by its success in blocking the construction of the Gabčikovo–Nágymoros Dam, public attention shifted to traditional political issues. By 1992 political and economic issues overshadowed environmental protection. In addition to the general climate and shift in priorities, the financial state of potential polluters also works against strict enforcement of regulations against them. According to a recent expert study, it is difficult to enforce standards and impose sanctions on two groups of polluters: state-owned manufacturing or service companies, and companies being transferred into local municipal ownership [*European Bank, 1993: 42*]. Generally, these firms do not make profits and tend to use outdated and inefficient technology. Given their marginal economic condition, vigorous enforcement of water quality and environ- mental protection regulations would meet the resistance of those concerned with maintaining sources of employment and potential tax revenues. On the other hand, there are indications that enterprises in private hands are more likely to operate with up-graded technology and make an honest effort to meet EU standards.

Waste Water Collection and Treatment

Collection and treatment of waste water is the responsibility of local self-government, either at the county level (for those areas, primarily rural, not served by municipal organisations) or in the towns and cities. It is the job of these governments to organise the provision of these services and to monitor discharges into the public sewer system. As we have seen, enforcement of these waste water discharge permits is also the task of local government, in cooperation with the economic organisation actually operating the collection system. Once again use can be made of the traditional instrument of the water management association to provide infrastructure for dealing with waste water collection and treatment.

This local activity is, of course, not completely free of national constraints and influence. The planning and constructing of these facilities is supervised by the national water authorities. Both national and regional plans for the development of water resources serve as the general framework within which local decisions regarding these services are taken. Capital financing also involves a number of national actors and funds. Of course, the effluent standards and the conditions of service and operations are also set by national policy and regulations. Here, too, these quality norms are enforced via the licensing system, while the district water offices exercise legal and technical supervision over the utilities providing the services. In short, the 'normal' water quality network is extended to include a number of important participants from local government plus actors supplying the financing for the capital investments involved.

Water Supply Networks in Hungary

From 1860 until 1950 both the provision and financing of water services were considered to be local responsibilities. Each water utility usually served a single community and was typically a joint stock corporation whose shares were entirely owned by the commune. Under the communists, all utility companies were nationalised. At first they were managed by the county councils, but in the mid-1960s they were brought under the control of the National Water Authority which then managed them through regional operating organisations formed by integrating the previously local operations. The tariffs were set by the central government. For political reasons these were not allowed to rise; consequently, the gap between revenue and real costs was filled by state subsidies [*Warren* et al., *1993: 69*]. During this period emphasis was place on extending the water supply and less attention was given to collecting and treating waste water and to environmental protection. Consequently there developed a substantial 'utility gap' – that is, the difference between the proportion of the population hooked up to piped water and the number of citizens served by public sewerage systems. This discrepancy has contributed greatly to the water pollution problem in Hungary [*Somlyody and Hock, 1991: 44*].

In 1990 responsibility for public water supply, sewage collection and treatment (as well as local flood control and drainage problems) was returned to local government, who also issue abstraction permits for near-surface wells. Although local governments now own 'local surface waters', these are not important for drinking water. Ownership of the utilities has also be returned to the municipalities. Privatisation has obviously reduced the occasions for – and thus the amount of – direct control and coordination of water services by the water management ministry and its regional offices. Under the previous regime, water utilities, with few exceptions, were the property of the state and under the control of the central government. The latter also determined the prices for these services. At present approximately 80 per cent of the water works have been privatised or are in municipal hands. The Ministry of Transport, Communications and Water Management retains control over only five large regional water works which sell water to counties and some smaller communities. Local government is responsible for granting planning permits for the construction of water works and sewerage system as well as for enforcing compliance with the waste water discharge permits. Water use and general allocation plans remain in the hands of the state water managers as does the granting of water use permits. Therefore, while the capital investments and operations involved in supplying water are in the hands of the local authorities, the normative parameters within which these services are organized are set and supervised by the state. Apart from the general regulatory framework within which these local services are provided, water services operations are supervised by the district water offices and, where relevant, the regional environmental inspectorates. To the extent that water utility associations are used, district water offices exercise legal supervision over these bodies. When questions of capital financing are involved, the water supply network is extended to include national funding agencies (or managers of funds) as well as local or regional banks.

In general then, in provision of local water services, the local actors, which have regained their autonomy and ownership of facilities, are embedded both in the emerging market for their services and in a system of national regulation specifying the relevant rights and obligations of the various parties involved. Once again it is quite clear that the networks for providing these services contain a number of influential 'non-water' actors. The resulting sets of complex relationships of local, regional, national water and non-water actors make it difficult to speak here of a single network. And certainly, there is no sign at the moment of a water services provision community.

The Dynamics of Network Development

The Breaching of a Semi-Closed Shop

The picture sketched in this study suggests that at least until 1990 there has been considerable continuity in the development of the state water management network in Hungary, organised around its core professional community of hydraulic engineers. The development of water management as task of central government, beginning in eighteenth century, reached its high point in the centralised system of state management during the socialist period. From the earlier 1950s until the collapse of the old regime, local actors were subordinated, consistent with the political logic of democratic centralism, to hierarchical state controls and the preeminence of state property. While the physical plant assets and daily operations remained at the local level, this activity was now part of the overall system of centrally controlled water services, managed through regional offices of the National Water Authority.

In the 1970s the growing importance of environmental protection and water quality appeared to represent a potential challenge to this dominance of a tightly integrated management network. However, the water management establishment responded by internalising this new issue and set of values into the existing structure. As we noted, this reaction was not that surprising since quality concerns were not total strangers to the water management community. Hungarian water managers point with pride to the fact that already in the water law of 1885 reference was made to the need to prevent contamination of the nation's waters. Furthermore, the water policy area was the first in which a special pollution fine was introduced. Consequently, by the time the new concern with quality crested in the 1970s – with passage of the Environmental Protection Act and the establishment of the National Office of Environmental Protection and Nature Conservation – the Hungarian water management community already had in place a rather well-developed monitoring and information system as well as a well-trained staff and laboratories to deal with water quality problems. In this sense, its response to the environmental challenge was to incorporate the values and concerns of water quality into its organisation and professional role definition.

Nevertheless, the environmental protection issue generated its own political dynamics and support system that went beyond water quality and sought to institutionalise environmental quality responsibilities in a separate administrative system that would effectively integrate the already existing fragmented and widely dispersed activities and tasks within the Hungarian government. The success of this movement was the merging of the already existing National Water Authority and the National Office of Environmental Protection and Natural Conservation to form the Ministry of Environmental

Protection and Water Management. At the same time, within the newly formed ministry the water managers continued to enjoy a dominant position with regard to water quality. Depending on how you look at it, the creation of the ministry for environmental protection can be seen as a victory for the environmentalists in bringing under their formal control an actor of crucial importance for the development and realisation of effective policy for environmental quality management. On the other hand, the continued dominance of water management – or its success in protecting its core activities – meant that the traditional water management policy network was able to maintain itself intact.

However, in spite of this initial success in salvaging a good deal of the autonomy of the earlier tightly-integrated policy community, even within the new ministry, water managers were now forced to share formal responsibilities with environmental protection officials and to open the network to other participants legitimated by the formal institutional arrangements created by the new structure. The problematic aspects of this new situation (and, ultimately, the threat to the vital interests of the water management network) can be seen in a small example of the kinds of conflicts that could arise between water and environmental quality: water management people planned to dredge silt from a stretch of river in order to improve the quality of the water while the environmental protection people were intent on protecting aquatic life along the same section of the river. Such disagreements were minor. The fundamental tensions quickly came to a head in the widespread public and political criticism of the water management establishment in connection with the hydro-electric project under construction on the Slovak–Hungarian border. Acknowledging that it could not effectively control the water managers, the environmental protectionists did the next best thing by breaking the formal, institutional alliance and taking away from the new water management ministry direct responsibilities for water quality.

New Rules, New Players: Redefining the Water Management Game

The traditional water management community was not penetrated from the outside (that is, the Ministry for Environmental Protection) by new sets of actors organised around the issue of environmental protection and water quality. In an important sense the call for more attention to the qualitative aspects of water management fell on receptive ears. However, as a result of the creation of two water-related ministries, the realisation of water quality policy objectives requires the cooperation of two groups of officials, with separate but overlapping domains.

Moreover, at the same time that it was forced to share regulatory space with Environmental Protection at the national and regional levels, more fundamental changes in the politico-administrative and economic system of

Hungary posed even more fundamental challenges to the centralised system of water management built up under socialism. More general policies with respect to privatisation, deregulation and decentralisation have worked to change the composition of these networks and the general conditions under which they operate. Property relations regarding bodies of water and service provision organisations have been redefined; the position of the state as a regulator of social and economic activities is undergoing change, along with the kinds of policy instruments with which they can work; and new and autonomous governmental actors have been (re-)introduced in the form of self-governing local communities. These changes have removed a number of important water management tasks from the direct control of state water managers and revived the role of local actors – both municipalities and water management associations – in the provision of water services.

But it has not only been changes in the formal division of institutional labour that make it necessary for water managers to seek effective cooperative relations with, in the first instance, their environmental protection colleagues and local governments. Perhaps much more important for the future development of water policy and administration in Hungary is the fact that the political and economic changes inaugurated with the fall of the socialist regime are redefining the broader politico-administrative and socio-economic context within which water policy and its mangers will operate. And these contextual changes, in turn, are redefining both the rules of the game(s) that will be played, and, more importantly, the range of players to be included and with whom water managers will need to cooperate. On the one hand, the move toward a market economy and the privatisation drive accompanying it are creating a multitude of new actors (and reshaping long-standing ones) in the water policy arena. The same is true of the more fundamental institutional and political changes the country is presently undergoing: the development of the institutions of parliamentary democracy along with the accompanying political infrastructure is creating new actors and channels of access to policy arenas for the formulation and implementation of water policy. The commitment to the market economy and the push for deregulation will also affect the kinds of instruments that water managers can effectively use in pursuing their objectives. Similarly, more general policy strategies based on pollution prevention and sustainable development (which can already be found in various general policy statements as well as in international agreements to which the government is a party) will put a premium on more cooperative relationships between government and target groups – at all levels – in co-producing the policy outputs desired. Under such conditions it is reasonable to assume that the need for inputs and cooperation from a broader range of independent actors as well as the redefinition of the relationships among them will open the water policy networks in the immediate future.

All these developments are likely to differentiate, expand and complicate the policy field and the assortment of both mandated and self-selected players. At the same time, there are a number of factors that could work to reduce the number of additional players in the water policy game. An initial reaction to the privatisation of state water services has led to a increase in the number of local water utilities and waste water treatment systems of one legal form or another. It would seem likely that the limited resources of many of these, particular smaller and medium-size communities, will force some kind of consolidation of these utilities. The same pressures for reducing the over-abundance of local economic organisations providing local water services can be expected from the exigencies of market survival: an emphasis on efficiency and need to capture economies of scale will also encourage various forms of inter-jurisdictional cooperation. Furthermore, there are reasons to believe that after the initial wave of defensive behaviour to protect and promote community autonomy and self-interest, local governments will begin to see the need for some kind of inter-municipal cooperation and coordination in order to provide the kinds of services that their citizens expect under conditions of limited resources and capacities. In general there seems to be a pressing need in Hungary for redefining the links joining state administration with local self-government in order to ensure the smooth transmission of national policy impulses and to create the capacity for coordinated action needed to deal with problems transcending local jurisdictions [*Bandi, 1993: 125–30*].

The general context within which water managers will go about their jobs and the conditions under which they will need to build effective relationships (networks) with the new actors inhabiting their policy field will also be influenced (defined) by more general policy developments regarding economic development and social transformation. In particular, water policy (together with environmental protection) will be hard put to mobilise the resources needed, given the problematic nature of the Hungarian economy. At the present moment, it will be impossible for Hungary to meet its commitments to reach EU quality standards by using advanced technical means. The money for these investment is simply not available. Similarly, effective enforcement policies will be difficult to carry out given the fragile position of many marginal firms which would not be able to make the required changes in product and production process, or to pay the fines that would need to be levied according to a strict interpretation of the rules. The renegotiation of the conditions under which water will be available and the specification of the degree to which industrial activities with impacts on quality of resources can be permitted will be sensitive issues at any time. Under present conditions, making these decisions will inevitably embroil water managers in severe conflicts with the immediately affected water users and the representatives of their interests. This situation also suggests that Hungarian water managers, like their counterparts in Western countries, will need to search for alternatives to instruments of direct regulation. New mixes of regulatory instruments also imply a more open network with new dynamics of negotiation and consensus building and division of labour between state regulators and the economic actors.

Hungary, like other countries, has well-developed institutional arrangements for the management of its water resources. There are formal administrative actors that function in regular and predictable ways, according to clear and accepted procedures and norms. These existing organisational relationships have been produced by fundamental political decisions regarding the position of the state and, more specifically, the way water management policy is to be made and carried out. At the same time, this administrative set-up is the cause of important problems of coordination, making conscious effort to achieve cooperative joint solutions a precondition for the effective functioning of the system. More important than the absence of unambiguous and non-overlapping grants of formal responsibility and authority, however, is the highly turbulent context within which water management is carried out. It is the context that is rewriting the rules of the game, producing new actors to join the play and, indeed, changing the political position of the water game relative to other policy issues and societal objectives. All of these developments make it almost impossible for the traditional water management community to maintain a closed and tightly-integrated network. It is clear that water policy in Hungary is now characterised by highly open and volatile processes of formulation and implementation in which a number of highly differentiated sub-networks are involved. It can be argued, on the basis of a rather brief examination of this emerging situation, that the networks for water policy that are presently taking shape are not, in the first instance, being shaped by changes in the formal structure of water management as by more fundamental changes in the constitutional and socio-economic contexts. Developments in these areas have 'embedded' water policy in a new political and social macro-context which makes it very difficult for the water management network to exercise effective control over sectoral processes.

A good deal of our argument concerning the changing context has to do with 'the dog that didn't bark', that is, those potential participants in water management networks which have up until now been absent or represented weakly in transitional form. Thus, we are arguing that it will be new economic actors, such as privately owned firms and farms, branch and other intermediary interest organisations, chambers of commerce and other non-governmental associations, as well as organisations representing the collective interests of major actors in the more traditional network, for example, Branch Association of Water Works and so on. The point is that: the water management establishment in Hungary is being penetrated by these larger developments, by new actors within the sector, as well as by a new pattern of inter-sectoral developments that will redefine the place and role of water policy in the total range of government activities in the new order.

Hungary and the Added Value of Network Analysis

The concept of 'network' is not, in the first instance, just another term for describing the division of labour between formal institutions and the fact that, normally, a number of governmental actors will have to work together in producing a given policy output. On the contrary, network analysis is touted as a way of getting at the fact that policy processes will involve interactions – both inside and outside formal governmental institutions – of a range of different public and private actors. In this sense, it is a further structural elaboration of the behavioural insight that an understanding of how policy is made (and delivered) requires that we look further than formal institutions alone. Network analysis attempts to follow and map the sets of relevant relationships involved in producing the actual decisions in a given phase of the policy process. In all this, formal institutions are not unimportant, even if they do not alone totally predetermine either the pattern of interactions or the decision dynamics within them. Formal institutional arrangements obviously define the need for cooperation across formally defined lines of responsibility and authority; they also define who legitimately can do what and in what way, thereby creating or blocking access to decision making and allocating resources among different participants. In turn, the weight of formal institutions will be affected by broader societal and political conditions determining both the context within which they function and the balance of power among the actors involved. Perhaps the relative weight of formal institutions and contextual factors will vary depending upon the degree of societal change or stability. Therefore, in a time of system transformation, contextual factors will affect the weight of formal institutions and the operative networks will be more unstable and less distinctly defined.

If we return to the question posed at the beginning of this article – will the networks of water management in Hungary have to await the final word on new formal institutions or will the operative networks that grow up to keep the system going during the transition period themselves 'pre-shape' the contours of the institutions to come – we can observe the following. Arguing that networks will evolve out of the need to hold or put things together in managing the everyday affairs of water policy is much like arguing that we should not mark out the footpaths of the park until we see where the visitors will actually walk (otherwise they will always be taking shortcuts through the flower beds). Once the patterns of real use have been established, the final paths can be put in to 'formalise' the interactions defined by daily need. Clearly, it is unlikely that governmental institutions are designed in such a rational manner. Moreover, other considerations and factors play a role in defining the division of labour among governmental actors, including the desire to promote certain values (environmental quality) even at the expense of overlap and parallel decision structures. The situation in Hungary should remind us that these things are more complicated. Hungarian water management is 'institutionalised' in a set of clearly defined and well-developed structures. A number of sub-networks have emerged around these formal institutions to join together the different actors involved in the different functional activities. At the same time, radical changes in the broader constitutional-political and socio-economic systems are transforming the rules of the game, the field of play and the composition of the teams of players involved in managing the affairs of the water sector.

Obviously much of this is reasonable speculation, given the likely impact of on-going socio-economic and institutional changes in the constitutional-political institutions. Clearly empirical research into the actual relationships among these different sets of actors with regard to the functional water networks is needed. Nevertheless, an overview of the formal division of labour among different agencies and levels of government gives, in any case, a clear picture of the number and variety of actors involved in the quantitative and qualitative management of water resources in Hungary. Likewise, a description of the allocation of authority and responsibilities suggests some of the occasions and ways in which they interact with one another.

To what extent can it be argued that, in Hungary (and by implication in other countries of Central and Eastern Europe), there is no clear network in place of the sort described in some of the other country studies in this volume? Of course the situation in Central European countries at the moment is not one in which formal institutions of government are lacking or do not function. It is true that the political and economic transformations currently being undertaken must, as we have noted, be formulated and carried out by institutional, and to a great extent, personnel holdovers from the previous regime. Once more, after the revolutionary dust has settled, most of these standard administrative and governmental actors will still be present. For example, the new water law which will determine the institutional arrangement for water management in the coming years does not contain any basic changes in the way the state management of water management is organised; nor has there been, as of yet, any political decision to reintegrate water and environmental protection, or to shift the locus of administrative responsibility for water quality policy. On the other hand, the institutional consequences of important modifications in the constitutional division of labour have been legally acknowledged to accommodate the new position of autonomous local governments.

What, then, do we have at the end of the day as an answer to the question: what comes first – the networks that mark out the way actually travelled in Central European countries, in the absence of clearly defined and articulated institutional arrangements for managing water resources? Or will there be a period of weakly developed, highly unstable networks in the transition toward a re-institutionalisation of the formal relationships between formal organisational actors? As far as the more traditional water management network is concerned, even the incomplete description of the basic institutional arrangements and the broader context of water management shows that a number of functional and political pressures – from within Hungary and abroad – have differentiated and pluralised the networks for formulating and implementing policy. The effective performance of even traditional tasks, let alone the new challenges of preventing pollution and sustainable resource management, requires bringing together players from different sectoral and institutional orders. Consequently, the institutional imperative is to break out of self-contained and isolated networks and to seek the required problem-solving capacity in flexible task-defined cooperative arrangements with other actors. Of course, the fact that a pattern of behaviour appears to be required by the imperatives of effective performance does not guarantee that it will be realised. Still, we have argued that the more closed relationships of the past will be 'forced open' by the dynamics of the changing policy context and population of policy-relevant actors.

From a management perspective, the growing functionally and politically defined need for a wider range and greater intensity of networked relationships focuses attention on the kinds of linking mechanisms that exist for consciously interrelating these actors in purposive cooperation. And here may be found a point of interface with already familiar analytical concepts and institutional forms. It would seem, therefore, that a focus on the dimension of issue network or policy community is somewhat limited. It may well be that in the longer run, once the new system settles in, a new policy community – more complex and differentiated than in the past – may establish itself. But even then, the interesting question will remain: by means of which mechanism are the actors interrelated in ways that are appropriate for the problems confronted by the policy area as a whole? While the dynamics of network change will continue to be of interest, equally important will be a better understanding of the decision-making processes through which at any given time the various functional activities of water management are fulfilled.

The Hungarian case, as an example of the kinds of challenges confronted in other Central and Eastern European countries, makes clear how broader system changes modify the context of sectoral networks and how these become embedded in larger political and societal structures. It is this set of more extensive changes that has created the need for new network relations and has, simultaneously, changed the rules and the conditions under which these will emerge. At the same time, a focus on the need actively to design and create such networks suggests the value in looking more closely at the nuts and bolts questions of how such cooperation can be brought about.

NOTES

1. There has not been much work done on the institutional arrangements for environmental and water policy in Hungary and other Central European countries. On the other hand, there is a growing literature on questions of privatisation and deregulation in these countries (see for example the book of case studies edited by Moran and Prosser [1994]). A good overview of some of the general problems of 'administrative modernisation' in Central and Eastern Europe can be found in Hesse [1993], while O'Toole [1994] looks at the relationship between effective privatisation and the need to development the necessary administrative capacities for implementing this policy. Markowski [1994] and Hanf [1994] discuss the relationship between economic change and environmental policy in these countries. In this .chapter use was made of information and material available in studies of the formal legal and administrative set-up in Hungary regarding water management, along with analyses of particular cases on water management and policy development. In addition to these documents, interviews were held with a few knowledgeable experts on water policy and management in Hungary and The Netherlands.
2. For a rather detailed description of the present division of labour between the different actors in the water management policy field, see Zotter [1993]. A short version of the institutional set-up can be found in Warren, et al. [1993].
3. This summary is based on the discussion presented in Zotter [1993].

REFERENCES

Bandi, G. (ed.) (1993), *Environmental Law and Management System in Hungary; Overview, Perspectives and Problems*, Budapest: Environmental Management and Law Association.

European Bank for Reconstruction and Development (1993), *Danube River Basin Environmental Programme*, Final Report, Copenhagen: Carl Bro Group.

Hanf, K. (1994), 'The Political Economy of Ecological Modernization: Creating a Regulated Market for Environmental Quality' in M. Moran and T. Prosser (eds.) (1994), *Privatization and Regulatory Change in Europe*, Buckingham Philadelphia: Open University Press, pp. 126–155.

Hesse, J.J. (ed.) (1993), 'Administrative Transformation in Central and Eastern Europe', Special Issue *Public Administration*, Vol. 71, Spring/Summer.

Hinrichsen, D. and G. Enyedi (eds) (1990), *State of the Hungarian Environment*, Budapest: Statistical Publishing House.

Karászi, K. (1991), 'Reflections on the Policy and Philosophy of the Water Sector in Hungary', *Journal of European Water Pollution Control*, Vol. 1 No. 3, Amsterdam: Elsevier, pp.29–32.

Markowski, T. (1994), 'Environmental Policy and Regulatory Change in Poland' in M. Moran and T. Prosser (eds), *Privatization and Regulatory Change in Europe*, Buckingham Philadelphia: Open University Press, pp. 96–110.

Moran, M. and T. Prosser (eds) 1994, *Privatization and Regulatory Change in Europe*, Buckingham Philadelphia: Open University Press.

O'Toole, L.J., Jr. (1994), 'Privatization in Hungary: Implementation Issues and Local Government Complications', in H. Blommenstein and B. Steuenberg (eds), *Governments and Markets: Economic, Political and Legal Aspects of Emerging Markets in Central and Eastern Europe*, Leiden: Kluwer Academic.

Somlyody, L. (1993), 'Water Quality Management in Urban Areas: The Challenge for Central and Eastern Europe', *Journal of European Water Pollution Control*, Volume 3, number 2, Amsterdam: Elsevier, pp. 26–31.

USAID (1992), *Point Source Pollution in the Danube Basin; report on data, management, institutional studies and priority projects*, Volume I, Water and Sanitation for Health Project (WASH), Europe Bureau.

Zotter, K. (1993), *Hungarian Water Legislation*, Annex E, PHARE 901/90, Budapest: Vituki Consult Rt.

Warren, S., N.G. Cartwright and T.F. Zabel (1993), *Public Administration of Water Management*, Final Report Part Two, PHARE 901/90, Medmenham, Marlow: Warren Environmental Services.

Networks and Water Policy: Conclusions and Implications for Research

HANS BRESSERS and LAURENCE J. O'TOOLE, JR

In this concluding essay, the overall findings of this comparative project are analysed. The article turns to the general questions providing the focus for each of the cases. Some of the variations across the cases are explored. However, particular attention is paid to similar patterns in most or all of the investigations, since the set of cases is consistent with a diverse case design. The similarities include similar arrays of 'layered' water policy networks in several countries. The pure types of issue network or policy community, prominent in the network literature, are not found in the actual water policy patterns. Similar water policy network developments across most of the cases include trends toward more network openness, more emulation of business behaviour, and less domination by traditional professional groups such as engineering. Network dynamics can be explained in part by the welfare state crisis and the environmental challenge. The impact of network arrangements on policy formation and implementation is more difficult to document, but some evidence suggests linkages worthy of further exploration. The overall assessment is that network approaches can be helpful in policy research, but that understanding some of the limitations of the perspective and the requirements for better empirical theory are requisites for fulfilling this potential.

The six cases reported in the preceding pages present findings on the composition, development, and operations of water policy networks in several settings. The studies include reports on water policy and the complex structures through which it is formulated and executed, thus clarifying matters of policy substance and process for an important environmental issue.

Several of the articles also raise explicitly some conceptual and theoretical issues related to the application of network ideas to policy action. For instance, the article on the Dutch case offers a tentative theoretical proposal, with some evidence from the national setting, regarding how characteristics of policy networks may be related to policy instruments used in water and other policy sectors. The contribution on England and Wales offers several

Hans Bressers is Professor of Policy Studies and Director of the Centre for Clean Technology and Environmental Policy at the University of Twente, The Netherlands; and Laurence O'Toole is Professor of Political Science at the University of Georgia, USA.

insights for scholars of policy – for instance, by pointing out that at crucial junctures key actors misperceived the composition of the network structure in which they were located, thus showing that even policy elites can make strategic errors in highly-networked contexts. And, to mention a further example, the article on the US pattern suggests that much of the extant scholarship on policy networks conflates several analytical dimensions in potentially confusing ways.

In this concluding article, we turn to the task of analysing the overall findings *across* the cases. This essay returns, therefore, to the initial questions posed in the opening selection and considers what has been learned about the broad issues raised there from the full set of empirical investigations.

The design of this comparative project should permit the development of some useful observations. The design might be termed a 'diverse case' approach. The instances under examination are not 'most different', in that all the nations included are at approximately the same level of development, and they face similar water problems: how to supply and dispose of an adequate amount of water at an acceptable standard (and an increasingly 'standardised' standard, particularly within the European Union, or EU) and for an acceptable price. But, as the initial contribution and the individual studies document, the cases are quite different on numerous other dimensions, including scale, specific water challenges, political alignments, and institutional-legal history. This variety permits certain inferences, as suggested below.

The set of studies is diverse not only in the sense that six different water policy settings are examined, but also in that the full assortment of studies reflects a considerable diversity of interests and approaches. Different contributors have brought a range of theoretical and substantive perspectives to bear.

This variety constitutes a strength of this combined effort, for at least two reasons. First, the diversity offers the possibility to build upon multiple strengths while also ensuring some degree of common purpose in the collective endeavour. Thus, the design of this project provides sufficient flexibility to allow identification of and reporting on interesting phenomena in each country (and at the level of the EU) that might otherwise be excluded in an application of a uniform case study protocol, while also assuring a certain common ground. And second, at this stage in the development of scholarship on the subject of policy networks, testable theories on the relations between network characteristics and their causes and effects are not yet clearly in place. Therefore, such a collaborative effort can generate promising ideas and insights for more systematic subsequent investigation.

To explore the conclusions and implications of this research effort, we proceed by organising points around the major questions identified in the opening essay. How can water policy networks in these settings be characterised?

How have they developed and what factors explain these dynamics? And how do the networks influence policy results? The following three sections of this contribution are devoted, respectively, to these issues. The fifth section of the study then provides an overall assessment of the utility and limitations of network perspectives as a way of understanding reality. The final part then points toward the kinds of additional investigations that would seem productive, given the results reported here.

Characterising Water Policy Networks

One important issue is how the networks examined in the six cases compare. The diverse case design means that, inevitably, many kinds of differences will be observable across the various cases. Some of these distinctions *are* important to discuss, particularly those related to the policy community-issue network dimension that was covered in the initial article. First, however, we turn to an examination of a different subject: not the obvious differences across the diverse cases but, instead, their similarities.

One strength of the diverse case design is that any correspondence observable across a collection of apparently-different instances points to a matter of likely interest. Here we focus on network characteristics. One correspondence across cases deserves special attention and is treated in the first subsection below. Some additional points are discussed in the second part of this section. Then distinctions that can be made across the countries, especially in terms of the issue network-policy community dimension, are examined. The section concludes with lessons for network characterisation and classification.

'Layered' Water Policy Networks

The most striking similarity across the national cases reported here, especially among the four nations not now in the midst of regime transformation, is that the water sectors are comprised of networked arrays that exhibit a degree of 'layering', an arrangement akin to concentric circles. In these several cases, researchers report relatively tightly-coupled clusters or 'cores', which operate interdependently with broader and more loosely-coupled structures. This parallel finding is evident, despite differences in the analytical language used in each article.

In some cases, the broader array has the appearance of a 'constellation': the actors are clearly interdependent but are dimly aware of the full picture and rarely deal directly with certain parts of the pattern. The US example clearly fits here, so much so that Heilman and colleagues make two points: there is *no* sectoral-wide network in United States water policy; and even sub-sectorally, the patterns consist of large numbers of loosely and sporadically linked participants: 'latent policy networks'. The arrangements in

England and Wales are different, according to Maloney and Richardson, but include 'sporadic interventionists' as well as the more regular and easily recognisable participants. The different layers, and more distanced but observable network patterns at some remove from the core, are also part of the depictions by researchers in Germany and the Netherlands.

The broader reaches of network arrays are documented, even if with some imprecision, in the foregoing essays. The more tightly-bound cores emerge more clearly from the analyses. The central portions of the national water networks are obviously influential in policy-making and execution. In addition, as the cases explain, the more peripheral network members also exert influence.

In the broadest sense, the cases document the point, raised in the contribution by Maloney and Richardson, that *contextual* and sometimes anticipatory effects of the broader network structure can be seen in the strategies and actions of those in the core (cf. Friedrich [*1940*] and Truman [*1971*]).

The sometimes-observable mutual and collective awareness on the part of the most central participants of the peripheral network elements is a feature of each case covered in this collection. This point does not mean that complex policy networks in the water sectors of these nations are easily adaptable and completely open. But it does suggest at least two forms of influence from the periphery, aside from sporadic direct involvement. First, the consciousness on the part of those in the core of the broader constellation can modify actions among the smaller set. And second, the broader network population – the pool of actors comprising the latent networks referred to in the depiction of the US case – not only arise on a temporary basis to alter the outcome on particular issues but also hold the potential to disturb the structure on a permanent or at least longer-term basis. The instances of the altered core composition in the Netherlands (to include the permanent involvement of important environmental actors) and the US (to introduce new professions like finance in water infrastructure development) illustrate this potential in action.

The water networks examined in this collection thus suggest a degree of stability and also – partially through the dynamics of peripheral involvement – the potential for adaptation.

Some further points of structural characterisation are of related interest. For instance, in several of the cases (clearly in the Dutch and German instances, apparently also in England and Wales) various segments of the water cycle are associated with identifiable sub-networks. (The US case also suggests a refinement, but of a somewhat different sort: in the American context, many water actors participate cross-sectorally in other patterns of networked interdependence.) And more generally, most cases contain various sub-sectoral networks even within a single phase of the water cycle. The more detailed features of these sub-arrays vary considerably across national settings.

All in all, then, the water policy networks in these cases exhibit complexity and variety, but also a set of structural similarities that are of potential importance to those concerned with understanding the role of the networks in policy making and implementation.

Additional Network Similarities

A few additional similarities across the cases can be mentioned briefly. In each examination of the water policy networks, the researchers note the importance of professionals in network activity. In all cases, distinctive professional groups have been part of the core for some period. Furthermore, the dominant profession in each case, particularly in the past, has been engineers and related groups such as hydrologists.

It should not be surprising that this policy field, which until fairly recently was treated as a focus of public works and resource extraction, has been dominated by such actors. What may be more striking is a set of developments clearly observable in recent years in all the countries investigated here towards, first, the representation of a more diverse array of professional specialities in the national networks, particularly with regard to business and finance professions, and/or broadened orientations among extant network participants and, secondly, a more general opening up of network membership toward a greater range of actors.

With regard to the former trend, the incorporation – indeed, in selected instances the domination – by finance professionals has accompanied increased budgetary stringency and a shift in policy instruments towards more businesslike mechanisms for addressing water-related needs. This point can in turn be linked to the theme of welfare-state crisis raised in the introductory essay. The point is addressed more carefully below.

The trend towards increased openness, extending beyond a simple proliferation of professions in the water sector, has been particularly conspicuous with regard to the role of those representing environmental interests. It would be an exaggeration to suggest that a universal trend has placed environmentalists at the core of water policy in these countries. And more generally, many of the networks continue to exhibit barriers to participation. But the direction of change is clear. Emphasising the shifts raises the question of network dynamics, which is examined in a later section of this study.

The opening of the sector has extended beyond these groups and perspectives as well, as the European Union and to some extent the US cases make clear. In the emergent EU constellations toxicologists and eco-toxicologists play important roles in debates about parameters and possibly in the agenda-setting process as well. In the US public health experts have appeared in some important water quality decision processes.

Beyond these points about network structure and membership, additional similarities can be identified among some of the cases. For instance, network features seem to be related to metapolicy characteristics, as mentioned at least in the US and England/Wales cases. Again, however, this issue of the relationship between network arrangement and causal forces is more appropriately discussed in the section on network development below.

Some Cross-Case Network Variations

The preceding subsections show that on some important structural issues, the cases exhibit similarities regarding network structure and membership. The cases do, however, differ. One of the most interesting dimensions of variation is the continuum between issue networks and policy community.

Despite similarities regarding layering, the network structures can be distinguished, with the interactor arrangements for groundwater at the level of the EU apparently at a pre-network stage. Similarly, in Hungary – examined as a representative case from central Europe – changed network structures as a result of the restructuring of society are only beginning to emerge.

Within the other national cases, considerable variation is apparent. The United States occupies perhaps the extreme point on the continuum. In the US, there is no sector-wide network – nor even an issue network – since portions of the sector do not relate even sporadically with each other. Rather, the US instance might be summarised as a set of arrays, most even more pliant than issue networks, with cores of varying composition significant but by no means dominant. In Germany too, the absence of sector-wide networks is notable, although the degree of structural integration appears somewhat greater than in the US case.

In England and Wales, shifts have restructured the interactor arrays. The former arrangements, consistent in most respects with the policy community concept referenced in the literature, have become less integrated, with the cosy pattern of earlier years having been displaced. Indeed, some of the most important actors in the network array are only now becoming aware of the shifts in their own structure of interdependence.

The Dutch case also documents transition, in particular shifts in network composition. And the depiction of sub-sectoral networks should serve as a caution that even in this instance, structural complexity is apparent. Nevertheless, the Dutch water policy networks exhibit more ties than do those in the other national settings. This point does not imply widespread agreement among the actors. Indeed, this case is one of several in which homogeneity has clearly declined in recent years.

With the 'seismic' shocks in the water sector in recent decades, and with the significant openings visible in most of the cases, the classic picture of pure policy communities – sometimes almost a caricature in the literature – does not hold for any of these cases. Rather, some formerly-tight clusters of interdependence have largely given way to looser, somewhat more ephemeral arrays. Meanwhile, newer sectoral settings (the European level, the regimes undergoing transformation in Central Europe) confront the need to begin *developing* ties among actors who must take account of each other's interests and influence. And analyses of network dynamics (see below) suggest processes of both differentiation and integration underway in the different cases.

The networks studied for this project differ, as well, on a number of other structural dimensions. It is clear that both within national water sectors and also across the cases, the arrangements vary on such features as density, openness, dominance, and other characteristics considered in several of the contributions. Any generalisation about 'networks' for policy is likely to be questionable – even, as we have seen, the generalisation that there *are* always networks in operation.

Toward Theoretically-Explicit Treatments of Policy Networks

The foregoing suggests a few points of importance, then, regarding the most fruitful lines of conceptual development concerning the network concept. It seems apparent that policy networks are important structures in much of today's water policy decision-making. It seems likely, as well, that they are consequential in other sectors. Further, the most often-used dimension of network characterisation, the policy community-issue network range, can be used to array different cases. However, the pure types often referred in the literature do not correspond to today's policy settings, at least in the cases documented here. Certainly, simple dichotomies are not particularly useful in empirical terms.

The range and complexity of network arrays documented in these instances, particularly when coupled with the recognition of the many dimensions of network characteristics offered in the case studies, suggest that efforts to classify networks into simple compartments are not particularly helpful. Underlying dimensions suggesting a range of structural possibilities should be the focus of empirical scholarship.

Which dimensions? We have explored one with some care in this volume, primarily because of its ubiquity in the literature. Additional dimensions have been referenced as well. The most useful course of action for those interested in further exploration of the network idea is to recognise that there is no inherently good or bad classification of networks. Rather, the dimensions at the focus of analyses should be selected on the basis of broader theoretical considerations.

In particular, the network concept needs to be linked clearly to factors explaining the development of networks (that is, networks as dependent variable) and to theoretical ideas regarding the effects of networks, for instance on policy (networks as independent or intervening variable). The network project, in sum, needs to be part of a theoretical agenda. And the dimensions of interest regarding network characterisations need to be related explicitly to this theoretical ambition.

Accordingly, we turn now to some observations regarding the development and effects of water policy networks, respectively, as evidenced in this collection.

Network Developments

The water policy networks described above show both remarkable similarities and intriguing differences. In this section we attempt to analyse how this came about. What trends can be observed in the countries under study and what dynamics of change were associated with them? An overall conclusion is that fairly similar trends evolved in the four countries with established water policy networks (that is, leaving aside Hungary), patterns basically emanating from more or less the same challenges, but modified by diverse initial situations and a number of rather stable factors that influence both these circumstances and the ways in which new challenges have been incorporated into network operations.

Developments

As can be concluded from the contributions in this collection and the coverage in the section above, in the four countries studied water policy networks generally have become, first, more open; secondly, more businesslike – in the sense that certain organisations such as water authorities try to behave more like businesses; and thirdly, less dominated by an engineering orientation. These trends seem to be related to each other.

The British case study showed, for instance, that the institutionalisation of the more businesslike identity of the water sector, culminating in large-scale privatisation, brought the sector into the midst of the public debate, increased the range of organisations involved, and made the sector more vulnerable to external influences than at any time in its previous history. The environmentalists, especially, gained influence, simply by being out there. Dealing with these and other interests forces the network actors to give more attention to social interactions and processes in their strategic considerations, and less to their older, predominantly-engineering orientation.

The growing openness of the sector is apparent even in the US case, which was already permeable to begin with. New professions have been included.

Even on the sub-national level the relationships among the actors involved are sufficiently loose so that even the concept of issue networks suggests more coherence than can be observed. In this case, as well, the entrance of new professions into the patterns is related to more business-like water management. The shift is reflected, in other ways, by the emergence of privatised services. These new professions also bring new orientations, for instance an emphasis on economic efficiency.

In the Dutch case both the water supply companies and the water boards, central actors in two rather separate sub-networks, have declined sharply in number. This shift has been induced by the pressure for viable and efficient entities which could be managed as modern businesses. While water boards have always been more or less autonomous, indeed even guaranteed independence by the national constitution, the water supply companies have become significantly more autonomous. Nevertheless both water supply companies and water boards face an increasing need to respond to various kinds of external demands. This trend forces them to be more communicative, thus acting more on the basis of a social interaction orientation and less from an engineering perspective. To achieve their new goals they have to negotiate with actors from outside 'the water world', actors that to some degree become thereby part of it. Thus far, this form of openness has not really endangered the coherence of the network core. In the case of the Dutch water supply network signs are actually evident that the companies have come to accept more coordination through their association, as they face another well-organised community: agriculture.

In Germany the water networks, separate for various parts of the water cycle and in various Länder, have remained relatively stable. Although here too environmentalists have participated in discussions on a regular basis, it remains to be seen to what extent environmental interests manage to establish themselves as members of water policy networks. Furthermore, all over Germany new public, and sometimes private, organisations with large discretion and independent management are apportioned a share of water management tasks. Water supply utilities are dependent on the success of groundwater and surface water protection. The tension between groundwater protection interests and agriculture has not had as many consequences for the decline in dominance of engineering as in the Netherlands because in Germany water management already had often been included in environmental management agencies.

The European Union case also exhibits the phenomenon of expansion in types of participants involved in water policy, even though these constellations are still in the process of formation. The developing links with potentially large numbers of diverse actors are exemplified in the broad list of the DG XI General Consultative Forum.

Change Agents

Apart from their mutual interaction, the developments described above can be related to a number of factors. Among these are the historic and geographical settings in which network developments have occurred, the impact of federalism in the US and Germany, German and European unification, and the notable lack of political salience of this sector in earlier years. Many of these, however, are more or less stable features of national context and cannot be invoked to explain network changes (though they may affect the fashion in which these changes occur). Their influence is felt more on the *ex ante* situation and as intervening variables between the real causal forces or 'change agents', and network developments.

What then are these change agents? Two complex factors seem to lie at the heart of many of the observable lines of influence over network evolution. The first is the welfare state crisis, especially in its public finance pressures, and the second is the environmental challenge. Both have empirical and ideological dimensions, which vary across the countries in specific detail and intensity but have presented substantial meta-challenges in North America and Northwestern Europe during the 1980s and 1990s. Together they have had an unmistakeable impact on the water sector: the time for 'pumping and billing' is over.

The welfare state crisis became manifest after the first and especially the second oil crisis, contributing to stagflation. The neo-conservative response of the Thatcher and Reagan administrations set the tone for the direction of policy response: more market, less government. In other countries such as the Netherlands and Germany, the ideological aspect of these policies was weaker. But less explicit, common-sense notions stemming from renewed confidence in the capabilities of private business spread in these countries as well. This shift resulted in the reorganisation of water tasks, and in some cases a reduction in financial support and an increase in expectations for more business-like management of public tasks – even to the extent of privatising the tasks in certain instances.

The environmental crisis emerged in two waves of public attention, one in the late 1960s and early 1970s, the other in the late 1980s and early 1990s. Though both these waves were triggered by 'epistemic communities' warning on the basis of scientific studies of imminent environmental decline, each also carried an ideological dimension. After each upsurge, public attention declined but stabilised at a higher level than before, in the process creating both new governmental and private organisations and bases of power for them. General environmental awareness rose, of course. And, in addition, some specific signs of environmental threats in the water sector increased the salience of the issues and added pressure for policy response. For instance, surface water pollution in such places as the Rhine had killed water life and had often prevented the use of these waters for water supply purposes. Groundwater sources, as well, had showed increasing amounts of pollution which threatened to make them useless for drinking water production. The water sector inevitably had to deal with these problems, and the sectoral responses themselves caused new pressures. More generally, the tendency has been for other actors in other sectors, such as agriculture, to be drawn into water policy issues and thus render the networked context even more diffuse.

Central propositions in this section, then, are that the public finance challenge prompted, in particular, institutional and cultural developments promoting more business-like management; that the environmental and scientific challenges encouraged a social interaction-orientation; and that both factors directly and indirectly forced more openness in the water sectors of the several countries.

Variety

Similar developments stimulated by similar factors may present a misleading picture of uniformity, one that is valid on only a very general level. Closer inspection reveals considerable variety. The fashion in which the two fundamental factors just discussed have influenced developments in the four countries excluding Hungary is influenced by features characteristic of each country. For example: in the Netherlands and Germany many of the benefits possible from privatisation were attained instead by greater autonomy and shifts in management culture among organisations in the water sector. The same process was happening in the United Kingdom, but other factors pushed the institutionalisation of autonomy further – to full privatisation – without there being a deliberate government policy toward this end. The British government became trapped in its own ideology. Though a four-case-study design is unlikely to demonstrate definitively the impact of these kinds of influences in a comparative fashion, some expected influences can be plausibly related to the observed differences in developments across the cases.

The highly legalistic culture of German policy-making, for instance, seems to have affected the nature of the actors involved (note the inclusion of law experts) and the kind of relationships among actors within the network (relatively inflexible). In fact, the changes in openness and orientation within the German water sector seem somewhat less significant than in the other countries covered in this collection.

So it is important to consider the significant differences in the *ex ante* situations across these four countries. In the preceding contributions, these initial conditions are related to similar kinds of variables, factors that both

help to determine the *ex ante* circumstances and also modify more directly
the relationship between the main agents of change reviewed earlier and the
network developments of interest. Factors such as natural or geophysical
differences, plus scale and degree of federalism, shape antecedent circumstances and newer developments alike.

Not all such factors with a general impact create variety. Two that do not
can be mentioned for purposes of the discussion below. The first of these is
water itself, which actually flows through its own natural cycle, thereby
suggesting and stimulating an 'undercurrent' of interest in more coordination
in the sector. Left to their own devices, the technical specialists of the sector
in each of these countries would integrate their efforts through the cycle's
phases. Thus factors promoting fragmentation never have an easy or permanent victory. Second, to a significant extent the water sector operates specific
technologies of its own. These encourage the sense that water engineers as a
professional group are both distinct from other professional groups and able
to harmonise water management throughout the developed world. The existence of such a tightly-knit and technically-specialised professional community has made it possible for the sector to be regarded as an apolitical,
management-focused cluster, during certain periods at least – although the
evidence from the EU is that newly-forming arrays in the current period are
likely to display more diverse characteristics even in the early stages.

One of the factors that does cause variation across the settings is the degree
of natural diversity present, especially in combination with each country's
history. The United States is home to almost every imaginable water circumstance. National uniformity cannot be a practicable aim under such conditions. Moreover, water policies present virtually no 'core politics' for the
federal level. Against this background, water policy issues have often been
used in package deals to accommodate regional interests, often interests
focused primarily on other issues. These separate bargains tended to stimulate
fragmentation even further. As an additional background feature, the
country's political culture views any division of authority as such in
favourable terms. The theme is even anchored in the constitution. So the
tension between repeated efforts to increase coordination (the undercurrent of
water policy), on the one hand, and the factors reinforcing fragmentation, on
the other, are as present in the US case as in the others. The balance between
the two, however, falls more on the side of diversity in this instance than in
the other countries. The debate on subsidiarity within the EU echoes this
theme, of course, with talk of repatriation of some water laws and of greater
flexibility for the member states.

There is a further factor which creates some variation between the United
States and the three Western European countries: the evolving European
Union. To some extent it might be considered a change agent itself, because

the impact, even interference, of European regulation with water policies of the member states is on the rise. The EU influence on the development of the water networks in these countries, however, seems more indirect and variegated. In Germany the reactions of the Länder to European regulation differ from that of the federal government. This range of response has the effect of rendering the European dimension visible in German water politics. In the United Kingdom institutional developments have made the European regulatory issue much more visible. Here, as well, the European dimension became highly visible as a consequence. In the Netherlands, on the contrary, European regulation is completely included without much debate into national policies and standards. Its visibility as an exogenous factor is therefore low during everyday elaboration into regional policies and implementation, and its influence on the structure of the network is not distinguishable from that of internal policy developments. Finally, and outside the current EU membership, nations such as Hungary are being influenced by European regulation as water networks develop and policies take hold; and such countries will, somehow, have to accommodate their policies and policy processes to the developing patterns as described in the European Union review.

The initial situations in the various countries also seem to have had some influence on the ways in which the prime change agents have influenced network developments. Network stability depends not only on the degree to which the structures adapt to new challenges, but also on the extent to which these emergent issues become integrated into the professional expertise and attitudes of those in the network. In all countries examined here, as well as in the EU, environmental considerations have become more prominent than ever. The manner in which this has occurred, however, has varied. In some nations' networks, environmental values were incorporated into the existing organisations; in others new organisations, with environmental issues as their prime focus, were added to the network. Access for new environmental organisations was not easy in any of the instances. In England and Wales their influence seems to stem primarily from others' taking them into account as a relevant outside force. In the Netherlands and Germany, the two most intact policy communities of the sample, environmental values seem to have been internalised to a larger extent by existing network organisations which have identified themselves with these new tasks. In the US both patterns are visible across the differentiated network 'waterscape', although the principal method has been the inclusion of new actors representing heretofore excluded or under-represented interests. The suggestion here is that the initial degree of network coherence reproduced itself in the ways in which environmental perspectives have been incorporated.

Even in the Dutch case more openness can be observed, but this shift has an impact mostly as a means to include new fields of expertise. The most typical pattern is one in which others are invited to participate in forums of the more established network participants. With considerably less frequency do the newer participants come alongside the older network, thus challenging it from the outside. This pattern is plausibly related to the fact that the Dutch networks to begin with are far less fragmented than the US ones.

Networks at Work

The cases presented in this collection offer considerable information regarding the characterisation of water policy networks in the several settings, and they also provide rich and somewhat complementary explanations for the development and evolution of these networks over time, as the preceding two sections of this essay explain. The cases, however, contain considerably less information on the third research question at the focus of this comparative investigation: how have the networks had impacts on the formation or implementation of policy, or both? On this theme, networks as independent or intervening variables in policy and implementation processes, the researchers report some, but limited, evidence.

Particular points on this score, developed as parts of the individual investigations reported in this collection, are mentioned below. Yet the fact that the discussion of the issue is relatively limited in this set of studies – and also in the broader literature on policy networks – raises questions of importance. Does this point suggest that the usefulness of the network concept, at least as a potential explanatory tool, is itself limited?

Three possibilities can be mentioned. It may be, first, that the notion requires careful incorporation into a theory and set of testable hypotheses before clear evidence can be gathered and assessed. An instance of how this task might be undertaken is presented in the Dutch case in this collection. A related point, secondly, is that it seems likely that measurement problems impose limitations on what can be documented and tested regarding networks as causal entities. This is a theme developed in particular in the US paper. Third, of course, it may be that, despite their near-ubiquity and the level of interest they have generated among scholars of policy, networks actually turn out to have relatively little impact on policy. This last possibility seems least likely.

Furthermore, it seems particularly appropriate that scholars of policy are devoting attention now to increasing the clarity of the network notion, since in western Europe as well network discussions are likely to increase in frequency as the European Union continues to seek influence over national actors in the water sector, as elsewhere. As Richardson documents, there currently are no clearly-discernible network-like arrays involving the EU in regular patterns of interaction with national decision-makers. However, the goal of the EU is policy (and implementation) change. As these efforts develop and intensify, should they be conceptualised as shifts engendered by exogenous forces, or as a set of altered network constellations resulting in (endogenous) policy consequences? Clearly, in at least some of the relevant countries, national actors and their heretofore-autonomous water sectors are coming under the influence of a different (and very messy) policy-making arena in Brussels. A question for policy researchers is whether to see these impacts as the products of network dynamics, or to conclude that the network notion itself is limited in such cases by failing to account for exogenous but significant impacts.

The studies in this collection do offer some evidence on the importance of networks for policy results. The cases imply, furthermore, additional questions and hypotheses on the subject. These deserve additional, more sustained follow-up in later research. Three articles here citing evidence of networks as causal forces are worth brief mention in this regard: the Dutch case arguing that network features may be related to certain policy characteristics; the US findings on the impact of network composition on the State Revolving Loan programme and implications regarding network effects; and the indication in the England/Wales case of contextual impacts on the actions of core policy-makers.

The Dutch case certainly does not constitute ironclad proof that networks determine policy instruments in patterned and predictable ways. Nevertheless, the evidence is suggestive and largely consistent with the theoretical propositions developed in more detail in Bressers [1993b]. It may be possible, then, to substantiate systematic relationships between broad network features and some kinds of policy results, even if difficult measurement problems are entailed in documenting the intervening behavioural or cognitive dynamics. In a related vein, the findings here suggest broad support for the themes of Sabatier and Jenkins-Smith in their model of policy change based on belief systems: the clusters of activists (Sabatier and Jenkins-Smith deal with advocacy coalitions and policy learning in several sectors) may have both short-term and long-term impacts on policy, including the instruments adopted by those involved [Sabatier and Jenkins-Smith, 1993].

The US case points to some limitations involved in demonstrating clear and measurable network impacts, but it also offers evidence regarding the relationship between a shift in network composition (towards involvement of private for-profit actors in wastewater infrastructure financing and development) and policy choices made (funding less environmentally pressing but also less financially risky projects).

Beyond this specific relationship, the US study suggests a broader – and thus far unanswered – question about the link between networks and policy change. The US water policy example represents, as the authors suggest, an extreme pluralistic case, at least among the countries in this collection. In documenting the lack of coordination characteristic of the US case, the analysis is reminiscent of arguments developed in other studies of pluralism: that high fragmentation facilitates only incremental changes. The coverage of the US water policy setting makes it clear that important policy changes have taken place over relatively brief periods, thus suggesting that the *degree* of change and the likelihood of *coordinated* change are different dimensions. This point implies, as well, the need for clarity and differentiation in the specification of dependent variables in network investigations.

What is more, the US case serves as a reminder that conventional ideas of pluralistic policy-making, which emphasise the difficulties of large-scale change, clash with some of the scholarship on policy networks, which proposes that more integrated structures of interdependence are likely to be more resistant to change (see, for instance, Rhodes and March [*1992: 197-98*]). Both views challenge the null hypothesis that there is no relationship between network features, on the one hand, and policy results, on the other; but they do so in different ways. It may be possible to render the two theoretical arguments consistent, provided that they be made more specific and perhaps narrower in focus.

The Dutch case also suggests the importance of specifying and distinguishing among the possible dependent variables influenced by network arrangements, in noting for wastewater pollution policy that the relationship between network complexity and implementation success is not necessarily negative (cf. Goggin *et al.* [*1990*]).

The findings for the case of England and Wales are suggestive in another fashion on the question of networks as causal forces. For the impact of increasing openness in policy settings, at least as documented in this instance, appears not only as reflected in the participation of more actors but also in the degree of influence that *ad hoc* participants can achieve, especially in the agenda-setting phase. As indicated above, the evidence suggests that the more sporadic participants can have important contextual effects on policy processes and contents even when there is no direct and observable interaction.

One additional theme may be mentioned usefully in this review of networks at work: networks in the implementation process. As the introduction to this collection indicated, structures of interdependence have clearly been recognised as a topic of potential importance by scholars studying implementation in numerous policy sectors. The point is emphasised in these studies of water policy networks as well. The Dutch findings on this subject have already been discussed. Similarly, but necessarily in a more speculative fashion, Hanf and Roijen point to the likely importance of network development in Central and Eastern Europe if the daunting water problems of that region are to be managed effectively.

A further, more general, theoretical issue is suggested by these analyses. It is worth considering, on the basis of the findings in these cases, how much openness can be expected in networks for implementation when compared with those for policy formation. The layered network concept, above, implies that when network cores for policy formation have characteristics similar to those associated with policy communities, the implementation network is likely to be more open and complex as core clusters of actors find they must deal with other interests during execution. The Dutch case illustrates this possibility. An opposing line of reasoning, however, would suggest that during the implementation phase the turbulence of policy-making is replaced by the more stable and technical activities of execution, with the full-timers and technocrats in control. In general, then, implementation networks in many cases could be expected to be somewhat narrower and closed, in practice, than the patterns of interdependence associated with the more visible phases of public decision (see O'Toole, Hanf and Hupe [*forthcoming*] for a general argument). In the water policy cases, this pattern might be visible in some of the European cases, at least until some actors complain to the EU and thus enlarge the pattern for strategic reasons. Note, in this regard, the possibility raised in the article by Maloney and Richardson that with some of the European developments currently underway, the distinction between formation and implementation networks might virtually disappear.

In short, when one examines how and whether networks for formation and implementation might differ according to the challenges with which they are faced, some intriguing possibilities emerge. This collection is more helpful in identifying these than in documenting clear patterns across the cases.

Overall, then, this set of studies documents limitations regarding what can be concluded clearly about networks as influences on policy. But evidence of impact is indeed available, and – perhaps more interestingly – the analyses serve as fruitful sources of ideas and preliminary hypotheses. A number of these ideas can be pursued in future investigations, although the limitations on conceptualisation and measurement noted above must also be borne in mind.

Networks as a Way of Understanding Reality

The preceding analysis has documented several fashions in which a network approach can be useful for the comparative examination of water policy. In most of these respects, a network perspective can also be expected to offer considerable potential in other sectors of policy, provided that it is used carefully and in accord with the lessons and limitations suggested from this set of studies. The general approach clearly offers promise. It is useful here, accordingly, to develop further some of the more cautionary notes that should be kept in mind by empirical researchers and theorists who seek to build on the possibilities sketched above, as the network notion has been applied to the water policy sector.

Network thinking tends to stress the issues at stake as the product of a negotiated reality. In such a view there is little room for external, direct central governmental intervention. Nevertheless, some such instances are visible in the cases examined here. In Germany the Emscher Co-operative Association and the Ruhr Association were formed by statute, thereby forcing all relevant actors to be members of a new organisation and thus compelling them to manage their own affairs without any direct state involvement in the operation. Although this action was taken at the beginning of this century, it is a form of network management that could be regarded as modern if applied today. It shows, however, not only the importance of networks, but also, in a sense, the opposite: that networks in some cases are themselves primarily a tool of government.

This example from an earlier period might not be very convincing evidence that such a possibility could be anticipated under present circumstances. But other, more recent instances can be found among the cases. For example, some crucial stages of the recent privatisation process in the United Kingdom were described by Maloney and Richardson as representing an opportunity to resort to an impositional policy style in which the policy community and the policy network as a whole were excluded by government. (Consider, as well, the instance of DG XI and its efforts to 'structure relationships' among non-governmental actors to 'make the process of consultation more effective *and manageable*' (emphasis added), as discussed in the contribution on the EU.) What is relevant here is that a network concept of reality seems to be not invariably helpful. Indeed, to some extent it can also disguise the fact that in at least some instances networking is not an inevitable course of action for modern government, but a choice. Descriptions of reality as being overwhelmingly networked might even become to some extent self-fulfilling in such cases. Therefore, again, careful attention to both the merits and the limits of network analysis seems appropriate.

Network analysis also faces some limitations in that it enlightens much but not all of the policy action that is of interest to scholars. Furthermore, alternative explanations can often be described in network terms or used independently. The impact of the Dutch effluent charge system – as the main financial institution of Dutch surface water quality management – on the processes of building treatment plants and negotiating cleaner industrial waste water can be described in network terms, but the relationships could be explained with alternative conceptual and theoretical approaches. The continuing subsidisation of water treatment in the US and Germany has a substantial impact on policy implementation. But is network analysis really needed to understand it?

More generally, network analysis as well as other approaches used in policy studies are characterised to some extent by an accent on both a real-world object of investigation (a 'locus') and also a certain perspective, in principle, on policy (a 'focus'; cf. Bressers [*1993a: 203*]). Thus, for instance, a policy-instruments approach would stress instruments and their characteristics as both objects of inquiry and also as a certain orientation to the policy process and its determinants. Conceived as perspectives, various approaches such as institutional analysis, network analysis, process analysis, resource analysis, and others, can produce complementary insights that may be usefully integrated. This synthesis is an essential step so that familiar insights are not simply rediscovered in other terms in a nearly endless fashion. The key question, then, is what have we learned by the end of the day? Only old wine in new bottles?

When the approach as partial object and the approach as perspective are mixed together, the integration runs the risk of using simultaneously concepts drawn from different approaches which relate in an unclear fashion. Therefore it is very important that the links between these concepts are further clarified so that analysts can be better able to assess the added value of network concepts for understanding public policy. There has been a tendency in scholarly explanations to use the network concept to refer not only to actors (that is, networks as a reworking of actors) but also with respect to institutions (constellations of rules) and processes, occasionally even with respect to characteristics of policy. A solid integration and clarification must inevitably restrict and tighten the use of the network concept in analytical terms.

Another difficulty can arise in efforts to use the network concept systematically in comparative investigations. There might be some disjunction between the scale of the subject (such as time-span, process, region, country) and the degree of coherence of the network related to that subject. Perhaps networks can be used as a meso-level concept. Although there is some evidence to the contrary, one could imagine that the lesser degree of integration of the water policy networks in the US compared with, for instance, the Netherlands could be a function of the size of the subject (in this case, countries) rather than a product of the difference in the way water matters are dealt with in the two countries. Trying to find 'the' water policy network of the European Union might pose similar, or even worse, problems. This problem of scale increases the importance of a very clear definition of the variables that are under study. Without such clarity, the temptation is to put different phenomena into similarly labelled boxes, because of similar functions being performed in the larger and smaller countries. Conclusions drawn from such comparisons might then easily be misleading. All in all, the usual methodological requisites of well-defined variables, explicit expectations, and precise measurements are certainly no less important in an application of a network approach. Again, then, a lesson to be stressed from the present set of investigations is the importance of designing empirical studies not around a general idea of networks, but by incorporating some underlying dimensions or variables of network types which are both measurable and plausibly related to causes or effects. The formulation and use of theories that are both empirically and logically based and cast light on the relationships between these variables and their causes and effects are of the utmost importance. Otherwise, network researchers risk getting stuck with vague insights that prove useful only as a preliminary eye-opener rather than as a crucial stage in the development of empirical network theory.

Concluding Perspective

The contributions to this collection have a broad common theme, beyond the substantive focus on water policy; it is that the concept of networks for the study of environmental politics is indeed promising (cf. Glasbergen [*1989*]), but that it also remains at this point a rather vague notion with many underlying dimensions. Separate case studies run the risk of using network analysis only as a language. Comparative analysis reveals that that is not enough to understand the causes and effects of network dynamics. It is not the adoption of the concept of networks *per se*, but more specifically the use of the various characteristics that networks can have that enables researchers to increase understanding of the relationships between these causes and effects. Though hardly surprising as such, this conclusion has not often informed the efforts of those who undertake comparative empirical studies. This symposium can be seen as a modest effort to do just that. Much careful comparative empirical analysis still has to be done, and should be guided by increasingly tight theoretical frameworks. The products of such analyses can be expected to enrich the theories in return.

The choice of the subject of water policies for this comparative effort has also been of considerable importance, from the perspective of the contributors to this symposium. In the past for the developed world, and also nowadays in developing countries, improving the availability and quality of water has probably been the single most important factor for increasing human life expectancy (see World Bank, [*1992: 99*]). Nevertheless, in today's Europe, and in North America as well, significant threats to an uninterrupted supply of high quality water have been identified [*Commission EC, 1992: 19-24*]. Water policy issues have gradually become recognised as an important component of the effort for sustainable development. On the other hand water policy *in toto* might be too broad a subject for an in-depth analysis of the relationships between network developments and policy processes. Therefore, as a next step in the develop of network analysis toward the end of understanding such policy developments, the research group represented in this volume has begun to pursue a new project on cross-sectoral connections: a systematic comparative analysis of water-agriculture linkages in several countries and the EU.

REFERENCES

Bressers, Hans Th.A. (1993a), 'Ontwikkelingen in het onderzoek naar beleidsinstrumenten' (Developments in the study of policy instruments), in: J.Th.A. Bressers, P. de Jong, P-J. Klok & A.F.A. Korsten (eds.), *Beleidsinstrumenten bestuurskundig beschouwd*, Assen: Van Gorcum, pp. 203-210.

Bressers, Hans Th.A. (1993b) 'Beleidsnetwerken en instrumentenkeuze'. *Beleidswetenschap*, Vol. 7, No.4, pp.309-330.

Commission of the European Communities (1992), *The State of the Environment in the European Community*, Brussels: EC.

Friedrich, Carl J. (1940), 'Public Policy and the Nature of Administrative Responsibility', *Public Policy*, Vol. 1, pp.3-24.

Glasbergen, P. (1989), *Beleidsnetwerken rond milieuproblemen* (Policy networks and environmental problems), inaugural speech, The Hague: VUGA.

Goggin, Malcolm L., Ann O'M. Bowman, James P. Lester, and Laurence J. O'Toole, Jr. (1990), *Implementation Theory and Practice: Toward a Third Generation*, Glenview, IL: Scott Foresman/Little Brown.

O'Toole, Laurence J. Jr., Kenneth I. Hanf, and Peter L. Hupe (forthcoming), 'Managing Policy Implementation in Complex Networks'. In Walter Kickert, Erik-Hans Klijn and Joop Koppenjan, eds., *Management in Complex Networks*.

Rhodes, R.A.W., and David Marsh (1992), 'New Directions in the Study of Policy Networks', *European Journal of Political Research*, Vol. 21, Nos. 1-2, pp.181-205.

Sabatier, Paul A. and Hank C. Jenkins-Smith (eds.) (1993), *Policy Change and Learning: An Advocacy Coalition Approach*, Boulder, CO: Westview Press.

Truman, David B. (1971), *The Governmental Process: Political Interests and Public Opinion*, 2d ed., New York: Knopf.

World Bank (1992), *World Development Report 1992: Development and the Environment*, Oxford: Oxford University Press.

Profile

The Electoral Breakthrough of the Irish Greens?[1]

One of the most spectacular results of the European elections of 1994 occurred in Ireland where two candidates from the Green Party – *Comhaontas Glas* – (Patricia McKenna and Nuala Ahern) were elected to the European Parliament. This success coincided with the accession of a Green councillor (John Gormley) to the Lord Mayorship of Dublin. The combination of these events has projected the Greens on to the national agenda. Public reaction, however, has been split between the belief that the party now has a major part to play in the nation's political life – 'Green Fortunes Set to Bloom!' was the *Sunday Tribune*'s post-election headline – and the familiar view that this represents a temporary rebellion against the political establishment – 'The Protest Vote of the Nineties!' – in the words of a defeated rival Euro-candidate. It is unclear whether the party's success in the European elections is the latest manifestation of a continuing political upswing or a short-lived expression of frustration with Ireland's main political parties.

It is the latter judgement which academic commentators on the party have generally adopted, arguing that green politics in Ireland is likely to remain marginal for a number of reasons. These include the unique nature of the Irish political system; the conservatism and continuity of political loyalties displayed by the Irish electorate; the lack of fragmented voting cleavages and post-material values in Ireland; and the absence of the severe environmental problems experienced elsewhere in Western Europe [*Baker, 1990; Farrell, 1989; Parkin, 1989; Whiteman, 1990*].

To understand the nature of the Party's apparent political breakthrough, it is worth considering the background to its recent success as well as the careers of the three representatives mentioned above. Whilst the Irish party is in many ways unique and atypical, its recent successes raise some interesting questions about the nature and definition of the political breakthrough which green parties seek.

The 1994 European Election Campaign

The party won 7.9 per cent of the first preference votes cast in the elections and proved the major beneficiary of the single transferrable voting system, receiving a large number of second preferences from the eliminated candidates of other small parties.

TABLE 1

STATISTICS OF GREEN PARTY VOTE IN EACH EURO CONSTITUENCY, JUNE 1994

Constituency	Candidate	First Prefs	Valid Poll	Per Cent	Final Vote	Seats Won
Connacht/Ulster	Richard Douthwaite	8628	232680	3.71	8628	0
Dublin	Patricia McKenna	40388	277844	14.54	57749	1
Leinster	Nuala Ahern	30997	262445	11.81	45821	1
Munster	Dan Boyle	10033	364571	2.75	11971	0

These results illustrate the importance of the urban/rural divide which cuts across Irish political life for the Greens. Their vote was markedly stronger in the urbanised context of Dublin and in County Leinster, a variegated region which includes suburban developments, affluent commuter towns and semi-rural districts. Elsewhere, in the country's rural hinterlands, the party's vote was almost negligible.

The results in Dublin and Leinster were generated by a combination of national and local factors. During the campaign the Greens focused on the Irish government's support for the European nuclear industry, highlighting the IR£43 million allocated through Euratom, as well as the embarrassing role played by the *Taoiseach* (prime minister), Albert Reynolds, in overseeing a European Union decision to fund nuclear processing. Behind these criticisms lay the spectre of the recently commissioned Thorp reprocessing plant at Sellafield in England, which lies a mere 35 miles across the Irish sea and has dominated the Greens' campaigning agenda since 1992. The party has repeatedly called for legal action against the British government to prevent this plant's operation.

In addition, *Comhaontas Glas* benefitted from a more professionally organised campaign than in previous years: Dublin was flooded with Green posters, whilst the party's only election broadcast focused on a single issue – the dangers posed by Sellafield. Other environmental themes which arose in the campaign included the need for an urban forestry programme and increased regulation of salmon farming, the environmental implications of the government's tourism projects, the weaknesses of its environmental impact assesssment methods, and the inadequacy of its deployment of EU structural funds.

Significantly, the party was determined to present a broad agenda beyond purely environmental issues, offering a radical set of economic proposals. Criticising the existing taxation-welfare system, the Greens repeatedly called for a revolution in conventional fiscal strategies, arguing for a shift from taxes on labour to levies on energy, and calling for the abolition of income tax in favour of taxes on the use of non-renewable resources, as well as more punitive property taxes. Criticising government failure to stem the increase in unemployment in recent years, the party proposed the institution of a non-means-tested basic income. If these ideas sound familiar, this is perhaps because one of the party's unsuccessful candidates in the elections was Richard Douthwaite, English-born author of the widely read book *The Growth Illusion* (in which a similar set of proposals are outlined). He has become an increasingly influential figure in the party. More generally, the emphasis placed on this seemingly utopian policy agenda illustrates the party's commitment to issues of social as well as environmental justice: Green activists have continually involved themselves in campaigns for civil and human rights throughout Ireland, and have been especially outspoken about the rights of travellers, gender inequality and the importance of nuclear disarmament. Politically, many Greens operate within a diverse network of voluntary and campaigning groups, especially in Dublin, which constitutes a small, yet vibrant, counterculture.

Furthermore, the party has reaped the rewards of its longstanding opposition to the Maastricht treaty – it calls for a decentralisted alternative – but general pro-Europeanism. The party's literature continally emphasises the achievements of Greens within the European Parliament. Simultaneously, though, its consistent defence of Irish neutrality has struck a chord with voters at a time when many are uneasy about the direction which Irish foreign policy has been taking under the guidance of the Labour leader, *Tánaiste* (Deputy Prime Minister) and Foreign Minister, Dick Spring, who has floated the suggestion that Ireland may be better off within co-operative international security structures.

Policies aside, after 1992 the party looked fresh and innocent in the wake of the disappointment associated with the *Fianna Fáil*/Labour ruling coalition which has failed to deliver the political and social reforms it promised; as well as the damage to the establishment wrought by the scandals which have emerged out of the Beef Tribunal. Interestingly, the success of the Greens appears to have surprised some of their rivals. This provides some indication of the increasingly self-enclosed and politically detached nature of the Irish political elite. The Greens' populist critique of the country's mainstream politicians, and their claim to be addressing the real concerns of Irish voters, carried some strength in this context.

Local issues were also important in the Greens' resurgence. In Dublin the party has made an impact with its succcessful campaign to make the city a smoke-free zone, as well as its trenchant criticisms of the water quality management plan for Dublin Bay and the waste management strategy being pursued by local officials. In the run-up to the European elections it exploited anxiety about plans for a motorway through the city and decried delays in the extension of the Dart, Dublin's environmentally benign railway system. In previous months it led a vocal campaign against plans to redevelop Dublin's zoo at an estimated cost of IR£15 million. The party's Dublin activists also highlighted the issues of gender discrimination and human rights abuse which appealed to the city's cosmopolitan and educated political classes. McKenna's campaign referred repeatedly to Dublin's housing crisis and to the question of women's safety. She presented herself as a candidate with integrity and intelligence, in contrast to the discredited members of the political elite against whom she stood. Yet, she was far from a novice in European and national politics. She became the first Irish co-secretary of the European Green Federation in 1990 and was leader of the East-West Dialogue Forum, an organisation committed to making contacts with small radical parties in Eastern Europe. Within Ireland she has been adviser to both Green TDs (Delegate to the Irish Parliament). She became widely known due to the party's High Court bid, in 1992, to prevent the government using the tax-payer's money to fund its party political campaign in favour of the Maastricht Treaty.

Nuala Ahern's success in County Wicklow was particularly interesting given the party's traditional weakness outside Dublin. Greens have come to the fore in this area through campaigns about waste disposal and recycling, and by calling attention to the dangers of pollution levels. Wicklow greens have been prominent in the *Stop Sellafield* campaign. This record of local activism seems to have offset the problem of scant resources which hampered the party's electoral efforts. The campaign in Wicklow spent only IR£6,500 and consisted of leaflet distribution and interviews with the local press. Ahern herself had been publicly critical of the absence of a proper conservation policy for the area and came to prominence, as a local councillor, in a campaign to improve the quality of river water. A couselling psychologist by profession, as well as a teacher of aromatheraphy, she was a founding member of the Women's Environmental Network and has been a longstanding activist within the Wicklow Environmental Group.

Elsewere, the Greens have struggled to gain a political foothold, with the exception of West Cork where a flourishing alternative political culture survives. Here, environmentalist campaigners have made a mark through their vigorous protests against the dangers posed by the local chemical industry. The results achieved by McKenna and Ahern were clearly not the products of candidate appeal alone. In the local electoral contests which occurred simultaneously, the Greens were also successful: at Balbriggan in County Dublin and Greystones in County Wicklow (a satellite town for Dublin), Green councillors were elected for the first time.

Mayor Gormley

The historic accession of a Green councillor to the Lord Mayorship of Dublin has combined with these victories to throw the national spotlight on the party. The position of Lord Mayor possesses little executive authority, though the post-holder can set up investigative commissions: Gormley has launched several, looking at the quality of the city's air and the future of its bay. The mayoralty is, however, imbued with symbolic value and ideal for political agenda-setting: he has, for example, set out ambitious plans for expansion of the city's cycle-ways (attracting attention for his decision to continue cycling to many official engagements, reserving the Volvo saloon which accompanies his office for 'appropriate' occasions), has ordered energy-saving light bulbs for the chandeliers of the official residence, insists that stationery is printed on recycled paper and has even introduced organic champagne for official receptions! Gormley is the beneficiary of the formation of the Civic Alliance, a loose coalition of political groups which was formed on Dublin City Council to break *Fianna Fáil*'s monopoly on the Mayorship. The Alliance ensures the rotation of this particular office amongst its constitutent parties.

Gormley's political career is fairly unusual. Born in Donnybrook in Dublin, he is a schoolteacher who spent several years living in Germany, where he worked as a builder, carpenter and coalminer. He subsequently studied at University College, Dublin, and then spent a year at Freiburg where he first became aware of the green movement. He joined *Die Grünen* in 1982 and *Comhaontas Glas* in 1983. Between 1987 and 1990 he served as the latter's campaigns director and played an influential part in the successful anti-smog campaign in Dublin. In 1991 he was elected as a local councillor for the suburb of Rathmines and was the victor, early in 1994, in the closed selection meeting held by the Greens to choose their mayoral candidate. His principal strengths lie in his relative youthfulness (he is 35 years old), populist political instincts, and ability to combine a modernising political sensibility with his environmental commitments. Misleadingly billed by his opponents as an inveterate enemy of the motor car and proponent of water charges for Dublin residents, his politics actually tilt towards the light green end of the ecological spectrum. His political outlook tallies closely with the party's strategic perpective: as he suggested in a recent newspaper interview, 'one of the problems for us has been that people perceive us as a single-issue party. The mayoralty, we hope, will give ... us an opportunity to make our views heard on many different issues' (*Irish Times*, 11 April 1994).

The Party's Electoral Fortunes, 1989–94

The first signs of an electoral breakthrough for the party appeared in the national elections of 1989, when its candidate, Trevor Sargent, polled 37,000 first preference votes in Dublin, defeating three high-profile rivals, though he failed to win a seat in the *Dáil*. At the same election Roger Garland won in Dublin South, gaining 8.8 per cent of the first preferences, whilst John Gormley came close in Dublin South East. Nationwide, the party contested 11 seats and won 1.5 per cent of the vote.

The party consolidated its advance in the County Council and Corporation elections of 1991, gaining ten seats in Dublin and three elsewhere (including Ahern on Wicklow council). Yet, the Greens' progress has not been linear: in the national elections of 1992, their agenda was marginalised by the furore generated by the Beef Tribunal scandals. The party lost its *Dáil* seat, in Dublin South, yet Trevor Sargent managed to win in Dublin North. According to many commentators, the Greens were a spent force. Their performance in these elections undoubtedly mirrored the decline of green parties elsewhere in Western Europe. Specifically Irish factors were also important, though, especially a swing to the left-of-centre Labour party which gained its highest ever vote (19.3 per cent), reversing a 20 year decline in its electoral fortunes. This was especially damaging for the Greens because of their intense competition with Labour for the young, urban, middle-class vote.

Problems Facing the Greens

Like their counterparts elsewhere, the Irish Greens have found that electoral success means that rival parties seek to appropriate aspects of the environmentalist agenda. Most spectacularly, after years of hostility to ecological values and a triumphant celebration of the benefits of economic growth, *Fianna Fáil* – the dominant party of government over the last 15 years – has responded more favourably to the Greens' agenda in recent years, most notably through the establishment of an Environmental Protection Agency as part of the Environmental Action Programme it announced in January 1990. This makes the political terrain more complicated for the Greens. Should they lobby this agency and press for greater regulation and enforcement, or view this as a reformist sop to alleviate environmentalist pressure? In practice, they have done both, calling for tougher regulations on issues such as land conservation and pollution, whilst highlighting the inadequacy and incoherence of *Fianna F*áil's approach to the environment.

Compared with other West European countries, concern for ecological issues remains relatively low in Ireland, though continuing public anxieties about Sellafield have considerably aided the Greens. There is limited evidence to suggest that environmentalist awareness has increased throughout the 1980s, providing one explanation for the Greens' electoral success. When asked to what extent the environment was an 'urgent and immediate problem', the percentage of survey respondents who agreed rose from 50 per cent in 1986, to 63 per cent in 1988, and 76 per cent in 1990, according to the results of the Eurobarometer surveys. A survey of attitudes and behaviour patterns in environmental matters commissioned by the Department of the Environment in 1991 suggested that green issues still rank some way below other concerns, notably unemployment, the cost of living and health (though one might perceive a connection with environmental questions here). The political and ideological climate is, therefore, far from favourable for the Greens.

Moreover, the party faces several problems which are particular to Irish politics: its success in establishing a more stable foothold in the country's political system depends on its ability to transcend these. First, the party remains riven by internal differences about its role and nature. Several months before the recent elections, a row broke out because Roger Garland, the party's former TD, backed an independent candidate against Ahern, decrying the party's move away from a green campaigning role. This is not an isolated instance of anxiety within the party about the dangers involved in penetrating too deeply into the conventional political system. Historically, the party has retained close links with outside campaigns and grassroots organisations; activists remain reluctant to channel all their energies into conventional political activity. Second, the party system in Ireland is notoriously inhospitable for new, small parties [*Chubb, 1982; Mair, 1987; Sinnott, 1992*]. The two main ruling parties, *Fine Gael* and *Fianna Fáil*, have become 'catch-all' organisations [*Carty, 1983*] whose political outlooks do not polarise on a clear left-right axis. This makes the ideological agenda of Irish politics unpredictable, whilst the broad political spectrum contained within these parties tends to squeeze the space available to competitors. Third, the party has been forced to take sides on a number of issues which touch on the sensitive question of its political identity. The constitutional debates over divorce, in 1992, and abortion in 1986, generated a great deal of discussion within its ranks. Whilst the response of its spokespeople illustrates its generally liberal-left leanings (it supported liberalisation in both cases), the party includes a religiously-inclined minority for whom such a stance is problematic. Similarly, the party supported Mary Robinson in her successful campaign for the Irish Presidency of 1990, yet party literature reveals that many activists are uncomfortable about the Greens being regarded as a left-wing party.

The biggest challenge facing *Comhaontas Glas* is to establish itself as more than a protest party against the prevailing political culture and system. There is little hard evidence to suggest that it has done this, a judgement which raises serious questions about its supposed 'breakthrough'. Its vote remains noticeably stronger in local and European than national elections, a frequent indication that a party appeals to protest voters. Its support is generally confined to a few urban centres, presenting a huge obstacle to further advance. Simultaneously, its internal organisation remains woefully inadequate for the pressures of sustained national representation.

On the other hand, there are some indications that the party has begun to establish a more secure place in the country's political life. Its core constituency remains urban, young and middle-class – the classic profile of 'post-materialist' support, as evidenced by the strength of environmentalist groups in the country's tertiary colleges. Yet, in the recent elections, the Greens constructed a more diverse electoral coalition – across social groups, geographical areas and age cohorts, which most commentators had hitherto thought impossible. Meanwhile, the evidence suggests that the party is becoming more effective in its fierce electoral competition with Labour, the Democratic Left and the Workers' Party for the support of a cohort of urban voters with liberal-left political leanings.

Conclusion

Assessing whether a particular Green party has achieved a political breakthrough is a relatively complex exercise. Whilst election results provide a useful indication of its standing at different moments, they do not constitute copper-bottomed evidence of success or failure. The challenge which a party poses to existing patterns of interest articulation and policy formation, as well as its impact on the national political agenda, are equally important criteria. Of course, the nature of green politics introduces specifically ecological factors which affect this judgement too. In Ireland, medium-term political gains have been secured through struggle on a range of fronts – involving ideological pressure, local campaigning and networking, and the lobbying of government. Yet, it still remains unclear whether the party has secured more than a precarious toe-hold in the wider political system.

The very uncertainty of the party's future, as well as the specificity of green politics in this semi-industrialised, peripheral economic context, makes the party an interesting object of research. Unfortunately, its particularities – for instance, its activists' immersion in different political countercultures – have yet to be captured adequately by its academic interpreters.

ROSEMARY HOLMES
University of Belfast
MICHAEL KENNY
University of Sheffield

NOTE

1. The authors would like to thank Bronwen Maher and Brian and Siobhan Doherty for their
   help in preparing this profile.

REFERENCES

Baker, S. (1990), 'The Evolution of the Irish Ecology Movement', in W. Rudig (ed.), *Green
    Politics One* (Edinburgh: Edinburgh University Press), pp. 47–81.
Carty, R.K. (1983), *Electoral Politics in Ireland*, Dingle: Brandon Books.
Chubb, B. (1982), *The Government and Politics of Ireland*, New York and London: Longman.
Douthwaite, R. (1992), *The Growth Illusion*, Bideford: Green Books.
Farrell, D. (1989), 'Ireland: The "Green Alliance"', in F. Muller-Rommel (ed.), *New Politics in
    Western Europe*, London: Westview Press, pp. 123–30.
Mair, P. (1987), *The Changing Irish Party System: Organisation, Ideology and Electoral
    Competition*, London: Pinter.
Parkin, S. (1989), 'Eire: Comhaontas Glas', in *Green Parties: An International Guide*, London:
    Heretic Books, pp. 68–75.
Sinnott, R. (1992), 'The Electoral System', in J. Coakley and M. Gallagher (ed.), *Politics in the
    Irish Republic*, Galway: PSAI Press, pp. 57–76.
Whiteman, D. (1990), 'The Progress and Potential of the Green Party in Ireland', *Irish Political
    Studies*, Vol. 5, No. ?, pp. 45–58.

Recent Developments in Dutch Environmental Policy

In 1989, the Dutch Minister of Environmental Affairs published the National Environment Policy Plan, which was generally seen as an ambitious, well-researched document aimed at achieving sustainable development in the Netherlands within a generation. However, the publication of a document is not the same as the implementation of environmental policies. Although the document was received with open arms, many argued that polluting industries and the related vested economic interests would not be willing to give up their favoured position [*Van der Straaten, 1992*].

At the end of 1993, the Minister for Housing, Regional Development and the Environment published the National Environmental Policy Plan 2. This provides an opportunity for analysing the impact of the ambitious environmental plans published in the first National Environmental Policy Plan in 1989. The central point of this paper is to discuss the degree to which vested economic interests have been able to neutralise the environmental plans of the Dutch government.

National Environmental Policy Plan 2 (NEPP-2)

The NEPP-2 is completely different from the NEPP-1. In the NEPP-1 a complete overview is given of all relevant environmental problems in the Netherlands. These problems are analysed and targets, aims and instruments are set out. The aim was to reduce most emissions by 80–90 per cent within a generation in order to achieve a sustainable society. The implementation of these targets was left till later. NEPP-1 only provides the framework of the policies to be implemented. The implementation itself was left till after the acceptance of the plan by Parliament.

The NEPP-1 was published in 1989, when environmental awareness was at its highest level in the Netherlands. The result was that the publication of this plan attracted a good deal of political interest. One of the proposals in the plan – concerning the financial position of commuters – was so controversial that the Cabinet fell.

As the policy aims had already been dealt with in the NEPP-1, the NEPP-2 could not include new policies. The aim of the environmental policies had already been set out in the first plan of 1989 where it had been stated that a sustainable society should be achieved within a generation. A reduction in emissions by 80–90 per cent was seen as the way to achieve that. The NEPP-2 focuses on the 'intensification of implementation; supplementary measures in cases where the aims cannot be achieved with current policies; and the prospect of sustainable production and consumption. In all cases special attention should be given to international aspects and economic development' [*Minister of Housing, Regional Development and the Environment, 1993: 7*]. In individual chapters, the problems of strategy, international environmental policies, environmental topics, target groups, instruments, and economic and spatial effects of environmental policy are discussed.

The publication of the NEPP-1 prompted a fundamental discussion in political circles and among environmental economists about the use of economic or market oriented instruments. Many economists argued that a command and control system with permits, in which norms are introduced, would not produce the desired results. It was argued that economic instruments, for example a levy on energy, would bring faster results which could be realised with lower costs. In the Netherlands, environmental groups became the advocates of the introduction of economic instruments. They came to the conclusion that results could only be achieved by increasing the prices for the use of resources and the emission of polluting substances. The polluting industries and industrial groups in general were against the introduction of economic instruments. They used traditional arguments to the effect that such an approach would increase their costs and would ultimately worsen the export position of Dutch industries.

During the preparation of the NEPP-1 it was rumoured that there was disagreement between the Minister of Economic Affairs and the Minister of the Environment about the introduction of economic instruments. In the NEPP-1 the suggestion is made that economic instruments should be given more attention. The preparation of the NEPP-2 repeated that situation. There was a delay in publication due to disagreements between the Minister of Economic Affairs and the Minister of the Environment again, about the implementation of economic instruments. In particular, the introduction of an energy tax was not accepted by the Minister of Economic Affairs. The result of this controversy was the same as in the first plan – the implementation of economic instruments would be studied.

Summarising, it can be concluded that the NEPP-2 does not contain new initiatives for improving the quality of environmental policies. In those areas where new policies could be formulated, such as an energy tax, only vague ideas were put forward.

National Environmental Investigation 1993–2015

In 1993, this research report was published by the *Rijksinstituut voor Volksgezondheid en Milieuhygiëne*, the research institute of the Ministry of Environmental Affairs. In this report an overview is given of the results of the policies which had been proposed in the NEPP-1. This report thus gives a great deal of information about the results of recent environmental policies.

It is said in the report that policies have had a positive effect on the environment. However, the targets to be achieved by 2000 will not be reached. There are three reasons for this. First, events regarding the use of energy, and increases in population and mobility are different from the assumptions made in the NEPP-1. Secondly, the effect of the measures taken have been considerably less than was assumed. Finally, only limited measures have been applied.

In particular, targets regarding the emissions of CO_2 have not been met. Given the current policies, the emissions in 2010 will be 50–60 per cent lower than was the case in 1985. However, in the NEPP-1 it was argued that in 2010 a decrease of 80–90 per cent would be necessary. This implies that policies have to be intensified and new instruments have to be developed. This, in particular, was missing in the NEPP-2.

Energy Use and the Greenhouse Effect

It is not possible to discuss here all the environmental issues that have been raised recently in Dutch policies. We will demonstrate current controversies in environmental policy using the example of the greenhouse effect. The greenhouse effect is caused by the use of fossil fuels. Some fuels such as natural gas have a lower percentage of carbon than coal. Thus, the substitution of fuels can result in a lower emission of carbon dioxide. The most significant contribution to lowering emissions can be obtained by using less energy. This implies that the actors involved should be those sectors with a high consumption of energy. The greenhouse effect is a global problem. The globe is the sink for carbon dioxide. The Dutch sectors responsible for the emissions can be tackled without paying attention to these global problems. All emitting sectors are in the same position. They have to lower their consumption of energy.

In this policy area, there was one topic on which attention was focused after 1989 – the introduction of an energy tax. It was argued that the current price of energy was too low. This low price resulted in a relatively high consumption of energy. The implementation of an energy tax was seen as an instrument for bringing prices to a more appropriate level. This proved to be a far from easy task. The environmental movement, in particular, was in favour of an energy tax.

The debate began in earnest in 1991 when it became clear that the Minister of Environmental Affairs intended to increase the levies on energy consumption. In 1991, the total amount of this levy was one billion guilders, and the intention was to increase the levies to 2.5 billion guilders in 1995. These levies were seen as a source of revenue for the Ministry of the Environment. Employer organisations and large corporations were against such an increase. They were afraid that there would be a strong tendency to increase these levies every year. However, this levy was not seen as a levy for lowering energy consumption. The aim of the levy was to finance the Ministry of the Environment.

The increase in the price of energy was sharply criticised by seven international companies which were large consumers of energy, such as AKZO, Shell and DSM. These companies wrote a letter to the Minister of Economic Affairs in which they stated that they would shift their investments to other countries if there was an increase in the price of energy. The right-wing liberal party sided with these companies. However, some points were not given sufficient attention. In the first place, it had always been the aim of the Dutch government to implement an energy tax in cooperation with other European countries. Secondly, the prices of energy for industrial purposes were the lowest in Europe, as can be seen from Figure 1.

The Minister of Environmental Affairs established the Wolfson Commission which included a number of well-known Dutch economists. The Minister argued that companies working in an international market should probably by exempted from an energy tax. In Parliament, most parties argued that concentrating on a tax on energy would not be the best way of dealing with environmental problems. It would be better to introduce a tax on the use of all natural resources including manure, groundwater and heavy metals.

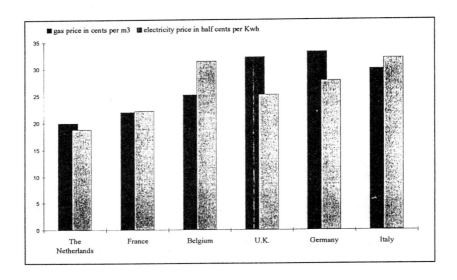

FIGURE 1
INDUSTRIAL ENERGY PRICES: THE NETHERLANDS COMPARED WITH
FIVE OTHER EUROPEAN COUNTRIES (DERIVED FROM HAUBEN, IN
DE VOLKSKRANT, 19 OCTOBER 1991)

At the request of the Wolfson Commission, the Central Planning Bureau investigated the effects of the implementation of an energy tax accompanied by a decrease in the taxes on labour. The argument was that a shift of taxes away from the abundant production factor labour, in the direction of the use of natural resources, would result in a better system of state financing, more in accordance with the relative scarcity of the production factors. Several scenarios were calculated by the Central Planning Bureau. It was concluded that in the most favourable scenario, the effects on employment would be neutral. In a scenario in which only the Netherlands implemented an energy tax, there would be a negative influence on employment figures.

These calculations by the Central Planning Bureau were used as an argument by the Minister of Economic Affairs who claimed that the results were so negative that he was quite against the implementation of any energy tax. In Parliament, there was little sympathy for the opinions of the Minister of

Economic Affairs. Deputies argued that the Minister should have waited until the publication of the Wolfson Commission report. Some environmental groups said that, from the political point of view, this behaviour on the part of a minister was unacceptable. Of course, the Dutch international companies used the opinions of the Minister of Economic Affairs to support their case.

The Wolfson Commission came to the conclusion that the Cabinet was divided on the implementation of an energy tax. They thus refused to continue their work. During a discussion with the Cabinet, the Commission decided to publish their results. These results led to many controversies. The assumptions in the model used by the Central Planning Bureau were criticised by many environmental groups. However, the views of the Minister of Economic Affairs were known before the publication of the report. This changed the political climate in such a way that, from the political perspective, the report was ignored. The implementation of an energy tax had become, due to the minister's statements, a political non-issue. The influence of the seven international companies mentioned previously had such a profound effect on the political debate that an energy tax could no longer be supported in the Cabinet and in Parliament.

After the publication of the Wolfson Commission report and the resulting political debate, no plans were developed to implement an energy tax. One of the most significant instruments which could have been used to reduce energy consumption was moved off the political agenda in the Netherlands.

The Kok Cabinet

It is clear that the goals set out by the NEPP-1 were not achieved. The example of the energy tax clearly demonstrates that vested economic interests were able to exercise considerable influence over environmental policies. The Minister of Economic Affairs also played a significant role. Moreover, it can be said that environmental issues have recently been relegated to a lower profile position in Dutch politics. During the preparation of the NEPP-1 the Cabinet was brought down because of environmental controversies. However, the presentation of the NEPP-2 did not lead to any real debate in Parliament. Nor was the Minister of Environmental Affairs attacked in Parliament for the failure of the policies formulated in the NEPP-1.

New elections were held in the spring of 1994. The Christian Democrats and the Social Democrats were the biggest losers. A new Cabinet was formed under the leadership of Social Democrat Wim Kok. This was difficult and took a long time. It is striking that during the formation of the Cabinet, many issues became politically relevant. However, environmental issues were never a serious point of discussion, although numerous failures and controversies could have been brought forward. This demonstrated clearly that environmental issues are no longer high on the agenda in the Netherlands.

REFERENCES

Minister of Housing, Regional Development and the Environment (1993), *Tweede Nationaal Milieubeleidsplan* (Second National Environment Policy Plan), Parliamentary Year 1993–1994, 23560, nrs. 1 and 2.

Rijksinstiuut voor Volksgezondheid en Milieuhygiëne (1993), *Nationale Milieuverkenning 3 1993*–2015 (National Environment Investigation 1993–2015), Alphen aan den Rijn: Samsom H.D. Tjeenk Willink.

Straaten, J. van der (1992), 'The Dutch National Environmental Policy Plan: to Choose or to Lose', *Environmental Politics*, Volume 1, No. 1, pp.45–71.

Jan van der Straaten
European Centre for Nature Conservation,
Tilburg University,
The Netherlands